D1606235

MASTER SPY

For my wife, Charlotte,
and my children: James, Margaret,
Dirk, Janette, and Laura
with Love

Edward Van Der Rhoer

MASTER SPY

A TRUE STORY OF
ALLIED ESPIONAGE
IN BOLSHEVIK RUSSIA

Charles Scribner's Sons
New York

Extracts from *The Curious Lottery,* by Walter Duranty, reprinted by permission of Coward, McCann & Geoghegan, Inc.

Extract from *Soviet-American Relations, 1917–1920,* Vol. II, *The Decision to Intervene,* by George F. Kennan (copyright © 1958 by George Kennan), reprinted by permission of Princeton University Press.

Extracts from *Memoirs of a British Agent,* by R. H. Bruce Lockhart, copyright R. H. Bruce Lockhart 1932, reproduced by permission of the author and Macmillan London Ltd.

Extracts from *Ace of Spies,* by Robin Bruce Lockhart, copyright © 1967 by Robin Bruce Lockhart, reprinted by permission of the author and Macdonald Futura Publications.

Extract from "Mr. Harrington's Washing," copyright 1928 by W. Somerset Maugham from *Ashenden.* Reprinted by permission of the Estate of W. Somerset Maugham and William Heinemann Ltd., and by permission of Doubleday & Company, Inc.

Extracts from *I Dreamt Revolution,* by William Reswick, reprinted by permission of Regnery Gateway, Inc., Suite 300, 116 S. Michigan Ave., Chicago, Illinois 60603.

Library of Congress Cataloging in Publication Data

Van Der Rhoer, Edward.
  Master spy.

    Bibliography: p.
    Includes index.
    1. Soviet Union—History—Revolution, 1917–1921
—Secret service. 2. Reilly, Sidney George, 1874–
1925. 3. Espionage, British—Soviet Union. 4. Spies
—Great Britain—Biography. 5. Spies—Soviet Union
—Biography. I. Title.
DK265.9.S4R448   327.1′2′0924 [B]   81–2279
ISBN 0–684–16870–7   AACR2

1 3 5 7 9 11 13 15 17 19 Y/C 20 18 16 14 12 10 8 6 4 2

Printed in the United States of America

Preface

THE WORLD OF ESPIONAGE is a reflection of the world of politics. It provides a truer barometer of the condition of international relations than alliances, treaties, summit meetings, conferences, and official declarations, all of which frequently reflect nothing more than expediency and hypocrisy on the international level. To think that spies pursue an independent path in defiance of the world's statesmen would be a serious or even fatal miscalculation of political realities.

This is the story of a secret agent who, from the time of the Russian Revolution, became identified with clandestine operations designed to overthrow the infant Soviet regime—to "smother Bolshevism in its cradle"—with consequences that are still important for us today. It is not necessary to whitewash the Soviet regime in order to recognize that, despite their public protestations of nonintervention in Russia, Western statesmen pursued diametrically opposite policies behind the scenes, policies that they sincerely believed (but would not publicly espouse) to be in the interest of their countries. They utilized secret agents to help in the execution of these policies, as in the case with which we are concerned.

The name of the secret agent was Sidney George Reilly. Because of his flamboyant character, he succeeded in placing himself in the forefront of these efforts, seeking to mobilize the support of responsible leaders and public opinion in the countries that had been Russia's World War I allies—Great Britain, France, Italy, and the United States—for an anti-Bolshevik crusade. In this, he and others of like mind were aided by the unremitting hostility and morbid suspicion that the Bolsheviks directed at all so-called capitalist and imperialist states, making no distinction between Russia's wartime allies and her enemies, such as Germany and Austria, which compelled the Soviet regime to sign a humiliating peace treaty. The concept of cold war—or "no war, no peace," as Trotsky said—had its inception with the Soviet leaders who made it clear from the beginning that they would be satisfied with nothing less than "international socialist revolution," a euphemism for the overthrow of all other states with different political systems.

Sidney Reilly wrote: "If civilization does not move fast to crush this monster while there is yet time, the monster will finally overwhelm civilization. . . . At any price, this foul obscenity which has been born in Russia must be crushed out of existence. . . . There is only one enemy. Mankind must unite in a holy alliance against this midnight terror!"

Yet if the rest of the world did not know how much to believe the Soviet leaders' self-professed aims or whether to regard those aims as immutable, it was never easy for Reilly's contemporaries to know how much to believe about Reilly and his own activities.

That Reilly existed there is no doubt. But from beginning to end his life was full of mystery. Indeed, he went to an extreme in carrying out the requirement of every professional spy to have a "cover story," a false identity that matched his own background as closely as possible without giving him away, by making a cover story of his whole life. Nothing illustrates this truth better than the fact that even the name by which he is known to the world was not his own, nor was he Irish as the name implies. Among the few certainties about Reilly are that he was born in Russia (in the Ukraine) and returned to die there—precisely when and how nobody knows.

The feats of the legendary Sidney Reilly rival those of fiction's most famous spy, James Bond, and are scarcely more credible. The difference is that in the case of the fictional Bond the reader may be willing to suspend disbelief, whereas in the case of Reilly the reader's credulousness reaches a limit. The Reilly legend has been perpetuated not only by his many admirers but by Reilly himself. Still, even if the legend cannot be accepted at face value, there were some parallels between Bond and Reilly. Like Bond, Reilly has been cailed a British spy, although he certainly worked for other intelligence services in the course of his career. Like Bond, who was registered as Agent 007, Reilly had a designation, S.T. 1, which he received from British Intelligence, the sector now known as MI6, then known as MI1C. Presumably, he was the first agent recruited to work against the "Soviet target." If some of the stories about him can be believed, Reilly also appears to have had a "license to kill." His ability to attract women and his numerous love affairs stand comparison with Bond's as well. There remain, however, troublesome questions that inevitably detract from the legend and raise a more fundamental question: Who was Reilly in reality?

The mysteries of Reilly's life cannot be wholly unraveled until the files of Soviet State Security, the secret police, are opened for public inspection by some future generation. And perhaps not even then. There is indeed reason to doubt that all or more information about Reilly will ever come to light. In the first place, Feliks Dzerzhinski, founder of the Soviet secret police, who died in the summer of 1926, and Jacob Peters, Dzerzhinski's deputy, who was later shot, would have been the best informed of all those who knew Reilly. However, Dzerzhinski, firmly believing in Schopenhauer's principle "never confide to a friend anything that you would conceal from an enemy," purposely did not maintain files about the most sensitive cases. His successors, who found their positions imperiled and their lives in grave danger, attempted to protect themselves by destroying existing records. In most cases, living witnesses did not long survive, either because they became victims themselves of successive purges of the secret police or because they knew too much and had to be eliminated.

Consequently, the whole truth about Reilly may never be known. All that is possible under the circumstances is to dig deeper into old records and source materials that still exist and to form certain hypotheses about his motives and actions that belong to the interplay of covert activities that ultimately solidified the basic hostility between the Soviet regime and the Western world. This hostility, with its underlying mutual suspicion, continues to this day and places enormous obstacles in the way of détente or any form of reconciliation of the conflicting interests of both sides.

This book is a reconstruction of the Reilly case and all its ramifications and follows the historical events and known facts as far as they go.

Prologue

SPIES, WHO NEED to hide their identities, come in many guises. One of the most audacious spies of all time was not above adopting a very humble guise in order to carry out one of his missions.

During the years of feverish rearmament that preceded World War I, a certain Karl Hahn, a welder by trade, went to Germany in search of a job. It was natural enough that he should go to the Ruhr, a vast industrial area filled with great chimneys and mountainous slag heaps—by day a depressing sight but at night, when the glow of its furnaces flickered against a dark and threatening sky, resembling nothing so much as hell. In the Ruhr, as the saying goes, Krupp was king, and in due course Karl Hahn applied for work with that outstanding arms manufacturer of Kaiser Wilhelm II's Germany, which was expanding rapidly to fill the orders of Imperial Germany's ever more powerful armed forces.

Hahn had a close-cropped Prussian haircut and callused, grimy hands. In his patched but neat clothes and substantial old boots, he created the impression of a conscientious man accustomed to hard work. He possessed excellent credentials, since his papers showed that he was an ethnic German from Revel (now Tallinn), the capital of Estonia, which then belonged to the Russian empire, and had been employed in the Putilov armament works in St. Petersburg. He spoke German and Russian fluently.

Hired by Alfred Krupp, Hahn proved to be an excellent worker. Like many dedicated workers, he did not limit himself to his job as a welder; when the plant sought volunteers for a fire-fighting force, which would also be available to work at night, he immediately offered his services.

Hahn's employers did not know that he had a stronger motive for volunteering to work as a fire fighter. Hahn had noticed that there were so many guards and watchmen stationed about the plant that he could not absent himself from his regular post and enter other areas without becoming conspicuous. It was different at night when he performed his work as a member of the fire brigade. He was able to move about freely and to enter any part of the plant. He succeeded in slipping away down a dark corridor on several successive nights, to pick the locks of a room in which confidential blueprints of Germany's most modern arms were stored.

Nevertheless, Hahn could find no opportunity to photograph the blueprints. At first he hoped to trace them, but this proved to be so time consuming that he decided to study the most important blueprints and to copy them section by section.

As things turned out, Hahn's curiosity about plans showing the layout of the Krupp works had already aroused suspicion. Krupp executives and local police officials questioned him about his prolonged absences from his duties on the night shift, but he was so adroit in his replies to this interrogation that he temporarily allayed their suspicion. He realized, however, that time was running out and that he had no option but to steal the blueprints if he hoped to accomplish his mission.

When all his preparations had been completed, Hahn went to work again on the night shift, knocked out the foreman assigned to watch him, and tied up the man with strips of cloth he had concealed in his work clothes. He then appropriated the vital blueprints, hid them on his person, and attempted to leave the plant. Stopped at the gate, Hahn found himself engaged in a fierce struggle with the stocky guard, who was middle-aged but still powerful. After absorbing some punishment, Hahn landed a vicious uppercut that knocked the guard unconscious. He quickly tied him up and made his escape.

Later he put the blueprints in envelopes he had prepared in advance and went to an all-night post office, where he mailed them to addresses in London, Paris, Brussels, and Amsterdam. Then he took a train from Essen to Dortmund, only twenty miles away, and went to a safe apartment where he had money, new clothes, and a passport waiting for him.

Karl Hahn disappeared forever, but another man took his place. The other man, who seemed taller than Hahn, perhaps because of his splendidly tailored Savile Row clothes and handsome black homburg, was smooth-shaven and imperious in manner, and had the aristocratic good looks that might have been thought appropriate to his British passport. A few days later he arrived in London like any upper-class Englishman returning from a well-deserved holiday on the Continent.

The distinguished-looking man was a notable spy named Sidney George Reilly, who would be remembered in history in connection with the Russian Revolution.

Chapter 1

Moscow, 1918. On the seventh of May, a raw spring day, a British officer walked up to the main gate of the Kremlin and surprised the sentries by asking to see Lenin, the new master of Russia.

The slovenly sentries regarded the British officer with suspicion, all the more because he spoke native Russian. But the officer, faultlessly turned out in a custom-made uniform, retained his self-possession while they summoned the sergeant of the guard. In reply to the sergeant's inquiry about his business, the British officer stated that he had been sent as a special emissary of the British prime minister, David Lloyd George, to speak with the Bolshevik leaders.

Bruce Lockhart, head of the British mission to the Soviet government then in Moscow, later said when he heard the story that the man's "sheer audacity took my breath away."[1]

While he waited, the British officer coolly looked up at the faded pink battlemented walls of the Kremlin surmounted by nearly twenty red and black towers. Behind those unfriendly walls rose the gold, pastel blue, or silver cupolas of Byzantine churches and steep-roofed gold and white palaces, under a high dark sky of storm clouds.

The Soviet government had moved its seat to the Kremlin barely two months earlier. Abandoning the previous capital, Petrograd,[2] the Bolshevik leaders sought greater security from the German armies, which remained in Russia and were advancing toward Petrograd to compel early Soviet signature of the Brest-Litovsk treaty (designed to bring about a separate peace between Russia and Germany). But the shift, pragmatic as it was, had its symbolism as well. In Petrograd the chimes of the time-honored Fortress of St. Peter and St. Paul, burial place of the czars, still played "*Bozhe Tsarya Khrani*" ("God Save the Czar"), but in Moscow, where the Soviet leaders now had gathered, the great Kremlin bells played instead the opening notes of the Internationale.

Lockhart first learned about the incident when Lev Mikhailovich Karakhan, a high official of the Soviet Foreign Office, telephoned him and asked him to come to his office at once. When they met, Karakhan told Lockhart that the British officer had identified himself as "Relli." Although he had requested a meeting with Lenin, "Relli" was received by Vladimir Bonch-Bruyevich, head of chancery of the Soviet of People's Commissars, who also happened to be one of Lenin's closest friends.

As he had already indicated on his arrival at the Kremlin, the British officer told Bonch-Bruyevich that he had been sent out on a special mission by prime minister Lloyd George to obtain firsthand information about the aims and views of the Bolshevik leaders, since the British government was dissatisfied with the reports Lockhart had been providing.

Karakhan came straight to the point with Lockhart. "Is this man an impostor?"

Lockhart checked his impulse to reply that the man could only be a Russian masquerading as a British officer. The man was either deranged or up to some devious game. But on second thought Lockhart decided that it would be wiser to avoid committing himself.

"I shall have to make inquiries," Lockhart said. "I'll advise you as soon as I have definite information on the subject."

Lockhart, a canny Scot who already had his share of diplomatic experience, including a tour as British consul general in Moscow under the czarist government, had experienced some doubts during his talk with Karakhan. In the past he had more than once received an unpleasant surprise from his superiors, who neglected to take him into their confidence or acted without his knowledge.

He checked with Ernest Boyce, the British Secret Intelligence Service chief in Russia, and learned to his chagrin that the man was a new agent named Reilly who had just been sent out from England.

"I blew up in a storm of indignation," Lockhart wrote, "and the next day the officer came to offer his explanation. He swore that the story Karakhan had told me was quite untrue. He admitted, however, that he had been to the Kremlin and had seen Bonch-Bruyevich. . . . I knew instinctively that on this occasion Karakhan had adhered strictly to the truth. Now I was faced with the unpleasant and even dangerous task of saving a British agent. . . . Fortunately I was able to arrange matters with Karakhan so that his suspicions were not unduly aroused."[3]

Only Sidney George Reilly, whose career as a spy had been marked by many daring exploits, could have made such a dramatic entrance on the stage of revolutionary Russia. Lockhart, meeting Reilly for the first time, could not foresee that his own career was to be seriously affected by Reilly's actions. The two men, who would be so closely associated in the next five or six months, were destined to play featured roles in risky, rashly conceived plots to overthrow the Bolshevik regime.

In 1918 Reilly was forty-four years old, about fourteen years older than Lockhart, bursting with energy, full of imaginative powers, a sleek, dark man—dark of hair, eyes, and skin—whom some of his colleagues described with the adjective "sinister" but whom women found irresistible. For Reilly, a cosmopolitan at home in many countries and languages, was a lover of the good life, which extended to good food and drink as well as the finest things. He collected books, paintings, and memorabilia of Napoleon, his idol;[4] he also collected women. He was a fascinating conversationalist, never dull. He radiated boundless charm, although he sometimes chilled people with a glance when, in his opinion, they encroached on his inner privacy.

Consequently, Lockhart was as ignorant as most other people about a background that Reilly preferred to shroud in mystery. Reilly was born on March 24, 1874, in Odessa, a Black Sea port that many Russians continue to regard as Russian while Ukrainians consider it a part of the Ukraine. Both are correct: Nominally the city is on the territory of the Ukrainian Soviet Socialist Republic, but the Russians control the Ukraine as they did under the czarist government. Nevertheless, the Ukraine also possessed historical ties to Poland, and Reilly, who was born Sigmund Georgievich Rosenblum, had Polish ties through his family.

The name Rosenblum, however, was one rarely used or acknowledged by Reilly. The little that is known about his family suggests that Reilly's father was a businessman situated in Odessa. But Reilly invented various fanciful stories about his origins that tended to exaggerate the status of his family and to lend a romantic aura to his departure from home, which involved a final break with the family.

Thus, on the rare occasions when he would discuss the subject, Reilly sometimes claimed that he was raised in a distinguished Russian family, that his father was an army colonel with an aristocratic background and his mother also of pure Russian upper-class origin. But he allegedly left his family after making the shattering discovery that his mother had conceived him as a result of an extramarital affair with her Jewish doctor, whose name was Rosenblum.

The truth appears to have been otherwise. The Rosenblums were well-to-do, and, contrary to laws restricting Jewish ownership of real estate, the czarist government seems to have winked at the fact that they owned large tracts of land, particularly in Poland. As a young man, Reilly was sent to study in Vienna, acquiring a good command of German, and there he became involved with a Marxist revolutionary group. When he returned to Russia carrying a concealed letter, he was arrested by the Okhrana, the Russian secret police.

The Rosenblum family's good connections with the czarist bureaucracy secured Reilly's eventual release, but he seems to have been disowned by his father, whose situation was threatened by the son's revolutionary activities, and sent abroad. In any case the break with his family was complete, and in the years to come, except for one chance meeting in France with his sister (unaccountably ending in the sister's fatal fall from a window), Reilly never saw or communicated with them again. He must have been very bitter as a result of this experience, since he hardly spoke of them even to his most intimate friends.

In later years Sidney Reilly liked to claim that, as a result of a love affair with Ethel Voynich, he became the hero, the revolutionary student Arthur, of her novel *Ovod* (*The Gadfly*), which acquired enormous popularity in Russia. Reilly's version once again appears to be more the product of his romantic imagination than reality, although it cannot be disproved.

Reilly's beginnings in intelligence work also remain mysterious. There are indications that, in the aftermath of his arrest by the Okhrana, he may have been recruited for secret work abroad. For most of his life, however, he was a free-lance spy. His services were presumably available to the highest bidder, except that he invariably refused to work against Russia and, on the other hand, was hostile to Germany and always ready to spy on the Germans.

During the first decade of the twentieth century Reilly carried out a number of missions for Britain's Secret Intelligence Service, SIS, but he continued to be unwilling to form any permanent ties with the British, although somewhere along the way he managed to obtain the status of a British subject.

He also acquired a wife, a woman whom he met in Russia, where she was traveling in the company of her husband, an elderly minister. Margaret Thomas, an attractive young redhead of Irish origin, had formerly worked as a housemaid in her husband's home. A torrid love affair, which began in Russia with Reilly following the couple from place to place and taking rooms on the same floor in their hotels, continued in London. When Margaret's affluent husband became ill, Reilly, who had a knowledge of chemistry from his student years, employed his related knowledge of medicine to prescribe for the old man. Nonetheless, the Reverend Mr. Thomas's condition worsened, and he finally made out a will bequeathing all his property to his young wife. At the last the couple, accompanied by Reilly, inexplicably decided to go to Europe, but Thomas died of an apparent heart attack before they left England. A few months later, on August 22, 1898,

Reilly married Margaret; when they registered the marriage at London's Holburn Register Office, he gave his name for the last time as Sigmund Georgievich Rosenblum. When the newly married couple set up housekeeping in the house bequeathed to Margaret by her late husband, Reilly also assumed his new name, which came from his wife's family.

On the eve of World War I Reilly accepted an SIS mission that took him to St. Petersburg, where he was supposed to collect information on German military and naval matters. It seems probable that in the process he must have arrived at an understanding with the Okhrana to provide them with the same information.

Russia was just then engaged in a huge naval shipbuilding program approved by the czar to replace the warships lost in the Russo-Japanese War. In view of the fact that Russian shipyards could handle only a small percentage of these orders, the major shipyards of the world, principally those of France, Germany, and England, were eagerly competing in the bidding. But it soon became clear that Germany, because of her influence at the czarist court and good commercial ties with Russia, would obtain the lion's share of the business.

Reilly had learned that the Blohm & Voss shipyard of Hamburg, which was likely to get most of the orders, had presented a list of three Russian firms from which the Russian Navy Ministry would choose one to act as Blohm & Voss's agent. With the Okhrana's help, Reilly secured a post with one of these firms, Mandrochovich & Lubensky, a company that was small enough to ensure that Reilly could soon maneuver himself into a key position. Reilly had also formed a friendship with Captain Massino, the navy minister's aide, and made certain that the choice of Blohm & Voss's agent would fall to Mandrochovich & Lubensky.

Once these arrangements went into effect, Reilly had no difficulty in secretly obtaining access to the latest German warship and arms designs requested by the Navy Ministry, since all these designs had to be forwarded by Blohm & Voss through its St. Petersburg agent. In this way, almost up to the outbreak of war, Reilly broke the seals of the packages, photographed the documents, reproduced the seals again, and forwarded them to the Navy Ministry. His copies of the designs were sent through the diplomatic pouch to England and ensured that the Royal Navy would not be caught offguard by some new German naval development in case of war.

By this time, Reilly's marriage to Margaret had long been in trouble. The ardor he had felt toward the red-haired woman had disappeared, while she, perhaps because of his neglect and frequent absences on SIS missions, including one lengthy stay in the Far East, had turned more and more to alcohol and had lost much of her beauty. At the beginning of his stay in St. Petersburg they were already separated, but Margaret heard about his new prosperity and hastened to join him, much to his annoyance.

Reilly was earning considerable sums of money through the contracts being handled by Mandrochovich & Lubensky on behalf of the big German shipyard in Hamburg. Pepita Bobadilla, whom he married at a later period of his life, described his situation at that time:

"He had a sumptuous flat, part of which was quite a museum of objects of Renaissance art, and his library of the finest editions extended to more than three thousand volumes. He drove the smartest equipages and had as fine horses as were to be found anywhere in Russia. Calm, dignified, immaculate, wherever he went he was the most observed of all observers."[4]

Reilly's relations with Margaret were further complicated by the fact that he had fallen in love with a striking brunette, Nadine Massino, Captain Massino's wife.

Nadine's husband, who had been so helpful to Reilly at the Navy Ministry, did not object to a divorce, particularly because Reilly had agreed to settle a large amount of money on him. Meanwhile Margaret remained firm in her refusal to give Reilly a divorce, rejecting a proposed settlement of ten thousand pounds, and fled the country when Reilly threatened to kill her.

The best that Reilly could do in the circumstances was to plant a false story of Margaret's death in a local newspaper. The newspaper reported that a "Mrs. Reilly" formerly resident in St. Petersburg had been killed in an automobile accident in Bulgaria.

When war broke out in 1914, Reilly left Russia with Nadine. They traveled across the country to the Pacific and took a ship to Japan. From Japan they crossed the Pacific to the United States. Reilly decided to establish himself in New York, where he had taken on the task of purchasing war supplies on behalf of Russia. The lovely Nadine was becoming restless because Reilly had so far failed to keep his promise to marry her. Reilly still hesitated to go through with the marriage, knowing that Margaret was alive. Nevertheless, Nadine's pressure finally became intolerable, and he married her in an Orthodox church ceremony in 1916. Thus Reilly, supposedly a widower, became in fact a bigamist.

Like many men in those years, Reilly began to fear that he would miss out on the adventure of war. He knew that there were few people better qualified than he to take part in espionage operations, which, dangerous as they were, required the kind of daring he possessed in abundance. He talked to Sir William Wiseman, who represented Britain's intelligence interests in the United States during the First World War much as William Stephenson, the "man called Intrepid," was to represent those interests during the Second. Wiseman placed Reilly in contact with the new head of SIS, Captain Mansfield Cumming, and "C," as the head of SIS was normally called in order to conceal his true name, welcomed Reilly back to the fold.

Leaving Nadine in New York to await the end of the war, Reilly joined the Royal Canadian Flying Corps as a military cover and, after a few months' training, returned to England, where he was immediately reassigned to SIS, or MI1C,[6] its designation at the time. During 1917, those critical months when revolution overthrew the Czar and Aleksandr Kerenski's Provisional Government was struggling for its existence and trying to keep Russia in the war, Reilly was undertaking a number of missions into Germany and German-held territory.

Returning from one of those operations, Reilly received a summons from "C" and learned, to his delight, that he was to be sent to Russia. He had not been able to keep abreast of the Russian situation, and Cumming now explained to him that the Allies feared the peace concluded by the Bolsheviks with the Germans could tip the military balance in favor of Germany by allowing her to transfer hundreds of thousands of troops to the western front and thus to win the war. Therefore, the Allies were seriously considering intervention in Russia. At the same time Lloyd George had asked Cumming to send a man to Russia to try to overthrow the Soviet regime from within.

This was Reilly's assignment, one which, in his view, set him to work not *against* Russia but *for* Russia.

Immediately following his visit to the Kremlin and his unpleasant interview with Bruce Lockhart, Reilly wasted no time in getting to work. Ignoring the international political and military equations and indifferent to long-range policy considerations, Reilly plunged into the stormy seas of Russia's immensely complicated internal situation, which verged on civil war.

Chapter 2

ON MAY 8, 1918, the day after Reilly's arrival in Moscow, a funeral attended by all the chief Allied representatives took place in the Soviet capital.

The deceased was Maddin Summers, the American consul general in Moscow. His untimely death, brought about by overwork and worry, was an ironic climax to the tug-of-war between Allied officials concerning policy toward Russia that had been in progress since the Bolsheviks carried out a coup d'etat against Kerenski's government and seized power in November 1917.

The funeral took place under a leaden gray, overcast sky on a cold and forbidding day. The pallbearers, U.S. Ambassador David R. Francis and the newly appointed Consul General DeWitt C. Poole among them, bore the coffin out of the church next to the American Consulate, where Summers had been married only a few years earlier, and placed it on a horse-drawn wagon. Then the cortege set out over a cobblestoned road toward the Cemetery for People of Other Faiths on the eastern outskirts of the city.

One American official was conspicuous by his absence from the funeral. He was Colonel Raymond Robins, chief of the American Red Cross mission in Russia. Ostensibly, Robins had journeyed just then to see Ambassador Francis in Vologda, where the Allied ambassadors had taken up residence, but Francis had left Vologda to attend the funeral. In the Allied community, Robins's absence occasioned critical shaking of heads because of the well-known conflict between Robins and Summers.

Raymond Robins, one of the most influential Americans in Russia, had held political office in the United States, taken a prominent part in Theodore Roosevelt's Bull Moose campaign for president in 1912, ran as the Progressive party candidate from Illinois for the U.S. Senate two years later, continued to be active in Republican politics on the national level, and also now possessed excellent connections in the Democratic White House. He looked upon himself as Woodrow Wilson's personal representative in dealings with the Bolsheviks.

But Robins was far more than a politician. He had made a fortune in mining, participating in the Alaska gold rush, and knew firsthand the rough and seamy side of life. He was a dramatic and colorful figure with a forceful personality distinguished by evangelical fervor, resulting from the religious conversion he experienced during his gold-mining days.

Physically, too, Robins was striking, with black hair and a long, beaked nose. His resemblance to an American Indian was not accidental, since he probably inherited Indian blood on his mother's side. Lockhart, who knew him intimately, described him in exactly those words: "An Indian chief with a Bible for a tomahawk."[1]

Robins became Summers's main antagonist in the cut-and-thrust of opposing factions among the Americans in Russia. Singling out Summers as an enemy because of their fundamental disagreements over the U.S. attitude toward the Bolshevik leadership, he drove Summers to the point of requesting, shortly before his sudden death, a transfer from his Moscow post. The State Department, however, encouraged Summers to remain in a message that failed to arrive until after his death.

From the moment the Bolsheviks seized power, the Allied representatives in Russia were deeply divided by apparently irreconcilable differences. American Ambassador Francis, a former governor of Missouri and successful businessman, was a man of advanced age whose views were understandably conservative. Nevertheless, Francis's suspicious attitude toward the Bolsheviks was shared by most high officials in Washington. Moreover, Francis was the faithful executor of the policy laid down by President Wilson and Secretary of State Robert Lansing that withheld U.S. recognition from the Bolshevik regime until it had obtained a democratic mandate from the Russian people in free elections.

Some of Francis's subordinates thought that the ambassador interpreted the policy too literally when he prohibited virtually any official contacts with the Bolsheviks. From a purely practical point of view, they reasoned, the embassy could not continue to function without at least maintaining contact with the Bolshevik authorities on housekeeping matters. Brigadier General William V. Judson, the military attaché, took the position that the security of the embassy could be assured only on the basis of cooperation with the authorities.

General Judson was a solidly built man of medium height with close-cropped gray hair, a dark mustache, and a round, ruddy Oriental face. If he had been wearing a mandarin robe instead of his mustard-brown tunic and leather boots, a casual observer would have taken him for a Chinese warlord. A direct and uncomplicated man, much like Francis, he openly disagreed with the ambassador on the question of recognition and set forth   still weightier reasons to support his position.

To anyone who would listen he argued along the following lines: There are two ways to force the Germans to keep their troops on the eastern front. The first is to kick out the Bolsheviks and induce their successors to pursue the war against Germany as before. The second way is to cooperate with the Bolsheviks. In my opinion, the first way won't work for two reasons: We can't succeed in overthrowing the Bolsheviks, and no one else stands a chance of getting the Russian people to fight. If we adopt the second way, we can work with the Bolsheviks and get them to insist as a condition of the peace treaty that no German troops are transferred from the eastern front to the west. And should the Germans resume hostilities in Russia, we can provide aid to the Bolsheviks who will know how to mobilize the population in fighting the Germans.[2]

The three principal Allies—the United States, Great Britain, and France—still were determined to withhold recognition from the Soviet regime, clinging to the hope that the Bolsheviks would be ousted and the Allies would be relieved of the distasteful necessity of dealing with them. In the absence of official contacts, the vacuum was filled in all three cases by men who moved outside the diplomatic framework.

On the American side, Raymond Robins took this task upon himself, although he always maintained that he had been authorized by the president to assume this role. Before the Soviet government moved from Petrograd to Moscow, General Judson looked for support to Robins, who was then based in Petrograd. Robins had no hesitation in acting independently and establishing close relations with the two most important figures among the Bolsheviks, Lenin and Trotsky.

Robins firmly believed that the Bolsheviks were the only effective political force in revolutionary Russia: The Bolsheviks knew exactly what they wanted, worked modestly and selflessly to achieve their goals, and ruthlessly subordinated all other considerations to rule of the party and implementation of its policies. Robins also believed that his personal influence on Lenin and Trotsky could move them in directions favorable to the interests of the United States.

Indeed, Robins was fascinated by the bald, high-domed, imperturbable Lenin, while Lenin, possibly less impressed by Robins, found it expedient to treat the American with special deference and, as Robins boasted, even gave Robins his private telephone number.

Robins saw even more of Trotsky, for whom he had only the highest praise. Trotsky was a "four kind son of a bitch, but the greatest Jew since Christ." Alluding to charges that the Bolsheviks were German agents, Robins added: "If the German General Staff bought Trotsky, they bought a lemon."[3]

Robins's unofficial activities inevitably brought about a collision with Ambassador Francis, who saw Washington's policies (and his own position) being undercut by Robins, Judson, and others. Robins was indignant about the hands-off attitude toward the Bolsheviks and embittered by the opportunities to win over the Soviet regime which, in his opinion, were slipping away.

For his part, Francis subscribed to the view prevalent in the State Department and the British and French Foreign Offices that the Bolsheviks were paid German agents. This view was based on the famous incident of the "sealed train," in which Lenin had been helped by the Germans to return to Russia, on vague reports that the Bolsheviks had received German money, and on the highly suspicious eagerness with which the Bolsheviks had sought a separate treaty with Germany as a means of taking Russia out of the war, thus violating an earlier Russian commitment *not* to conclude a separate peace.

Ironically, Robins contributed to the evidence that seemed to confirm this view by turning over documents he had received from clandestine sources to his friend Edgar Sisson, a professional journalist who had come to Petrograd on behalf of the U.S. government's Committee on Public Information. Sisson's job was to launch a major propaganda campaign designed to keep Russia in the war. The two men became close friends and ate breakfast together every morning, but the documents that Robins turned over to Sisson led to a bitter confrontation and a complete break between them. The documents, later called the Sisson papers, purported to show that the Bolsheviks were in fact German agents who acted in accordance with instructions from Berlin.

Sisson forgot all about his original mission and became obsessed with the papers, making every effort to purchase additional documents from the same clandestine sources. Robins, of course, considered the documents spurious, while Sisson, convinced of their authenticity, found them so important that he accompanied the documents back to the United States early in March 1918, after the final break between the two men.

A curious sidelight to this incident was later allegations that the so-called Sisson papers had first fallen into the hands of the British, when Sidney Reilly supposedly pronounced them forgeries and suggested that SIS recoup its investment by selling the papers to the Americans. Since Reilly did not arrive in Russia until the beginning of May, about two months after Sisson's departure, it appears improbable that he could have seen the papers at that time. If the British, perhaps in the person of Major Stephen Alley, who was the head of British Intelligence in Russia until April, passed off the documents on Sisson, the motivation would have been less a question of money than a desire to harden the American attitude toward the Bolsheviks, which was never as extreme as that of the British and French.

Sisson's extraordinary efforts brought about a subsidiary conflict within American official circles that raged over the question of whether the documents were genuine. U.S. policy toward the Soviet government was bound to be influenced by the answer to this question. If the Bolsheviks were really hirelings and puppets of the Germans, the extreme measures against the Soviet regime contemplated by the Allies would have been justified in order to wage war against Germany. It turned out, however, that the Sisson papers were actually forgeries—but it was not discovered until long after the war when the disarray in American foreign policy had already done its damage.

Yet it would not be surprising if the Bolsheviks had accepted German aid in various forms, including money. Lenin was always cynically willing to accept aid from any source as long as he and his associates were able to pursue their goals unswervingly. Traditionally, Soviet leaders have followed Lenin's example in all their dealings with outsiders; they are prepared to use others but remain firmly determined not to allow others to use them.

This also became a tradition of Russian émigré organizations, which have sought badly needed foreign aid but struggled to avoid becoming tools of foreign governments and their intelligence services. During World War II, anti-Soviet émigré groups of Russians and other nationalities, as well as the Vlasov Army, "cooperated" with Nazi Germany, their only possible source of aid, only to be stigmatized later as collaborators. The tradition was an old one even if it was not understood by the Soviet Union's World War II allies in the West.

Finding themselves completely at loggerheads with the ambassador, Robins and Judson worked together assiduously through back channels in an effort to undermine Francis and secure his ouster. Robins, who detested Francis, even cherished the hope of replacing the old man as ambassador.

Their efforts failed. Judson was recalled, Robins suffered a rebuff, and Ambassador Francis received a new vote of confidence from Washington. Circumstances then combined to separate Francis and Robins geographically, since the Soviet government's evacuation of Petrograd forced a relocation of most of the foreign community as well. As dean of the diplomatic corps, Francis was able to influence a removal of most of the remaining ambassadors to the small and undistinguished town of Vologda, safely out of the Germans' reach and remote from the Soviet capital. When the Soviet government chose to move to Moscow, Robins also decided to go to Moscow.

Like many others, Robins had underestimated Francis. The ambassador was a product of the American frontier, displaying all the robust virtues and faults of his milieu. Those who judged men solely by the yardstick of education and sophistication looked down on him, but he was nobody's fool. He possessed practical common sense as well as native shrewdness which, combined with his experience of life, made him a sounder judge of situations and events than most of his colleagues appreciated.

But Francis had been sent to a country he did not know and whose languages he did not understand. As Lockhart said, "Old Francis doesn't know a Left Social Revolutionary from a potato."[4]

A quite handsome man with good eyes and a hawk nose sometimes adorned with a pince-nez, Francis wore his white hair neatly parted in the middle and a full mustache. He had piercing eyes which could make those who displeased him very uncomfortable.

Leaving his family at home in the United States, Francis journeyed to Russia in the company of a black man, Philip Jordan, who acted as his chauffeur, valet, and general factotum. Francis had not particularly sought an ambassadorial appointment but, once appointed, took his position and his duties very seriously. He became a familiar figure in Petrograd, driven everywhere in a Ford touring car by Jordan. To his polished diplomatic peers he was a somewhat jarring, eccentric, and oddly provincial soul about whom all sorts of stories circulated in the foreign colony.

Francis owned a portable spittoon, a mechanical monster with a clanging lid, which supposedly accompanied him everywhere. His idea of a pleasant evening was to gather some cronies, with a plentiful supply of good bourbon and cigars, to play poker in informal surroundings. He abhorred diplomatic receptions, formal dinners, and all the other social duties deemed important in the world of diplomacy. His ambassadorial colleagues viewed him with haughty disdain, not only because of his lack of finesse but also because of his presumed ignorance of the affairs of state. When he was obliged to entertain these colleagues, he showed a certain tight-fistedness, giving small dinners served by Jordan, who had to interrupt his efforts at table to wind the Victrola that played music behind a screen during the repast.

Many criticized Francis's decision to move the embassy to the insignificant timber-working town of Vologda, some 350 miles to the east, because of the isolation in which the embassy now found itself. Nevertheless, the ambassador had his own view of that. Vologda had two chief distinctions in his eyes: its strategic location on two railroad lines, one connecting Moscow with the northern ports and the other crossing Russia from west to east along the Trans-Siberian Railway to reach Vladivostok on the Pacific; and its remoteness from the center of Soviet power, which enabled the embassy to continue its wait-and-see policy.

While still in Petrograd, Robins had been joined by a like-minded colleague, Bruce Lockhart, who had been sent out by Lloyd George over the objections of the British Foreign Office to see what could be done about keeping Russia in the war. It was a typically British solution to the problem of recognition: On the one hand, the Lloyd George government adhered to its official policy of nonrecognition of the Soviet government, and on the other, it bypassed British Embassy Chargé d'Affaires Lindley by dispatching Lockhart as a semiofficial emissary to the Bolsheviks. Lockhart enthusiastically set about his task, establishing contact with the Bolshevik leaders and soon discovering a worthy ally in Robins. The two men, greatly respecting and liking one another, felt that their joint efforts were being truly rounded out on behalf of the Allies when Jacques Sadoul, a Socialist politician who happened to be attached to the French Military Mission as a result of a wartime commission, associated himself with their approaches to the Soviet regime.

At first, all three men—Robins, Lockhart, and Sadoul—recognized the need to build their liaison with the Soviet government on a solid foundation. They had frequent contacts with the top Soviet leaders, Lenin and Trotsky, but dealt most often with Trotsky while he was still commissar of foreign affairs, and then later with Trotsky's successor in that post, Georgi Vasilievich Chicherin.

Both Robins and Lockhart hoped initially that the Soviet government could be dissuaded from going ahead with the Brest-Litovsk Treaty if the American and British governments would make an unqualified promise of aid to the Bolsheviks and also commit themselves not to intervene unilaterally in Russia. Lenin and Trotsky hinted that they might change their positions on the treaty with Germany and Austria if this were done. Despite the hopes cherished by Robins and Lockhart, it seems that the Soviet leaders never seriously entertained these proposals, while Washington and London never even came to the point of considering the suggestions advanced by the two men.

After the German advance on Petrograd, which finally resulted in the signing of the Brest-Litovsk Treaty in early March 1918, Robins, Lockhart, and Sadoul realized that Allied military intervention in Russia had become a real possibility, particularly if the Germans should continue their advance. Thus, they bent all their efforts—directly with the Soviet leaders as well as through their own channels to their respective governments—toward an intervention that would take place with Soviet agreement. For two months, from March to May, the question of an intervention based on Soviet approval was to occupy the thoughts of Allied officials on many levels.

Meanwhile, however, Robins and Lockhart continued to develop their contacts with the Bolsheviks in close harmony and remained in constant touch with one another. Lockhart leaves a vivid description of Robins as guest of honor at a luncheon to which Lockhart invited the staff of the British Embassy and other British representatives in Petrograd at the very time Soviet representatives were negotiating with the Germans at Brest-Litovsk.

After luncheon the guests assembled in the smoking room, where Robins stood at the mantelpiece and movingly called for Allied assistance to the Bolsheviks on behalf of the suffering Russian people faced with a mighty German military machine. "He became almost indignant at the folly of the Allies in 'playing the German game in Russia,' " wrote Lockhart.[5]

> Then he stopped dramatically and took a piece of paper from the flap pocket of his uniform. I can see him now. Consciously or not, he had provided himself with an almost perfect setting. Before him a semi-circle of stolid Englishmen. Behind him the roaring log-fire, its tongues of flame reflected in weird shadows on the yellow-papered walls. Outside, through the window, the glorious view of the slender spire of Peter and Paul with the great fire-ball of the setting sun casting rays of blood on the snow-clad waters of the Neva. Once again he pushed his hair back with his hand and shook his head like a lion. "Have any of you read this?" he asked. "I found it this morning in one of your 'noospapers.' "

Then in a low voice, quivering with emotion, he read Major McCrae's poem:

"We are the Dead. Short days ago
We lived, felt dawn, saw sunset glow,
Loved and were loved, and now we lie
    In Flanders Fields.
Take up our quarrel with the foe:
To you from failing hands we throw
The torch; be yours to hold it high.
If ye break faith with us who die
We shall not sleep, though Poppies grow
    In Flanders Fields."

When he had finished, there was an almost deathly silence. For what seemed an eternity Robins himself turned away and looked out of the window. Then, squaring his shoulders, he came back to us. "Boys!" he said. "I guess we're all here for one purpose—to see that the German General Staff don't win this war."

Three quick strides, and he was by my side. He wrung my hand. "Good-bye, Lockhart," he said. Four more strides, and he was gone.

Always a dramatic presence,[6] Robins was, as another writer has written, a "character out of Jack London." In the natural course of things he carried on his struggle for those Allied policies that he thought correct with the help of Lockhart and Sadoul, after all three had followed the Soviet government to Moscow. Robins, however, was like a man in the Klondike, ready to continue the struggle alone. Since he was physically separated from Ambassador Francis, he found a new antagonist in Maddin Summers, the American consul general in Moscow, who equaled Francis in his suspicion and dislike of the Bolsheviks.

Summers, a handsome, heavyset man, had been a fixture for years in prominent social and business circles of Moscow. He had married a Russian lady of excellent background with similar connections. His instincts were conservative. Apart from that, he had been shocked by the excesses of the Bolsheviks during their seizure of power in Moscow—the Bolsheviks *he* knew were cut from different cloth than those in Petrograd who had lived for lengthy periods in exile abroad. During the coup d'etat, there had been severe fighting in the center of Moscow; Summers, his assistant

Poole, and the rest of the staff were under virtual siege for several days in the American Consulate General building on the Bryusovsky Pereulok, whose facade still bore the scars of shell and rifle fire. None of these circumstances was conducive to an objective attitude toward the new rulers.

All in all, Summers was inclined to give undue weight to the involvement of the Bolsheviks with the Germans, which caused him to regard them as little more than German tools. For this reason, he consistently supported a policy of opposition to the Soviet regime and intervention in Russia on the side of its enemies. In contrast to Robins, who believed that the Bolsheviks were consolidating their position, Summers believed they were in a precarious position and would soon be overthrown.

Therefore, Summers was completely in sympathy with the policy of the State Department, while Robins with heart and soul opposed that policy. If the conflict between the two men had been fought out on that level, it would have been bitter enough. Robins, however, did his utmost to undermine Summers's position by communicating his complaints to Francis. Already overburdened with work as a result of the war, Summers was harassed by Robins on far more insignificant matters that he had to handle as consul general.

One such incident involved the anarchists who were making the streets of Moscow unsafe, even for Soviet officials. They robbed and looted, seized houses, automobiles, and other property, carried out many acts of brutality, and engaged in drunken debauchery. They refused to accept any discipline and defied all authority. The Soviet leaders were reluctant to take steps against them, however, because the anarchists were ideologically close to the Bolsheviks and had been regarded as harmless nuisances.

When an anarchist group entered a mansion and occupied the ornate rooms of the American military attaché's office, Summers protested vehemently to the authorities, but the Moscow municipal officials supported the anarchists. For his part, Robins made a complaint to Ambassador Francis, claiming that the whole affair involved the attempt by foreign diplomats to protect the palace of a Russian prince, which, in his view, constituted a misuse of the American flag.

But a few days later Robins's car was "confiscated" by a group of anarchists. Robins lost no time in protesting to Chicherin, who was in charge of foreign affairs, and Feliks Dzerzhinski, who, as head of the Extraordinary Commission to Fight Counterrevolution and Sabotage (or Cheka, its usual abbreviation), had created a Soviet secret police. Robins made the return of his automobile a test of the Bolsheviks' authority and their freedom from German control. By this time the Bolshevik leaders had exhausted their patience with the anarchists and were ready to crack down on them anyway, so Dzerzhinski promised to secure the return of the car to Robins.

On April 12 at 3 A.M., raids were carried out all over Moscow against the anarchist strongholds. More than a hundred people were killed and some five hundred were arrested. Ironically, Jacob Peters, Dzerzhinski's deputy, invited Lockhart (whom he would later interrogate after Lockhart's arrest) and Robins to accompany him on a tour of the scenes of these raids. Lockhart drew a lifelike picture of what he saw:

> The anarchists had appropriated the finest houses in Moscow. On the Povarskaya where the rich merchants lived, we entered house after house. The filth was indescribable. Broken bottles littered the floors. The magnificent ceilings were perforated with bullet-holes. Wine stains and human excrement blotched the Aubusson carpets. Priceless pictures had been slashed to strips. The dead still lay where they had fallen. They included officers in guards' uniform, students—young boys of twenty—and men who belonged obviously to the criminal class and whom the revolution had released from prison. In the luxurious drawing room of the House Gracheva the anarchists had been surprised in the middle of an orgy. The long table which had supported the feast had been overturned, and broken plates, glasses, champagne bottles made unsavory islands in a pool of blood and spilt wine. On the floor lay a young woman face downwards. Peters turned her over. Her hair was dishevelled. She had been shot through the neck, and the blood had congealed in a sinister purple clump. She could not have been more than twenty. Peters shrugged his shoulders. "Prostitutka," he said. "Perhaps it is for the best."[7]

Robins got back his automobile, but its recovery was the last triumph he celebrated in Russia.

The State Department's reply to Summers's request for a transfer, rejecting the request and urging him to remain at his post, had been framed with the knowledge that the Red Cross was about to recall Robins to the United States.

On May 3 Consul General Summers complained of being unwell and returned to his home to rest. On the following day he died, evidently believing that the Germans had poisoned him, although his death seems to have been due to a stroke.

Nevertheless, the cause for which Robins and Lockhart had fought was already lost. Sadoul had been neutralized by French Ambassador Joseph Noulens, who deprived him of his separate channel to Paris, and Robins was on the point of being withdrawn. In London, Lockhart was under heavy attack for being "pro-Bolshevik" and also faced the danger of a humiliating recall to England.

Before long Lockhart was summoned to Vologda, where a virtually united front of Allied ambassadors confronted him. French Ambassador Noulens smoothly presented a compromise formula for the Allied position: The Bolsheviks would be asked to consent to an Allied military intervention; if they refused, the Allies would carry out an intervention without their consent. Recognizing that the other ambassadors had already agreed or could be expected to agree to the formula, Lockhart capitulated.

It was hardly coincidental that Sidney Reilly appeared on the scene at this time with an assignment to bring about the downfall of the Soviet regime.

Strangely enough, however, Reilly was to have little to do with Boyce, head of the British Secret Intelligence Service in Russia and his nominal boss, and would, to the extent he confided his plans to anyone, carry on the work under the guidance of Lockhart, the man who was considered soft on Bolshevism.

Chapter 3

THERE ARE TWO branches of the Cheka," Sidney Reilly once wrote. "The political secret police of which Dzerzhinski was the head, the most diabolical organization in the history of the world, and the criminal branch answering to the civic police in a civilized country."[1]

It was Dzerzhinski's secret police that constituted the greatest menace to Reilly and to other Allied agents in their operations. Dzerzhinski was assigned the task of creating the new organization in December 1917, immediately after the Bolshevik takeover. As a first step, he gathered the remnants of the Okhrana, the czarist secret service, which Kerenski had dissolved in the conviction that repression would be unnecessary under a democratic form of government. Many of the Okhrana files had been destroyed and Okhrana personnel had been scattered to the winds. Dzerzhinski did his best to salvage what he could, but he recruited the nucleus of his staff among experienced Bolsheviks who had been tested in the underground battle with the Okhrana and who were well schooled in espionage and subversion.

As a result, in part, of administrative reorganization over a period of fifty years, the Cheka became the Vecheka and then acquired a succession of designations, a virtual alphabet soup: GPU, OGPU, NKVD, NKGB, MGB, and KGB, to be succeeded in due time by others. While reorganization partly explained the new titles, the changes also came about because of the evil reputation of the secret police and the revulsion that the different sets of letters ultimately inspired in the people.

The full names are in themselves instructive: Extraordinary Commission to Fight Counterrevolution and Sabotage; All-Russian Extraordinary Commission, etc.; State Political Administration; United State Political Administration; Chief Administration for State Security; People's Commissariat for Internal Affairs; People's Commissariat for State Security; Ministry for State Security; Committee for State Security. Not a word about police or intelligence suggesting the true function of this organization—understandable, perhaps, in a country where even the uniformed police is called the militia and a policeman is a militiaman.

Feliks Edmundovich Dzerzhinski was a tall, spare man with blond hair, Polish by birth, and a lover of music, especially that of his countryman Chopin. Unfortunately, his love of music did not soften his heart toward human beings. He started out in his youth as a religious fanatic and later, abandoning religion, became a Communist fanatic; like the masters of the Inquisition, he could send countless people to their deaths for the sake of a dogma, thus gaining a dubious reputation as the "sword of the revolution."

Lockhart, who met him personally, called Dzerzhinski a "man of correct manners and quiet speech but without a ray of humor in his character. The most remarkable thing about him was his eyes. Deeply sunk, they blazed with a steady fire of fanaticism. They never twitched. He had spent most of his life in Siberia and bore the traces of his exile on his face."[2]

Sidney Reilly never explained why he paid a visit to the Kremlin on his arrival in Moscow. If he hoped to establish himself on a footing of intimacy with the Soviet leaders by revealing London's loss of confidence in Lockhart and offering himself as a replacement, he succeeded only in arousing suspicion. Apart from that, he could hardly have chosen a way that was more certain to attract the attention of Dzerzhinski and the Cheka to himself.

That sort of attention could not be reconciled with a secret mission, but Reilly managed, so it appeared, to sink back into the anonymity of a clandestine agent. He immediately began to meet with members of the Russian opposition in order to prepare for the counterrevolution that the Cheka was designed to prevent.

The Germans were represented in Moscow by an embassy with Count Wilhelm von Mirbach in charge. Aside from Lockhart's British mission, the Allied side was represented by American Consul General Poole and French Consul General Grenard, as well as a large French Military Mission under General J. Lavergne, a smaller Italian Military Mission under General Romei, and an American military group commanded by Major E. Francis Riggs.

Reilly noted: "Furthermore there were Allied agents in the city, an American Kalamatiano and a French de Vertemont. But though I had been informed of their presence I judged it best to keep clear of them, thinking that my mission could be best fulfilled if I worked on my own and employed the assistance of Russian accomplices only."[3]

The Russian "accomplices" Reilly had in mind were mainly Social Revolutionaries, or SRs as they were called in Russia. But the Social Revolutionary party had split into two factions: the Left SRs who supported the Soviet government and the Right SRs belonging to the Russian opposition, which by this time had been outlawed by the Soviet regime.

Reilly pinned his hopes to recent developments that had opened up opportunities for future action against the Bolsheviks. The Left SRs were becoming more and more violent in denouncing the Bolsheviks, owing to the latter's treatment of the peasants, and the Germans, with whom they demanded renewed war. They threatened to withdraw their support of the Soviet government and take direct action if their protests were ignored.

Meanwhile, Boris Savinkov was also busily plotting against the Bolsheviks. Savinkov was one of the oldest SR members in point of service and a renowned terrorist who had participated in the assassinations of Czarist Minister of the Interior Wenzel von Plehwe and Grand Duke Sergei Aleksandrovich as well as unsuccessful attempts on Nicholas II's life. He was the moving spirit and prime organizer of a conspiratorial movement dedicated to the overthrow of the new regime. The organization, the Union for Defense of Fatherland and Freedom, was composed for the most part of former officers and possessed branches in a number of cities outside Moscow and Petrograd.

But Reilly was already thinking ahead to the government that would take power after the defeat of the Bolsheviks. He proposed that Boris Savinkov, who had functioned as Kerenski's minister of war, should become prime minister. The former czarist general Nikolai Yudenich had already agreed to become commander-in-chief of the armed forces and interim minister of war. According to Reilly, thousands of officers in the Moscow area would instantly respond to a call by Yudenich. There were three other men personally known to him who would also assume cabinet posts: Reilly's old friend Aleksandr Grammatikov, a lawyer, to be minister for internal affairs; a former judge named Vyacheslav Orlovsky, now chairman of the Cheka's criminal police, whom Reilly had met through Grammatikov, to be minister of justice; and E. P. Shubersky, Reilly's business associate from his St. Petersburg days, a railroad director under the czarist regime and head of the railroad administration in the ministry of communications under the Provisional Government, to be minister of communications.

To his fellow conspirators Reilly explained: "The essential first step is to plan for the government that will take over. A qualified man must be ready and willing to assume each cabinet post before we actually start a coup. Otherwise valuable time will be lost at the most critical moment—right after the seizure of power. That loss of time, resulting from inaction or hesitation during those first hours, may make the difference between final success and failure."

Some of Reilly's new friends expressed doubt about Savinkov, believing that the former terrorist had been discredited by his connection with Kerenski and the Provisional Government whose weakness and failure to gain popular support led to its overthrow.

Captain George Hill, whom Reilly met at this time, was a British officer advising Trotsky, the commissar for war, on the formation of a Soviet counterespionage organization and using this activity as a cover for his intelligence work. "I never liked Boris Savinkov," Hill wrote many years later. "My distrust of him was a matter of frequent contention between myself and Sidney Reilly, who had a blind belief in the man and spent a fortune in helping him to fight Bolshevism."[4]

In beginning his conspiratorial work, Reilly naturally gave first priority to the task of providing himself with safe houses in both Moscow and Petrograd, where the main uprisings were planned. He found a solution to the problem very easily in both cases.

In Moscow, Reilly had the address of Grammatikov's niece Dagmara, a dancer at the Moscow Art Theater. Dagmara K. lived with two actresses from the same theater at Number 8 Sheremetyevsky Pereulok, apartment 85, a huge block containing some three hundred flats. The three young women were enchanted by the dark, foreign-looking man with perfect manners and immaculate grooming, who was always handsomely dressed. They found him both exciting and a little frightening, with his glittering eyes and pantherlike step. One of the actresses, Yelizaveta Yemelyanovna Otten, normally called Elizabeth by her friends, fell in love with him at first sight. Reilly was also strongly attracted to the girl, who had long blond hair that fell to her waist when she let it down, a full-bosomed figure, and innocent bright blue eyes. Still, he did not neglect the other two women, finding time to dally with them as well without arousing anybody's jealousy, and within a short time they all had invited him to move into their large apartment. He was able to use the place as a safe house without too many questions being asked. Moreover, the women volunteered to help him in his work whenever he needed it.

In Petrograd the business was even simpler. Although a large part of the population had deserted the city, Reilly quickly located one of his former girlfriends with whom he had had an affair before the war. Her name was Yelena Mikhailovna Bozozhevskaya, a still attractive brunette. Yelena Mikhailovna readily agreed to allow Reilly to use her home at Number 10 Torgovaya Street, apartment 10, as a safe house whenever he was in Petrograd.

Using forged papers, Reilly lived under false identities in both cities. In Moscow he called himself Constantine and claimed to be a Greek merchant; in Petrograd, with his penchant for adopting the former names of his wives, he employed the name Massino and pretended to be a Turkish trader with interests in the Far East. In addition, he obtained a document identifying him as Sigmund Georgievich Rellinsky, an official of the Cheka's criminal investigation department, through Orlovsky, its head, who was himself hiding his past as a judge under the czarist regime.

Possessing these various documents, Reilly traveled back and forth between Moscow and Petrograd and lived in both places with comparative freedom. There were constant checks by the Cheka's own troops, known as Chasti Osobovo Naznacheniya or Special Purpose Troops (abbreviated as Chon), but since many of these soldiers were illiterate and had difficulty reading internal passports and similar documents, they were easily deceived. In a pinch, too, Reilly could fall back on his Cheka identity document, which never failed to produce a strong impression, allowing him to go anywhere without question.

The ease of movement enjoyed by Reilly and other foreign agents in postrevolutionary Russia contrasts markedly with the extraordinary controls preventing such movement in today's Soviet Union. The circumstances at that earlier time, which not only made it simple to move around but also to cross the border into and out of the country illegally, were due in large measure to the newness of the Bolshevik regime, its inexperience, and its still unconsolidated power. But in 1918 the basic elements of the present Soviet security system were already in place: Soviet patrols to prevent illegal border crossing in both directions; the Cheka's sudden descent on "anti-Soviet" groups and individuals, resulting in arrests, interrogations, and imprisonment; document checks and block-by-block searches of residential areas by the Chon; and a spreading net of informers.

George Hill described the use of *dvornik*s, janitors or hall porters, to maintain the Cheka's pervasive controls.

"No one is allowed to stay in a house without the *dvornik* being informed and given the passport of the visitor or, as in my case, the lodger, which he takes to the local commissariat for registration," Hill wrote. "The Bolsheviks had complicated the life of people like myself by forming House Committees which, under the guidance of the Cheka, pried into the doings and sayings of the people living in every block. The House Committees also issued the ration cards."[5]

Nevertheless, the system leaked like a sieve, and knowledgeable persons, intelligence agents like Reilly or citizens on the run, had no trouble slipping through the holes.

A half-century later, after the Soviet regime had gradually

strengthened its grip on the country and the people, the present security system became almost watertight. Playing on the fear of foreign espionage, the regime had effectively deprived the people of virtually all their liberties. With the overlapping documentation for residence, place of work, travel, etc.; with Soviet State Security's far-flung system of spies and informers extending to fellow workers, students, friends, and relatives; with the arbitrary arrests by State Security, which carried automatic conviction and imprisonment in "corrective labor" camps; with the other reprisals short of arrest at the disposal of the Soviet authorities, such as dismissal from work, withdrawal of permission to live in certain cities as well as exile to less desirable regions, and the loss of other normal rights enjoyed in civilized countries—with all of this, Soviet citizens have no rights at all, but only "privileges" contingent on their supposed good behavior and depending on the favor of the bureaucracy or individual bureaucrats.

Foreigners visiting the country or temporarily resident in the Soviet Union are subject to both visual and audio surveillance, spying, searches of their effects, entrapment for recruiting by State Security, and even, in some cases, arrests on trumped-up charges or, more rarely, the administration of poison or acid to incapacitate them.

In the beginning, Reilly avoided other Allied intelligence agents. Prominent among them was the American Secret Service chief, Xenophon (Russian spelling: *Ksenofont*) Dmitrievich Kalamatiano, who has remained even more of a mystery man than Sidney Reilly.

Kalamatiano was a smallish man with graying professorial locks, fussy and precise in manner, with very small, delicate, and well-formed hands and feet. His gray-green half-opened eyes seemed to see everything. With his fine walking stick and gray spats over elegant black shoes, he did not mind being taken for a pillar of the old regime, which brought him some hostile glances from workers in black blouses and caps.

Kalamatiano's origins were obscure. It appears that his ancestors must have been numbered among the Greeks who settled in southern Russia on the shores of the Black Sea many centuries earlier. His parents obviously intended him to remember these origins, naming him after Xenophon, the Greek historian, essayist, and soldier who lived in the third or fourth century B.C. In his later work in Russia, Kalamatiano's sympathies lay with the monarchists, appropriately, one might think, in view of the historian Xenophon's hatred of Athenian democracy and sympathy toward the aristocracy. Kalamatiano's Greek background was further characterized by his surname, which recalled the *kalamatianos*, a form of the *syrtos*, the Greek national chain dance.

But Kalamatiano, who was born in Russia, had spent most of his life in that country. It is not clear when he emigrated to the United States. In any case, he became an American citizen, married, and was the father of at least one child, a daughter named Verra who, after her own marriage, published a book of Russian fairy tales in the English language.

At some point, perhaps at the beginning of World War I, Kalamatiano was recruited by the American Secret Service and sent back to Russia. The Secret Service was subordinate to the Treasury Department, but in practice Kalamatiano, who used commercial cover in Russia, received his instructions through State Department channels. This came about because all U.S. wartime intelligence activities were coordinated by a small group at the top of the State Department. In Moscow he kept in touch with the American consul general, who also bore the responsibility for supervising the work of a number of consulates scattered about the country.

Unlike Reilly, Kalamatiano did not engage in any plots to overthrow the Soviet regime. He understood his mission to be exclusively devoted to intelligence gathering, and consequently he undertook to recruit a network of agents who could supply him with confidential information.

As the ostensible representative of an American company, Kalamatiano made his headquarters in Moscow but traveled frequently on business. His commercial activities gave him an excuse to meet occasionally with Consul General DeWitt C. Poole[6] as well as the consuls who happened to be stationed in cities he visited.

From Poole's point of view, the reporting by consulates under his overall direction adequately served the need of the United States for information from those areas. Therefore he advised Kalamatiano to concentrate on other areas and recruit agents in cities where Americans were not located.

Kalamatiano built up his network to the point where he was running about thirty agents. This represented a heavy responsibility, and, urgently needing help, Kalamatiano recruited a principal agent, Colonel Aleksandr Vladimirovich Friede, who was working at that time in the Red Army's Main Administration of Military Communications. While his position made it possible for him to supply Kalamatiano with travel documents, Friede's primary job was to maintain contact with Kalamatiano's agents and handle their reports. He also processed the reports before Kalamatiano enciphered them for transmission via the Consulate General's telegraphic facilities. Friede's sister Mariya soon joined the Kalamatiano group, performing duties as a courier.

In Moscow Kalamatiano's agents included a major general, Aleksandr Andreyevich Zagryazhsky, and a former colonel of the general staff, Evgeny Mikhailovich Golitsyn. Both of them provided high-level military intelligence. Another valuable man was Agent No. 26. He was Pavel Maksimovich Solyus, a graduate of the historical-philosophical faculty of Moscow University, who at first worked in the Moscow customhouse. Later he moved to Petrograd and collected economic and political information in that area. He also sent in reports on local transportation and the movements of German forces. Washington expressed appreciation to Kalamatiano for a couple of reports from Solyus, one on the Sestroretsk arms plant and the other on the anti-Soviet mood of the peasantry. Information on transport and economic matters in the Smolensk area originated from Agent No. 10, whose name was Aleksey Vasilievich Potemkin.

At the end of May 1918, Kalamatiano had to make a trip to Samara and Ufa in response to an urgent request from Washington. Czechoslovak troops had seized most of the Trans-Siberian Railway, much to everybody's astonishment, and Washington wanted a firsthand report on the situation, which could have enormous repercussions both inside and outside Russia.

The Czech Legion, as the group was called, had a curious history. While the czar still ruled, the Russian government had no desire to promote the dissolution of any empire, even among Russia's enemies, and therefore did not encourage the Czechoslovaks in their strivings for freedom and independence. After the czar's fall, however, the Provisional Government felt no such inhibitions, approving the formation of two divisions of Czechoslovaks made up of prisoners and deserters on the eastern front who wanted to fight for the liberation of their homeland from the Austrian Empire. Thereafter the Czechoslovaks went into battle side by side with their Slav big brothers, the Russians.

With the disintegration of the Russian armies that set in after their disastrous offensive in the summer of 1917, the Czech Legion remained the only unified, disciplined force on the eastern front, distinguished, moreover, by its loyalty to the Allied cause. When the Bolsheviks seized power, they were inclined to regard the Legion with suspicion, but the Czechoslovaks immediately declared their neutrality in Russia's internal struggle.

Meanwhile, the Allies concluded that it would be desirable to extricate the Czech Legion from Russia, evacuate it by way of Vladivostok, and transport it to France where it could be united with a Czechoslovak army already in being on the western front. Negotiations to this end were undertaken with the Bolsheviks, but before the conclusion of the Brest-Litovsk Treaty the Soviet leaders would not risk the wrath of the Germans by agreeing to such a step.

The Czech Legion continued to hold its base area in the Ukraine, where it protected arms depots and incidentally improved its own armaments. Its position, however, was unexpectedly menaced after the conclusion of a separate peace treaty between the Ukrainian Rada and the Central Powers. Then the German armies began a new advance into the Ukraine when negotiations with the Bolsheviks broke down. There was no time to be lost. With or without the Bolsheviks' agreement, the Czech Legion decided on a withdrawal to the east.

In withdrawing, the Czechoslovaks had to fight a fierce rearguard action. At times they found themselves fighting side by side with the Bolsheviks; finally they succeeded in breaking out of encirclement.

Once they were free, there seemed to be no further obstacle to their evacuation via the Trans-Siberian Railway. Initially the Soviet leaders offered no objections. On the local level as well, the Czechoslovaks and the Bolsheviks reached amicable agreements concerning the evacuation.

Nevertheless, Soviet leaders continued to regard the Czechoslovaks with suspicion, and their suspicion was exacerbated by a Japanese landing at Vladivostok in April. They realistically saw the danger of possible foreign military intervention in a link-up between the Japanese and the well-armed Czechoslovaks.

The Soviet fears were well founded. Many Allied officials, particularly the British and French occupying key posts in Russia, strongly favored intervention. They were urging Japanese intervention in the Far East and combined British, French, American, and Italian intervention in the North. The unwitting Czechoslovaks became a key factor in the thinking of the Allies about intervention in Russia.

These considerations led Allied representatives to propose an important alteration in the plans for evacuation of the Czech Legion. They suggested that the withdrawal of the Czechoslovaks could be facilitated by dividing the force: Those units which were already *east* of the Urals would continue on their journey to Vladivostok, while the remaining units *west* of the Urals would be diverted to Murmansk and Archangel.

To most, if not all, of the Allied statesmen, and to the Bolsheviks and Czechoslovaks as well, the new plan seemed logical. But there were Allied leaders who secretly thought that, divided in this manner, the Czechoslovak troops could provide critical assistance in case of intervention in the Far East and the North.

Before the new plan actually went into effect, however, a minor incident brought about a radical change in the situation. Shots were exchanged between the Reds and the Czechoslovaks at one point on the railway. The incident resulted from a misunderstanding, but Trotsky, the commissar for war, immediately ordered the Czechoslovaks to turn over their arms to the Soviet authorities. The Czechoslovaks refused. Trotsky then ordered the local Soviets to disarm the Czechoslovaks, either drafting them into the Red Army or organizing them into labor groups.

Fighting broke out on May 26, with the Reds being repulsed everywhere, and within a few days the Czechoslovaks, who were spread out all along the rail line, took control of most of the railway from Samara to Irkutsk, a distance of more than two thousand miles.

When he returned from his trip, during which he conferred with Czechoslovak commanders, Kalamatiano reported that the situation was highly unstable. In the absence of Allied pledges of support, the Czechoslovaks appeared likely to lose heart and give up their resistance. On the basis of Kalamatiano's report, Consul General Poole later took action without authorization from Washington that brought him severe criticism in some quarters.

Sidney Reilly was of course aware of the situation involving the Czechoslovaks, and although it had no direct effect on his plans, he expressed pleasure over this new complication, which was bound to increase the Bolsheviks' troubles. The possibility of Allied military intervention also entered into his calculations for an uprising by Boris Savinkov's conspiratorial organization.

Reilly knew little about Kalamatiano's operations, but he had a general awareness of the other man's intelligence-gathering activities, which did not interest him at all. In the course of developing his own plans for an uprising, however, he discovered that the French Secret Service chief, de Vertemont, was fishing in the same waters.

Colonel Henri de Vertemont had a brief that was very similar to Reilly's own. Both the British and the French were working feverishly along separate but parallel lines for an uprising against the Soviet regime. De Vertemont, who bore a faint resemblance to Kalamatiano, was attached to the French Military Mission under the command of the fiery General Lavergne.

Owing to the close connection between the French and the Czechoslovaks, de Vertemont had been involved with the Czech Legion long before the current crisis, and the idea of using the Czechoslovaks had been in his mind for some time. Like Reilly, de Vertemont was involved in the plotting for an uprising by Savinkov's organization as well as other Russian opposition groups, and was supplying them with liberal amounts of money.

When the Germans tried to force the Bolsheviks to sign the Brest-Litovsk Treaty with threats of a renewed offensive, de Vertemont and his men offered their assistance to the Bolsheviks in blowing up bridges and tunnels to delay the German advance. Later, after the Bolsheviks made their separate peace with Germany, the French, who could not forgive the Bolsheviks for aiding the Germans by allowing them to shift large armies to the western front against France, turned their efforts against the Bolsheviks. Possessing large stores of dynamite and other explosives, de Vertemont began a campaign to blow up the same railroad lines, bridges, and tunnels and to dynamite or burn down storage warehouses, aiming to worsen the food situation in Russia and increase the people's opposition to the Bolsheviks.

While he was not interested in sabotage of this type, Sidney Reilly came to the conclusion that he needed to establish closer liaison with de Vertemont in preparations for an uprising against the Bolsheviks.

Reilly liked to recall the obscure Corsican lieutenant who took over a revolution and left his stamp on Europe and the world. Napoleon remained his ideal, in spite of his failure in Russia. Reilly thought that men like de Vertemont and himself were better qualified than the generals to accomplish great deeds.

"Generals know how to command *armies*," he would say, "but lieutenants know how to command *men*. That's far more important."

Chapter 4

THROUGHOUT THE MONTH of June 1918, the word *intervention* was on the lips of everyone—the Allied representatives, the Russian opposition, the Bolsheviks, and even the man in the street.

While Sidney Reilly and Colonel de Vertemont were holding separate meetings with Savinkov at secret places in Moscow to discuss plans for an uprising, the Allies leaned more and more seriously toward military intervention. Only President Wilson was holding back. He would consider intervention only in terms of protecting Allied arms supplies that supposedly had been stored in the Murmansk area; he also grew more favorable to a possible intervention at Vladivostok when it appeared that the Czechoslovaks would need Allied assistance in their evacuation. He was unaware that there were Allied leaders who had ulterior motives for intervention, hoping thereby to bring about the overthrow of the Soviet government.

The Soviet leaders realistically appraised the dangers and desperately sought to find ways to delay or, if necessary, to counter Allied military moves. Above all, they recognized the immediate threat posed by the armed resistance of the Czechoslovaks. At the same time, groups of the Russian opposition, encouraged by these developments, become increasingly active. The violently anti-Bolshevik French ambassador, Noulens, recklessly came to Moscow from Vologda in mid-June to meet with opposition leaders, in spite of the fact that their parties had been outlawed by the Soviet regime. Noulens later addressed a letter to these leaders, spelling out the conditions to be met, in his view, if Allied support was to be forthcoming. By implication, his conditions included the expulsion of the Bolsheviks.

During June the Soviet leadership faced other difficulties: strikes in factories in Moscow and Petrograd; disturbances on the Nicholas line between these two major cities and in workshops of the Alexander railroad; and a rebellion in Tambov southeast of Moscow, which had to be put down by force. The Cheka was already on the trail of Boris Savinkov's conspiratorial organization, the Union for the Defense of Fatherland and Freedom, in Moscow itself and in Kazan but had so far failed to uncover another sizable part of the organization in Yaroslavl, a city on the Volga northeast of Moscow.

Early that month, after receiving Kalamatiano's report, Consul General DeWitt C. Poole continued to worry about the situation of the Czechoslovaks.

Poole was a clever, alert, and vigorous young man. He wore glasses and parted his dark hair neatly on one side, and with his high starched collar, thin black tie, and sober black coat, he looked more like a promising high school principal than a diplomat. He had only recently succeeded to the position held by his late chief, Maddin Summers, and still felt unsure of himself, but he enjoyed a fuller measure of Ambassador Francis's confidence. Francis had respected Summers but never was completely comfortable with him; he felt more at ease with Poole, who came from the Midwest and had roots similar to his own.

Francis made a point of taking Poole into his confidence. Poole learned that the Allied ambassadors in Vologda had recommended intervention in the north of Russia to their governments (the idea of first asking for Soviet consent had apparently been dropped). A decision was expected in the next few weeks. The British and the

French had also told Poole that intervention in Siberia appeared to be definitely in the cards. If an intervention took place, no one could doubt that the participation of the Czechoslovaks was highly desirable.

At that very moment the situation in France was critical. The big German offensive then under way on the western front could decide the outcome of the war. Artillery fire at the front was clearly audible in Paris. To Poole as well as other Allied representatives in Russia, there was an urgent necessity to keep the Germans from withdrawing more troops from Russia and sending them to the west. The best way to accomplish this was to reopen an eastern front against the Germans.

Acting on Francis's instructions, Poole called on Chicherin, the commissar for foreign affairs, and informed him: "The Soviet government's use of force against the Czechoslovaks or attempt to punish them in any way would be very regrettable. The United States government would regard such an action as inspired by Germany or at least by a hostile sentiment toward the Allies."

Chicherin, round-shouldered and nearsighted, his eyes red-rimmed from lack of sleep, shook his head. "This trouble is not the responsibility of the Soviet government."

"Regardless of the cause of the trouble," Poole repeated, "any use of force by the Soviet government would be regrettable."

Chicherin stared at the young man. "We shall take your government's views into consideration."

After his interview with Chicherin, fearing that, as Kalamatiano had projected, the Czechoslovaks might become discouraged and give in to Soviet demands, Poole sent off a message to the Czechoslovaks by way of Vice-Consul George W. Williams in Samara. In his message Poole requested the Czechoslovaks to hold their positions on the Trans-Siberian Railway until they received further official word from the Allies. Poole knew that he was exceeding his authority by sending such a message, but he was convinced that delay would be fatal and that he had to take action at once or not at all.

As it became obvious that Allied intervention at Archangel was not far off, Boris Savinkov's meetings with Reilly and de Vertemont became more frequent. As Lockhart said, "More even than most Russians, Savinkov was a schemer—a man who could sit up all night drinking brandy and discussing what he would do the next day." Lockhart added cynically: "And, when the morrow came, he left the action to others."[1] But this time, at least, Savinkov *was* prepared to act.

Among the three men it was agreed that Savinkov should organize an uprising in the city of Yaroslavl, strategically situated between Moscow and Vologda. The assumption was that the Allied forces would advance rapidly down the rail line from Archangel to Vologda on the northern branch of the Trans-Siberian Railway. Meanwhile, Savinkov's organization was to occupy a blocking position at Yaroslavl across the rail line leading north from Moscow, thus preventing the Red Army from reinforcing their units in immediate contact with the Allied forces.

Boris Savinkov, whom Winston Churchill once characterized as a "terrorist for moderate aims," had spent only one brief period of his life inside the government, as minister of war under Kerenski. He was never happy in that role. As a lifelong terrorist, he seemed to find it far more congenial to be in opposition, particularly when he was a hunted man. Under the czarist regime he had used assassination as a weapon in order to bring about a democracy along the lines of the United States or England. He saw nothing incongruous in a recipe for a democratic society based on such ingredients as blood and scorched flesh.

Churchill, who met him after the war, described Savinkov in these terms: "Small in stature; moving as little as possible, and that noiselessly and with deliberation; remarkable gray-green eyes in a face of almost deathly pallor; speaking in a calm, low, even voice, almost a monotone; innumerable cigarettes."[2]

Savinkov unconsciously gave a clue to his character when he related an incident involving Kerenski that filled him with anger and aversion. As prime minister of the Provisional Government, Kerenski was showing one of the czar's palaces to a number of foreign dignitaries. While speaking to the visitors, Kerenski kept plucking at a button on the czar's uniform, which hung in a cupboard. "That was disgusting," Savinkov said. "Czars may be killed, but familiarity even with the uniform of a dead czar cannot be tolerated."[3]

Once it had been settled that Savinkov would organize an uprising in Yaroslavl, the question of timing became crucial. First of all, the uprising had to take place at or near the time of the Allied landing in Archangel. De Vertemont promised to notify Savinkov well in advance of the landing. Reilly also assured Savinkov in their meetings that he would provide information on Allied plans.

But the timing of the uprising was complicated by another factor. Toward the end of June it became known that the Bolsheviks intended to convoke the Fifth All-Russian Congress of Soviets early in July. Since all other parties had been declared illegal, the Left Social Revolutionaries would be the only party to be represented at the Congress aside from the Bolsheviks. And the Left SRs had already arrived at a fateful decision: They planned to organize an uprising of their own in Moscow to coincide with the Congress. At that time they hoped to swoop down on the Bolshoi Theater, the site of the Congress, and capture the whole Bolshevik leadership at one blow.

It is not known whether Boris Savinkov had reestablished contact with some of his old party comrades among the Left SRs. Certainly that was to be expected in view of the disenchantment of the Left SRs with the Bolsheviks. In any event, Sidney Reilly was in touch with the Left SR leaders. It could hardly have been coincidental that Savinkov carried out a series of uprisings in Yaroslavl and other cities on July 6, the very day that the Left SRs struck in Moscow.

Years later Jacob Peters, Dzerzhinski's Cheka deputy, wrote: "It is perhaps understandable now, after Savinkov's explanation that the Left SRs also received money from the French, that in the drafting of the plan for the Yaroslavl uprising by General Lavergne, Moscow was not included. Possibly the French even then considered that in the general plan Moscow was to be assigned to the Left SRs."[4]

Savinkov subsequently claimed that he had been misled by the French, who told him that the Allied landing at Archangel would take place between the 5th and the 15th of July. Whether or not this was true, it remains a fact that the delay in the landing, which was postponed until the beginning of August, had a fatal effect on Savinkov's chances.

As the Fifth All-Russian Congress of Soviets approached, Sidney Reilly continued to travel back and forth between Petrograd and Moscow, where he met with opposition leaders.

In Petrograd he also saw Commander Ernest Boyce, the British Secret Intelligence Service chief in Russia, who was absorbed in operations against the Germans, and Captain Francis N. A. Cromie, British naval attaché, who remained at the Embassy after most of the staff had left. Cromie's primary task was to ensure that the Russian Baltic Fleet did not fall into the Germans' hands. Cromie, described by Lockhart as a "tall, dark Byronesque figure with heavy eyebrows and side-whiskers," was busy recruiting Russian naval personnel for the job of scuttling the warships. Nevertheless, Cromie did not hesitate to help Reilly in planning the uprising in Petrograd.

In Moscow, Reilly tried to limit the number of his meetings with Lockhart, who lived in the Hotel Elite.[5] Allegedly he wished to avoid compromising Lockhart, but infrequent meetings made it easier for him to keep the leader of the British mission in the dark about his doings. Yet a certain amount of contact with Lockhart was inescapable. Lockhart was supplying Reilly with the huge sums of rubles, which Reilly kept in his safe apartment at Sheremetyevsky Pereulok, in order to finance his operations.

On the eve of the Congress, *Pravda*, the official Communist party newspaper, published an article entitled "Deep into Russia?" that was carefully noted by Allied representatives in Moscow:

> When Balfour and Asquith asserted in the English parliament that the English imperialists fervently seek nothing more than the "development of patriotism and self-consciousness in the Russian people," they failed to say by what means they hoped to achieve this. Their agents in Russia and a whole array of facts reveal the answer to this puzzle.
>
> It turns out that the plan is very simple.
>
> In order to smash German imperialism, it is necessary to force it to penetrate still deeper into Russia. Then the victory desired by English and French imperialism will be easily achieved because Russian space and tracklessness will swallow up the German army.
>
> How can this plan be realized?
>
> The English landing at Murmansk and the Czechoslovaks in the east will compel the Germans to advance deeper into Russia. If, moreover, they succeed in the "development of patriotism" in Russia through contact with the Mensheviks and the Right SRs and overthrow Soviet rule, then the cause of the Anglo-French imperialists will have won, and the cause of German imperialism will have been defeated.

All of this is brilliantly simple. And judging from the facts, this simple but brilliant plan is already being executed with great energy.

We already know how French millions have united the counterrevolutionaries, Mensheviks, SRs, and Czechoslovaks, and they are trying by their mutual efforts to overthrow Soviet rule.

Now an English landing has taken place at Murmansk! This landing is supposed to overthrow Soviet rule and suck the Germans into the wastes of Olonets and Archangel at the same time that the Czechoslovaks lure them to the Urals.

That the Germans will be such fools as to fall for this venture and create for themselves a second front is highly questionable. . . .[6]

Eager for action, Reilly read this article with equanimity only because he knew that the uprisings by the Left SRs in Moscow and by Savinkov's organization (largely representing the Right SRs) in Yaroslavl and other cities were only days away. He also knew that the murder of Count Wilhelm von Mirbach, the German Ambassador, was to be the signal for the Left SR revolt. The Left SRs, who wanted a revolutionary war against the Germans, confidently expected that Germany would be provoked by the murder of her ambassador into renewing hostilities on the eastern front.

Chapter 5

ON THE FOURTH OF JULY, a hot, muggy day in Moscow, Sidney Reilly set out through streets drenched in bright sunshine in the direction of the Bolshoi Theater, where the Congress of Soviets was about to open. He did not bother looking for an *izvoshchik*, since the regulations laid down for the Congress banned automobiles and other conveyances after one P.M. from the streets around the theater. Moreover, the streetcar stop opposite the theater would not be in use during sessions of the Congress.

The few pedestrians Reilly met in those deserted streets resembled actors on a vast, empty stage. Despite the fine weather, a dead hand seemed to have descended on Moscow. Famine stalked those avenues, accentuated not only by crippled soldiers with pinched faces, squatting on the sidewalk while they tried to sell single cigarettes or sunflower seeds, but also by the signs on bakery doors, "No bread on sale today." The Bolsheviks had made a special effort to bring food into the city in the days preceding the Congress, hoping to create a favorable atmosphere. According to a secret report that had reached Reilly, Stalin, as "Director-General of Food Supplies for the South of Russia," had gone off to Tsaritsyn[1] to requisition foodstuffs. That action was sure to fuel the anger of the Left Social Revolutionaries, who had been driven to revolt partly by the Bolsheviks' penchant for squeezing the peasants. And yet, despite these efforts, the food situation in Moscow remained bad.

The area around the Bolshoi Theater was cordoned off by Red Army special troops under Cheka command, the Chon, who examined the tickets and other documents of delegates, visitors, and officials before letting them through. Reilly presented his papers to a soldier with a shaved head who studied them for long minutes, mouthing the words, struggling valiantly to read every word. With an impatient gesture and a scowl, the soldier finally waved Reilly through.

Facing the theater with its Corinthian columns, Reilly was surprised to see small numbers of Latvian sharpshooters, the toughest and best disciplined of Soviet troops, at all the doors. Again his passport and the ticket supplied by Lockhart secured admission to the building itself.

The interior of the Bolshoi Theater was unchanged, with ornate gilt everywhere and red velvet drapes suspended from row upon row of boxes on each side from floor to roof. The Imperial box had been assigned to correspondents of the official press. Lockhart, Lavergne, and the Italian general Romei together with other Allied representatives occupied a large box on the ground level. Above them were the representatives of the Central Powers—the German ambassador, Count von Mirbach, accompanied by his embassy counselor, Dr. Riezler, and surrounded by the Austrian, Bulgarian, and Turkish envoys.

Reilly stopped off in Lockhart's box to greet him and the other Allied representatives. Then he went to his seat in an adjoining box. Although he had no way of seeing the man in the box above him, he could not have been unconscious of the presence of Rudolf Bauer, chief of the German Intelligence Service in Russia, a man who sat like a statue, with a face chipped out of stone.

Mirbach and Bauer represented antipodes of German policy toward Russia. On the one hand, Germany found it expedient to establish diplomatic relations with Soviet Russia after the March

1918 signing of the Brest-Litovsk Treaty. For this they relied on the proper Mirbach, an average, pleasant man with no special qualifications for the post but who accepted it as his due in view of his noble lineage. On the other hand, the German government was using its intelligence operatives, led by Bauer, to support opposition groups against the Soviet regime. In contrast to the Allies, however, the Germans funneled their aid to Russian monarchist and extreme right-wing elements.

The delegates to the Congress had their places in the orchestra or parterre while their friends and supporters filled the remaining boxes and balcony seats to overflowing, those lacking seats perched on railings or sitting on the floor. Delegates belonging to opposing political factions could be distinguished by their dress: on the right the Bolsheviks, uniformed soldiers and sailors as well as workers in black blouses; on the left the Left Social Revolutionaries, rough men in peasant blouses, with long, untidy hair and beards, outnumbered two to one by the Bolsheviks. In the theater it was already hot, and the atmosphere became even more heated as the afternoon wore on. Under the bright lights the odor of unwashed bodies, overpowering in itself, combined with a cloud of blue cigarette smoke to oppress the more sensitive members of the audience. Watching the proceedings, Reilly turned to one of the Allied military officers seated next to him. "I remember the time I saw Chaliapin singing the role of Boris Godunov on this stage," he said with a smile.

But scenery, opera singers, ballet dancers were absent from this stage. In the front row on the stage sat the Presidium, with Sverdlov, the chairman, in the center; members of the Central Executive Committee filled the ranks behind the Presidium. These were the real leaders of the Soviet regime. Reilly spotted Lenin's bald head and caught sight of Trotsky, with his fiery eyes and bush of black hair. He also noticed the Left SR leaders, terrorists of the same stamp as Boris Savinkov, one of their former comrades. Foremost among them were the robust and jovial Boris D. Kamkov; Vladimir Aleksandrovich Karelin, an emaciated, spiritual figure; Yury Vladimirovich Sablin, a young man from an aristocratic family who had made a name for himself as the leader of a Red Guard detachment in battles with Lavr Georgievich Kornilov and Pyotr Nikolaievich Krasnov, and who had recently been making speeches in which he used the slogan "No war, but rebellion," calling for a

renewed, undeclared war against Germany; and Mariya Spiridonova, a heroine of the revolutionary movement who had been
sentenced to life imprisonment under the czarist regime for an
assassination. She had won widespread admiration for the fortitude
with which she had endured her punishment, made all the more
horrifying when, in the tradition of Russian prisons, she had been
raped repeatedly by her jailors.

Although the first session was to be limited on the whole to
procedural questions, Kamkov took the offensive before Sverdlov,
the Bolshevik chairman of the Presidium, could even formally open
the Congress. Kamkov sprang to the podium, pushing aside the
black-bearded Sverdlov, and demanded a vote on the admission of
Ukrainian peasants from German-occupied areas to full participation in the Congress.

During a lull in the proceedings Reilly wandered about the
lobby, keeping himself apart from the people who stood there in
small groups, engaged in vigorous discussion. One young woman
stood apart from the others, like himself, looking out at the empty
square in front of the theater. He saw a slender, well-formed
figure, a wistful expression, and friendly, lively brown eyes. Her
brown hair was tied in a single braid behind her shapely head. Now
looking around, she met his interested glance and saw a man whose
good looks impressed her at once. Those familiar with a later generation of actors would have been astonished by his uncanny physical resemblance to Humphrey Bogart. He had a dark, oval face and
a high, intellectual forehead; but the black probing eyes, the lines
that came down in arcs from each side of his sharp nose to the
corners of a thin mouth, and the expression on his lips all
hinted at certain socially equivocal qualities like sensuality and
ruthlessness.

Reilly smiled across the lobby at the woman, but she did not
return the smile. He crossed over to her with swift steps and said
something, but she replied with an averted gaze. He spoke again,
and this time the woman's face was transformed by a sweet smile.
He took her arm and led her to the buffet, where people were already sipping drinks.

Reilly ordered Georgian champagne. He handed a glass to the
woman, bowing slightly to her at the same time.

"Do you work for a Soviet institution?" she asked.

He noticed that she was looking at his finely tailored suit and bow tie. "Yes," he said, "Narkomindel."

Apparently his mention of the People's Commissariat for Foreign Affairs allayed her curiosity about his appearance, for she nodded.

"Where do *you* work?"

Her face grew a little pink. "I'm only a typist."

"*Only* a typist!" Reilly laughed. "I just have to look at you to know—what*ever* you are—that you're a very *special* person. Where do you work?"

"The Central Executive Committee. In the administrative section."

Reilly looked at her as if seeing her for the first time. "And you say you're *only* a typist! It must be quite an honor to work with such important personalities."

She shyly lowered her gaze. "I rarely see any of those important personalities."

"You're too modest," Reilly said. "Allow me to introduce myself. Rellinsky—Konstantin Georgievich."

She took Reilly's outstretched hand. "Starzhevskaya—Olga Dmitrievna."

"Well, Olga Dmitrievna, to your health!" Reilly said, raising his glass. "Or better still, to our friendship!"

On the second day of the Congress, the storm that had threatened on the first day broke with full fury. First Sverdlov spoke in defense of the Bolshevik position, but the atmosphere, already heavily charged, reached new heights of tension when Mariya Spiridonova rose to speak. She was a small woman clad in a black dress with a gray apron. Her face deathly pale, her black hair brushed straight back, a pince-nez on her nose, she fiercely challenged the Bolsheviks, daring to attack Lenin himself. Her anger made her voice quaver, but she emphasized every word with chopping motions of her right hand as she talked about the Bolsheviks' forced requisitioning of grain in the villages by armed detachments that seized everything and left the peasants to starve.

Reilly leaned over to speak to his neighbor. "She reminds me of Olga, the schoolteacher, in *Three Sisters*."

His neighbor nodded but did not take the time to reply. At this moment Spiridonova turned and looked directly with angry eyes at Lenin, but he ignored her, calmly continuing to take notes while she was speaking. Accusing Lenin of betraying the peasants and using them for his own opportunistic purposes, she said to her peasant followers in the audience:

"In Lenin's philosophy, you are only dung—only manure. When the peasants, the Bolshevik peasants, the Left SR peasants, and the nonparty peasants are alike humiliated, oppressed, and crushed—crushed as peasants—in my hand you will find the same pistol, the same bomb which once forced me to defend . . ."

A Bolshevik delegate shouted an obscene name at her as general pandemonium broke out. The Left SR delegates were standing up, shaking their fists and screaming; the Bolshevik delegates responded with angry cries and insults. Trotsky, his face contorted with rage, rushed to the podium and tried to speak, but he was shouted down. Sverdlov, the chairman, rang his bell for order in vain and finally threatened to have the theater cleared.

Then Lenin strolled toward the podium, patting Sverdlov on the shoulder in a friendly manner and telling him to put away his bell. He stood in front of the audience, holding the lapels of his coat, and began to speak calmly and objectively, in the manner of a professor delivering a lecture to students.

Shaking his head, Lenin rejected the accusations of the Left SRs. "To want to tear up the Brest-Litovsk Treaty is to put the peasants' neck into the big landlords' noose," he said. "It is essential to gain time. The Republic is getting stronger, the rival imperialisms are at their last gasp. Civil war is necessary to socialism, but the parties must base themselves not on the standpoint of the starving individual, but on that of socialism. The Left SRs are setting the peasantry against us: merciless war upon those socialists who desert us while some people are cornering all the grain and others are dying of hunger! We shall not shrink from any struggle whatever. . . ."

As soon as Lenin had finished, Kamkov seized the opportunity to reply. Abandoning his usual joviality, he spoke to the delegates in harsh, biting language: "What is happening on the southern border is not the work of provocateurs. It is the work of Russian revolutionary peasants who see their comrades in the Ukraine murdered before their eyes while you commissars calmly sit there and declare that you are restrained by treaties. This is an unmistakable sign of the revolutionary indignation of Russian workers and peasants."

Kamkov walked to and fro on the stage, finally coming to a stop directly opposite the box occupied by Mirbach and the other ambassadors of the Central Powers. He pointed a finger at Mirbach, at the same time sweeping the multitude of delegates with his angry glance. "The dictatorship of the proletariat has developed into a dictatorship of Mirbach. In spite of all our warnings the policy of Lenin remains the same, and we have become, not an independent power, but the lackeys of the German imperialists, who have the audacity to show their faces even in this theater."

Kamkov was obviously whipping himself into a rage. "Do you believe," he cried, "that our peasants in uniform on the southern border will idly stand by and allow their brothers to be executed before their eyes by these barbarians?"

The Left SR delegates leaped to their feet, screaming defiance and shaking their fists at the German ambassador. There were cries of "Down with Mirbach! Away with the German butchers! Away with the hangman's noose of Brest!" Reilly noticed that de Vertemont in the next box had also jumped to his feet and was loudly applauding. Sverdlov hastily rang his bell and declared the session closed as the excited delegates continued to shout and then, reluctantly, began to move toward the exits.

Saturday, July 6, was glorious, the kind of day in Moscow's short summer when the city's inhabitants headed for the country to spend their time among white birches and shaded streams, hunting for mushrooms in the cool woods to allay their hunger. The next session of the Congress was also scheduled to take place, but Sidney Reilly had other plans during the early part of the day, anticipating the Left SR uprising that would soon begin.

First of all, Reilly went to de Vertemont's apartment at Milyutinsky Pereulok Number 18, where the French had set up a command post. Here messengers were constantly coming and going. Then an excited courier arrived with news that caused the grim faces of the French officers to relax into smiles. Reilly and de Vertemont exchanged fervid congratulations. For the unpredictable and volatile Left SRs, adhering to their plan for an uprising, had struck the first blow against the hated German enemy.

At an earlier point the Left Social Revolutionary party's Central Committee had decided to withdraw its representatives from all branches of the Soviet government. There was, however, one important exception: the Left SR members retained their posts in the Cheka. Contemplating even then an attempt to topple the Bolsheviks, the Left SRs believed that they could neutralilze countermeasures of the secret police and, at the same time, use the Cheka as a springboard to power. Thus the Cheka became a key element in the Left SR plot against the Soviet regime.

Shortly before 3 P.M. on that Saturday afternoon, two Left SRs who were officers of the Cheka drove to the German Embassy situated on a quiet side street in the Arbat district of Moscow. One of the most elegant residences in the city, the house was known to most Muscovites as the Berg palace, recalling the sugar magnate who had been its original owner. After the signing of the Brest-Litovsk Treaty, the Soviet government turned over the Berg palace to Germany for use as an embassy.

The two Russians rang the bell and identified themselves as representatives of the Cheka to the servant in livery who opened the door. The servant admitted them into the front hall and summoned a German member of the staff. One of the Russians, who carried a briefcase, took out a letter of authorization and showed it to the German official. The letter stated:

> The All-Russian Extraordinary Commission authorizes its member Yakov Blyumkin and representative of the Revolutionary Tribunal Nikolai Andreyev to enter into negotiations with His Excellency the German Ambassador to the Russian Republic concerning a matter having a direct relationship to the Ambassador. Chairman of the All-Russian Extraordinary Commission: F. Dzerzhinski. Secretary: I. Xenophontov.[2]

"This is a matter of the greatest importance," said Blyumkin, the man with the briefcase. "We must speak to the Ambassador personally."

After a short interval the two men were conducted through an anteroom hung with Gobelin tapestries, across a spacious ballroom that had two imposing crystal chandeliers suspended from a painted ceiling, into a lovely drawing room. It was a room that might have been found in an eighteenth-century palace of some German court. The walls were covered with crimson silk, heavy gold brocade drapes framed the front windows, and a thick Oriental rug muffled the men's footsteps as they entered the room. The only things missing were ornate framed paintings by Dutch and Italian masters.

Dr. Riezler, counselor of the embassy, and the ambassador's military aide, Lieutenant Mueller—a "tree-long" man, in the German phrase, towering over six feet—received the Cheka emissaries. Dr. Riezler, dignified and self-important, was still showing signs of irritation due to the insulting treatment of German diplomats attending the Congress. "The Ambassador is still at lunch," Riezler said. "Can I be of assistance to you?"

Blyumkin shook his head.

Riezler frowned. "He is bidding farewell to his guests. It should only be a few minutes. Please take a seat."

Riezler pointed toward a heavy marble table with elaborate brass ornamentation that stood near one wall in front of a sofa. Blyumkin occupied a chair opposite the sofa with his back to the windows. His associate, Andreyev, unexpectedly pulled out a chair beside folding doors leading into the ballroom and sat down. Since only one chair remained at the end of the table for the ambassador himself, Riezler and Mueller had no alternative but to sit on the sofa, sinking down into deep cushions, partly blinded by the glare of the sun slanting through the windows directly opposite them.

Blyumkin did not speak, and the Germans made no effort to engage in small talk with the two strangers from the Cheka.

Then Count Mirbach entered the room with a firm step, obviously curious to see these representatives of the dreaded Cheka. He shook hands with Blyumkin, nodded to Andreyev, and sat down in the vacant chair at the end of the table.

Once again Blyumkin produced his letter of authorization. The ambassador barely glanced at it before he returned it.

Blyumkin's cold expression never changed, even when he shook hands with the ambassador. "Mr. Ambassador," he said, "you will be interested to learn that a German officer, a certain Count Mirbach, is in one of our prisoner-of-war camps. He appears to be a relative of yours."

Mirbach nodded. "That's entirely possible. The Count Mirbach to whom you refer belongs to a distant—Protestant—branch of my family. My immediate family is Catholic."

"If it is your wish, my government is prepared to repatriate your relative at an early date."

"Nothing would please me more," the ambassador replied. He

waited a moment and then went on: "I appreciate your kindness in raising this family matter with me. Can I be of service to you in any other way?"

Blyumkin stared at Count Mirbach for a few seconds. Then he nodded, starting to open his briefcase. "There is another matter of a much more serious nature. The Extraordinary Commission has recently received information concerning a terrorist plot against your life. I have here some papers to show you . . ."

Blyumkin reached into the briefcase as if to draw out the papers, but when he withdrew his hand he was holding a Browning automatic. Without another word, he stood up, dumping the briefcase on the floor, and pointed the gun at the ambassador. He fired quickly and, as the two Germans on the sofa gave involuntary shouts of alarm, turned and fired two more shots at them.

To everyone's surprise, all three shots missed.

Dr. Riezler, stunned, still sat in the same position on the sofa while the huge Mueller, like a great fish just landed from the water, floundered to reach an upright position. The ambassador, however, reacted more swiftly. He jumped up and made a wild dash for safety. He lurched through the folding doors and ran across the ballroom toward the back of the house.

Up to this point the other Chekist, Andreyev, had remained only an observer. As Count Mirbach ran, Andreyev stood up, pulling a small gun out of his pocket. He aimed carefully and fired a single shot at the fleeing ambassador.

Count Mirbach reacted as if he had been struck on the back of his head by a gigantic fist. The shot from Andreyev's pistol had gone through the back of his head and come out at his nose. He collapsed on the hardwood floor at a spot over which thousands of couples had danced in the course of the years. Lying there in a pool of blood, he died almost immediately.

The two assassins now set about making their escape. Each hurled a grenade into the ballroom to add to the confusion and fear of the moment while hindering pursuit. The subsequent explosions shattered the stately chandeliers. Threatening Dr. Riezler and Lieutenant Mueller with their guns, the Chekists opened a front window and, one after the other, jumped out.

Andreyev landed safely on the ground, but Blyumkin fell heavily and clumsily, breaking his leg. Andreyev helped him to climb over the iron fence and dragged him to the waiting car. The car roared away and disappeared before the embassy's shocked staff could make any attempt to intervene.

Blyumkin and Andreyev drove to the Pokrovsky Barracks, where the Left SR leaders had set up their headquarters. It was here, too, that a detachment of Chon troops, commanded by Aleksei Popov, a Left SR, had concentrated its strength. To the Popov detachment came small groups of Left SRs assembled from as far away as Petrograd as well as anarchists and Black Sea Fleet sailors. Reilly had left de Vertemont's apartment and also made his way to the Pokrovsky Barracks. He estimated the total strength of the mutineers at close to two thousand riflemen and one hundred cavalrymen. They had at their disposal forty-eight machine guns, eight field guns, and three armored cars.

By late afternoon Popov had set up defensive positions— trenches and machine gun posts—on the approaches to the barracks from the directions of the Pokrovsky Gates, Chistye Prudy, and Yauzky Boulevard. In the early evening the principal nucleus of the Left SR forces under Popov took the offensive at several points in the city. They captured the Lubianka, headquarters of the Cheka, and the main post office, from which they sent telegrams all over the country announcing that thenceforth the Social Revolutionary party was to be the only governing party.

Meanwhile, Dzerzhinski had gone to the Pokrovsky Barracks, allegedly to confront the rebels in person, and was being held as a hostage. Another high-ranking official of the Cheka, Martyn Latsis, was arrested when the Left SRs captured the Lubianka.

Reilly took the time to visit one of the trenches manned by Black Sea sailors. He asked them if they had seen any sign of the enemy, and one of them pointed to a building in the distance in which, he said, there were Bolshevik snipers. Reilly borrowed the sailor's rifle and fired a couple of shots at the building, although he could see no one. When he left, he sensed an uneasiness among the sailors and wondered if they were up to any real fighting.

At the Left SR headquarters Reilly caught a glimpse of Dzerzhinski, sitting by himself in dignified silence with several sailors lounging nearby, guarding him. Encountering Kamkov a short time later, Reilly said: "What are you going to do with Feliks Edmundovich?"

"Do? What should I do?"

"Well, I wouldn't shoot him. You may need to exchange him."

Kamkov looked strangely at Reilly, mumbled something, and hurried off.

Despite the Left SRs' early successes, it soon became clear to Reilly that the revolt had sputtered to a halt. The main objective as projected in plans for the revolt had been the capture of the Bolshoi Theater with the whole Bolshevik leadership. But the Popov detachment had made only a weak attempt at advancing toward the theater and then retired when they discovered that the Bolsheviks had strongly reinforced the Latvian sharpshooters with elements of the Red Army, a Hungarian "international" brigade, and the rest of Vatsetis's Latvian division. Reilly quickly realized that the failure to capture the Bolshoi Theater doomed the whole operation.

He made his way by back streets to the theater and was admitted without difficulty on the strength of his ticket, although he became aware from remarks made by the Latvian guards that the theater was about to be surrounded.

Lockhart was sitting in his box with his assistant, Captain Will Hicks, and greeted Reilly with surprise. "I didn't expect to see you here."

"Have they made any announcement yet?"

"No. What has happened?"

"I'll tell you in a minute," Reilly said, surveying the stage. "Aren't any of the Bolshevik leaders here?"

Lockhart shook his head. "They haven't been here all day."

The speaker at the podium was a blond sailor, probably one of those heroes of the Baltic Fleet already immortalized by Soviet propaganda. He did his best in a halting way to expound the Bolshevik line, although no one bothered to listen.

"Comrades!" the sailor cried. "We are faced with a hard summer. The armed ring of fronts is moving toward us from all sides. Murmansk in the north, the Czechoslovak front in the east, Turkestan, Baku, and Astrakhan in the south. Not to mention the invisible front here in Moscow, in Petrograd, in other cities under Soviet rule. Plots, rebellions, espionage, diversions. The political strike called by the Mensheviks and the Right SRs has just ended in abysmal failure. Now it is the turn of the Left SRs to fish in troubled waters. . . ."

The audience suddenly came to life, and the peasants, hearing the mention of the Left SRs, drowned out the speaker with jeers and catcalls. Refusing to give in, the sailor kept on speaking.

Just then de Vertemont appeared in Lockhart's box and rapidly exchanged a few words with Reilly.

"What has happened?" Lockhart asked again.

Lockhart later related:

> At six o'clock Sidney Reilly came into our box with the news that the theater was surrounded by troops and that all exits were barred. He had only the vaguest idea of what had occurred. He knew, however, that there had been fighting in the streets. Something had gone wrong. . . . Fearful that the Bolsheviks might search them before they were allowed to leave the theater, Reilly and a French agent began to examine their pockets for compromising documents. Some they tore up into tiny pieces and shoved down the lining of the sofa cushions. Others, doubtless more dangerous, they swallowed. The situation was too tense for us to appreciate its comic side, and, deciding that in this case inaction was the best policy, we sat down to await the dénouement with as brave a show of patience as we could assume.[3]

An hour later Karl Radek, a Bolshevik leader, showed up and gave the Allied representatives an account of the day's events. At about 8 P.M. the Bolshevik commandant of the Fifth All-Russian Congress of Soviets, a man named Strizhak, announced that no one would be permitted to leave the theater until further notice. Around midnight the commandant reappeared and said that foreign representatives, journalists, and the Bolshevik delegates would be allowed to leave after their documents had been checked.

As an official announcement stated the next day, "all delegates of the party of Left SRs at the Fifth Congress in the Bolshoi Theater were detained as hostages by the Soviet authorities."

Reilly was up early on the following day, Sunday, July 7, and ventured forth to see for himself what was going on. *Izvestiya* had appeared but consisted of only a single page. It contained a proclamation by the Soviet of People's Commissars calling on the population to remain calm and support the All-Russian Congress. The Left SRs were called political infants who had to be curbed before it was too late; the alternative would be a formal war with Germany for which Russia was not militarily prepared.

Reilly heard some firing in the distance. He later learned that the Left SRs had opened up their battery of field guns and lobbed shells into the Kremlin from their position in the Trekhsvyatitel'sky Pereulok. There were some hits on the Maly Dvorets, or Small Palace, although the Soviet authorities claimed that the palace suffered only minor damage.

About 11 A.M., however, the houses began to shake from a tremendous barrage of guns belonging to a Latvian light artillery battalion[4] that had moved into position during the night. As Reilly found out later, the Latvians had taken direct aim on the Left SR headquarters at the Pokrovsky Barracks. The guns blasted holes in the barracks buildings, sending the SRs into a panicky flight past the Kursk railroad station and the Taganka.

Trying to cross Moscow's main business street, the Tverskaya,[5] Reilly found his way was blocked by artillery and infantry units loyal to the Bolsheviks. He made a long detour to the main post office, which had already been recaptured by a brigade of former Hungarian POWs commanded by the communist Béla Kun.[6]

By midday the revolt had been crushed. Three hundred of the SRs had been captured. A number of SR leaders were summarily shot, including twenty of the hostages from the Bolshoi Theater. Mariya Spiridonova became a prisoner in the Kremlin.

A less optimistic man than Sidney Reilly would have been depressed and discouraged. But Reilly was already making new plans. With Lockhart he analyzed the reasons for the failure of the Left SR revolt and drew from this failure certain lessons which he intended to apply in the future.

In any case, all was not lost, for Boris Savinkov had captured Yaroslavl and continued to hold the city as he waited for the Allied landing at Archangel.

Chapter 6

FOR SEVERAL DAYS after the failure of the Left SRs' attempted coup d'etat, Moscow remained virtually in a state of siege. There was increased patrolling of the streets, and travel into and out of the city came to a temporary halt. Meanwhile the Bolsheviks trumpeted their victory by all conceivable means: meetings, speeches, banners hanging from public buildings, posters plastered on every available inch of wall space.

Sidney Reilly was careful in his comings and goings during this period. He saw de Vertemont a few times and they exchanged information on the Yaroslavl uprising. By Tuesday, July 9, they had received a message from Boris Savinkov pleading for Allied assistance to the insurgents. Reilly urged de Vertemont to provide more money, as he was doing, to Savinkov. De Vertemont finally acceded, although he pointed out that only additional arms and men, which could not be purchased on short notice, would be of any help to Savinkov.

Reilly was ignorant of the fact, but the Allied ambassadors at

Vologda were already urging that the Archangel landing be expedited. Mirbach's murder had sent a shiver of fear down their backs, reminding them of the personal hazard to themselves. The Germans might be provoked to advance to Moscow, increasing the likelihood that the disorder in Yaroslavl, between Moscow and Vologda, would soon reach Vologda. Only the early arrival of Allied forces seemed to hold out hope of adequate security.

On July 7, the same night that Left SR resistance collapsed in Moscow, Ambassador Francis sent off a cable urging Washington to advance the date of the Archangel landing. The cable never arrived. Shortly thereafter, however, the four principal Allied envoys in Vologda agreed on a joint message to Admiral Thomas W. Kemp, the British naval commander at Murmansk, in which they stressed the vital necessity of an early landing at Archangel.

Nevertheless, all these appeals reflected the same misconception. They assumed that the Allies had really decided on a broadly based intervention in the North which involved a rapid advance toward the center of Russia. It was true that such an idea had been seriously contemplated by the British, who desired an Allied expansion from beachheads at Murmansk and Archangel to link up with Czechoslovak forces advancing west along the northern branch of the Trans-Siberian Railway, with the possibility of an eventual drive on Moscow. But their idea was remote from the understanding or intention of President Wilson. He was not prepared to have the Americans "take part in organized intervention in adequate force from . . . Murmansk and Archangel."[1] And the remaining Allies were not prepared to carry out a full-scale intervention without American participation.

Thus the Supreme War Council of the Allies had approved a plan early in June to send forces to Murmansk and Archangel for the purpose of guarding supply depots. It was a plan to which Woodrow Wilson reluctantly acceded, against his own and his military advisers' better judgment, only for the sake of maintaining Allied unity. Possibly Wilson gave his agreement in the belief that the four to six battalions of American, British, and French troops envisaged for this task could hardly be employed in any larger intervention. Yet he may have miscalculated, since there is evidence that the British, who had no intention of abandoning their plan, regarded this as only the opening wedge.

Reilly knew from both Boyce and Cromie that there were

British agents in Archangel engaged in preparing an anti-Bolshevik uprising timed to coincide with the Allied landing. He had no precise information about the projected date of the landing, but there appeared to be a good possibility that it would come soon enough to help Savinkov.

Be that as it may, the first troops to reach Murmansk in accordance with the Supreme War Council's decision did not arrive until July 26, and they consisted of only a few hundred French soldiers. In the circumstances, it was utterly unrealistic to advance the date of the Archangel landing, and the Allied leaders in Murmansk who were responsible for the landing rightly ignored all such suggestions.

For two weeks—from July 6 to July 20—the issue at Yaroslavl hung in the balance. The fighting was bitter, executions took place daily on both sides, and the battle proved in a sense to be a forerunner of the bloody civil war in which the Reds and the Whites gave no quarter. The expected Allied landing at Archangel still did not occur (and would not occur for another two weeks). In the end Savinkov and his men could not withstand heavy Red Army reinforcements. Savinkov himself was able to flee, but some four hundred of his followers suffered execution at the hands of the vengeful Bolsheviks.

In the middle of July, at about the same time that the Red Army succeeded in suppressing the revolt at Yaroslavl, the Bolsheviks cold-bloodedly executed Czar Nicholas II and his family. These executions were an indirect result of the formal request by General Sir F. Cuthbert Poole, British commander of the Allied forces in northern Russia, to the Czechoslovak command for a westward advance aimed at a junction with Allied forces, which he hoped would soon be advancing from Archangel. When the Czechoslovak forces threatened to capture Ekaterinburg,[2] where the czar and his family were imprisoned, the Bolsheviks feared that they would be liberated and therefore carried out the execution without delay.

Sidney Reilly showed no sign of losing heart because of these events. Indeed, he could calculate that the murder of the czarist family might spur the monarchists to seek revenge. General Nikolai Yudenich, whom he had once considered as an interim minister of war or commander-in-chief, was now at the head of a monarchist organization supported by the Germans. In spite of that, the monarchists could still be useful for diversionary purposes. In the meantime Reilly continued to possess most of his operational assets, having committed little more than money to the Left SRs and Boris Savinkov. During these days he devoted much attention to his agent network, weeding out agents who might have been compromised by the recent setbacks.

Although firm evidence does not exist, it appears certain that Reilly at this time developed a burning interest in the Latvian sharpshooters, whom George F. Kennan characterized as the "most radical, the most devoted politically to the Bolsheviki, and the most trigger-happy of all the armed forces in the area."[3] The division of these Latvian sharpshooters commanded by Ioakim Ioakimovich Vatsetis constituted in fact the praetorian guard of the Bolshevik leadership.

No less an authority than the Cheka's Jacob Peters, himself a Latvian, wrote the following about them:

> In the first moment of the revolution the Lettish rifle regiments were almost the only units of the old army which remained whole and did not disintegrate. This is explained by a number of factors but, to my mind, mainly by the fact that the Lettish rifle regiments had no place to go (Latvia was occupied by the Germans) while at that time Russian units headed home to the countryside. Whatever the case, these military units represented a combat-ready force, and this force seriously interested Lockhart, interested him for the sake of bringing about its disintegration.[4]

Peters neglected to explain a far more cogent reason for the Latvians' support of the Bolsheviks. It is true, of course, that the Latvians could not go home at the time. Many of their commanders had spent their whole careers in the czarist army and remained loyal to the old regime. After the revolution, however, the Latvian troops mutinied against these commanders and replaced them with other men who shared their attachment to Bolshevism. The attachment stemmed from the fact that the Bolsheviks—alone among all the Russian revolutionary organizations—held out the promise of breaking up the Russian empire and allowing national self-determination, which would have given Latvia her independence. The true attitude of the Bolsheviks and their successors has been demonstrated by subsequent developments: Under the Versailles peace settlement imposed by the Western Allies, Latvia and the other Baltic states became independent; on the eve of World War II the Soviet Union seized Latvia and neighboring states, incorporating them into her territory; after World War II, when the Germans were driven out, the Soviet Union once again seized Latvia. The qualitative difference between incorporation into the *Soviet* as opposed to the *Russian* empire does not appear to be very great.

Reilly must have discussed his ideas about the Latvian sharpshooters with Lockhart as well as Boyce and Cromie. He apparently let it be known through his agents that he was looking for a Latvian—not just any Latvian, but a Latvian who had good connections with the Lettish rifle regiments.

While Reilly was following this new strategy, Kalamatiano had problems of his own. Since the beginning of July the Consulate General in Moscow had been unable to send or receive any messages. The telegraph relay point was located at Murmansk; when the Allies assumed control there, the Consulate General's communications were severed. As a result, Kalamatiano could not send off his secret reports. As the translated and enciphered reports accumulated, he began to investigate the possibility of organizing a courier system for the purpose of conveying the reports to some place such as Murmansk, from which they could be forwarded to their destination in Washington.

The general situation in Moscow continued to deteriorate. Rumors circulated that the Allied landing at Archangel was about to take place. Despite the crushing of the Left SR revolt, the Soviet authorities showed their nervousness by stationing armored cars at a number of key points close to the Kremlin. And Soviet threats directed at the Allied representatives became constantly louder and uglier.

The Soviet government was also putting increased pressure on the Allied ambassadors at Vologda to move to Moscow. The ambassadors firmly resisted, since they had no intention of allowing themselves to become hostages of the Bolsheviks. Matters seemed to be coming to a head, however, when the Soviet of People's Commissars dispatched Karl Radek to Vologda.

Radek, a brilliant intellectual who spoke Russian, German, and Polish with equal fluency, was also notable for his nasty and abrasive manner, although he had a puckish sense of humor that somewhat diminished his disagreeable side. He was a remarkably ugly man with a monkeylike fringe of beard.

In Vologda the disagreeable aspects of Radek came to the fore. He had been sent there to cajole, wheedle, and intimidate in an effort to get the ambassadors to move to Moscow, but finally, with a huge pistol strapped to his hip, he resorted to threats. When all of this failed, Radek returned to Moscow. His visit, however, had had one effect: The ambassadors knew that they could not remain in Vologda much longer.

On July 25 the Allied ambassadors, including U.S. Ambassador Francis, entrained for Archangel. They left Soviet territory three days later to cross the White Sea, where they found safety with the Allied command at Murmansk. At about the same time the chief Allied representatives in Moscow requested permission from the Soviet government for the departure of all Allied military personnel by way of Archangel. This permission was refused, and they learned shortly afterward that all the Allied personnel were considered hostages.

A speech by Lenin on July 29 sounded like a declaration of war on the Allies. "The uprising of the kulaks, the Czechoslovak mutiny, the Murmansk movement," said Lenin, "this is all one war, descending upon Russia. . . . We have again gotten into war, we *are* at war, and this war is not only a civil war—it is now Anglo-French imperialism which opposes us."[5]

Unlike Kalamatiano, who was worried about the fate of his agents, Reilly went about his business as if nothing had changed. And it was about this time that he received an exciting piece of news, which came in the form of a summons from Cromie to come to Petrograd at once. Suspecting that the urgent summons concerned the Latvian agent he had been seeking, he set out eagerly on his journey.

Reilly loved St. Petersburg as much as he loathed Moscow (in contrast to Lockhart, who felt just the opposite). It would always be St. Petersburg to him, he said, for he found Petrograd, its new name, absolutely ugly. But St. Petersburg, at least in his memory, remained a city of grand architecture, of sweeping prospects, of soul-stirring music and art and literature, and of enchanting women. A city situated on the Neva, the most beautiful river of all —broad and smooth, like a sheet of shimmering liquid gold under the sun. He did not see the great emptiness left by the departure of half a million people fleeing starvation, or the grass growing through the pavement, or the furtiveness of the life that was still there.

Arriving in Petrograd, Reilly immediately went to the British Embassy, where he found Cromie, the naval attaché, and was delighted to learn that he had guessed correctly. Cromie's Russian contacts had introduced him to *two* Latvians, both former officers in the Lettish rifle regiments. Although they had left their regiments because of hostility to Bolshevism, they still kept in touch with many of their military comrades on a personal basis.

Cromie had set up a meeting with the Latvians that evening in the Hotel Frantsuzkaya, where he had taken a room for that purpose. When Cromie and Reilly reached the hotel, they discovered that several of their Russian friends were with the Latvians. Reilly, who acted as host, offered the others some cognac, but after a little sociability he succeeded in dismissing the Russians. He and Cromie were left alone with the two young Latvians, whose names were Sprogis and Shmidkhen.

It soon became obvious that Shmidkhen was by far the more intelligent and communicative of the two men. A short, pale man in his twenties, he made a favorable impression, speaking in a husky voice that throbbed with conviction. He was not opposed to the revolution, he said. On the contrary, he welcomed it because he wanted freedom for his people.

"Some more brandy?" Reilly asked. When Shmidkhen shook his head, Reilly filled the other three glasses. He looked down at his glass, speaking with deliberation. "Mr. Shmidkhen, why do the Lettish regiments support the Bolsheviks?"

Sprogis stirred in his chair but did not speak, watching his companion. "My old comrades have been misled," Shmidkhen replied. "They believe all the Bolshevik claims about a new and better world. They are idealists. In particular, they think that only the Bolsheviks will allow our country to be free."

"How do you feel about the Allies?" Cromie said.

"Now that the old regime is gone and Russia is no longer in the war, I think that the Allies will support Latvian independence. I'm judging, for example, by Mr. Wilson's Fourteen Points. Our enemies are Germany and Russia. Neither of them wants us to be free. And for us the choice between Russian and German domination is no choice at all."

Cromie nodded. "Since the Allies will win the war, you don't have to worry about Germany."

"No, and I don't trust the Bolsheviks, who, after all, are mostly Russians," Shmidkhen said. "Therefore we anti-Bolshevik Latvians are on the side of the Allies. They are our only hope."

"How do you think the *pro*-Bolshevik Latvians regard the Allies?" Reilly asked.

"They will also refuse to fight against the Allies."

"Does that mean they would be neutral if it should come to war between the Bolsheviks and the Allies?"

"No, no. They would go over to the side of the Allies."

Under persistent questioning by Reilly, Shmidkhen admitted that he had good contacts among the officers serving in Lettish regiments that supported the Soviet regime, but he seemed reluctant to accept any task involving his former comrades. Reilly managed to elicit from him the opinion that some officers might be induced to come over to the Allied side by political arguments, but other officers, realistically or selfishly looking out for their own interests, would demand tangible material benefits.

"Bribes?" Reilly asked.

"Money," Shmidkhen answered.

After due deliberation, Cromie and Reilly came to the conclusion that nothing further could be done without Lockhart's active assistance. Lockhart alone had the authority to raise the large sums of money needed for the bribery of the Latvian officers. Reilly persuaded Shmidkhen, who was on his way to Moscow, to deliver a letter from Cromie to Lockhart. He also hinted to Shmidkhen that his services could be extremely valuable to the Allies.

The night before Shmidkhen and Sprogis left for Moscow, Reilly called at their room in the Hotel Select. "Will there be any difficulty in handing over the letter to Lockhart? Do you need my assistance?" Reilly asked politely. It was no secret to anyone that Reilly was checking up on the Latvians.

Shmidkhen repeated his promise to bring the letter to Lockhart without delay.

"Thank you," Reilly said in farewell. "I'm sure we'll be seeing one another again in Moscow."

Chapter 7

T. S. ELIOT WROTE THAT "April is the cruelest month," but August must surely have a claim to the same infamous distinction, for two world wars have started in that month. And August 1918 in Moscow brought its own share of cruelty.

While Sidney Reilly was going about his business in Petrograd, there was a growing sense of nervousness on all sides about a future that seemed more than ever unpredictable. There was also growing fear among Allied representatives responsible for the safety of their nationals due to the equivocation of the Soviet authorities, themselves apparently divided on the matter. While the Commissariat for Foreign Affairs was in favor of letting the Allied nationals depart, the Cheka strongly felt that they should be held as hostages.

The Cheka's attitude was best expressed by Jacob Peters, who had exchanged his conservative suit for a leather jacket and khaki trousers and a Mauser strapped to his waist.

"We have no intention of shooting these foreign agents of imperialism if they don't force us to do so," Peters said. "No, we shall be kind to them. We shall keep them in jail and exchange them for our comrades who are rotting in capitalist jails."[1]

Thus Peters was one of the first Soviet officials to enunciate a principle that, to this day, governs the USSR's approach to the problem of Soviet spies who get caught and receive prison sentences abroad. In this way a Wynne is exchanged for a Lonsdale and a Powers for an Abel. Nevertheless, present-day Soviet leaders have added one refinement to Peters's formula. If no Western spy happens to be on hand in a Soviet prison, a spy can be "manufactured"—a prison sentence for alleged espionage can be given to some innocent traveler within the confines of the USSR who trespasses against a Soviet law of which he is unaware or who may be arrested on completely false charges.

In the light of Ambassador Francis's departure and the expected landing at Archangel which, unknown to DeWitt Poole, was finally taking place, the consul general invited all Americans residing in Moscow to a meeting. Nearly one hundred people assembled on Saturday, August 3, in a conference room on the second floor of the Consulate General. They included officials, military officers, employees of the National City Bank, representatives of the American Red Cross, and a sprinkling of permanent residents in private business or with other personal reasons for their presence in Moscow. Kalamatiano was among those present. Since chairs were in short supply, people stood two and three deep around the sides of the room, and even with all the windows wide open the atmosphere in the room became almost suffocating.

Poole sat at the end of a long table, holding a pencil in one hand. His thin face with its long, angled nose bore the half-smile to which Kalamatiano was accustomed, but red spots in his cheeks and on his forehead pointed to repressed excitement. He tapped with the pencil on the table, and the babble of voices within the room ceased immediately. Straightening his tie within the detachable starched linen collar of his shirt, he hesitantly began to speak.

"I have requested you all to come here today because of a crisis in our relations with the Soviet government." Poole paused and glanced around the room as if half expecting some interruption, but no one spoke. "As you may have heard, the Allied ambassadors, including Ambassador Francis, have already left

Soviet territory. It appears that an Allied military force will land at Archangel in the next few days. I have no way of knowing whether that force will contain any American soldiers"—there was a buzz in the audience and Poole waved his hand for silence—"but we are certain to be blamed by the Soviet government whether or not we're directly involved in a military intervention by our allies. The Soviet spokesmen are sure to point out that an intervention could not have occurred without the explicit or tacit approval of our government."

A heavyset bald man who was unknown to Kalamatiano suddenly spoke up in a harsh voice: "Mr. Poole, I find it hard to believe that the U.S. government has not informed you of its plans."

Poole's half-smile became a little broader. "I wish it were so, Mr. Dodge. The fact is that I have been out of touch with Washington during the past few weeks." As Dodge started to speak again, Poole held up his hand. "And the other foreign missions here are no better off. Our telegraphic channels have been cut."

"What about radio communications?" the bald man persisted.

Poole ignored him and continued: "I have brought you together to urge you all to prepare for early departure from Russia."

"Is that an order?" someone behind Kalamatiano shouted.

Poole left a long silence. "I'm afraid we aren't going to have any choice."

The meeting broke up after some aimless discussion that brought forth antagonistic views from other participants and ended with Poole's statement that he would be in contact with the Soviet authorities concerning plans for the evacuation of American citizens. He would inform all those present as soon as the details had been worked out.

The next day there was intense excitement all over Moscow as the news spread that the Allies had landed in Archangel. It turned out that all this excitement was based on only the vaguest information. Everyone was talking about the landing, even those people, mostly women, some with babies in their arms, who were standing in queues outside stores that had virtually no food to sell. All kinds of rumors were circulating about the size of the Allied force and its objectives. A few knowing souls insisted that the allies had already begun a lightning advance toward Moscow.

Kalamatiano was greatly encouraged by all this talk. The Soviet officials with whom he came in contact seemed frightened and dispirited. Lockhart reported: "Even the Bolsheviks lost their heads and, in despair, began to pack their archives. In the middle of this crisis I saw Karakhan. He spoke of the Bolsheviks as lost. They would, however, never surrender. They would go underground and continue the struggle to the last."[2]

If there was any doubt about how the Soviet government would react to the Allied landing, Kalamatiano and the others did not have long to wait for the Bolsheviks' countermeasures. In the early hours of Monday morning, August 5, the Cheka rounded up about two hundred British and French nationals and confined them in a building on Smolensky Boulevard. The Chekists also raided the British and French consulates as well as the French Military Mission's quarters. British consular officials succeeded in burning their confidential papers before they were arrested.

These actions convinced Consul General Poole that a similar fate awaited the Americans. On that Tuesday he called the consulate's American personnel together. Although the French and British consular officers had been released the same day, he informed his staff that, in his opinion, the U.S. Consulate General could no longer function in the circumstances. After burning his codes, he was placing the premises under the protection of the Norwegian mission, which would also be requested to arrange for the early departure of all American citizens.

Sidney Reilly, who had returned from Petrograd in the meantime, succeeded in escaping the Cheka's roundup by staying at the Sheremetyevsky Pereulok safe apartment. De Vertemont also escaped the roundup by taking refuge at a French girls' lycée where he received shelter from the headmistress, Jeanne Morans. While Americans so far had not been molested, Kalamatiano took the precaution of staying in a safe apartment of his own just off the Tverskoy Boulevard.

Nevertheless, DeWitt Poole was able to contact the three men and invite them to a meeting at the American Consulate General, which was by then officially closed. The small group gathered around Poole's massive desk and waited for him to speak.

Poole said, "I think I can dispense with introductions, as each of you knows who the others are. First of all, let me say that what I have to tell you has been cleared with Lockhart and Consul General Grenard. Any questions so far?"

The three men remained silent. Poole studied their faces and then went on: "Gentlemen, you're fully aware of the situation. From now on Allied representatives will be treated as enemies on Soviet territory. If we're fortunate, the Soviet government will permit us to depart in due course. If we're unfortunate, we may wind up in Soviet jails—or worse. Much depends, naturally, on the Allied troops that have landed at Archangel."

"According to rumors I've heard, there are a hundred thousand men in the Allied force," Kalamatiano said.

De Vertemont shook his head. "I don't think there's any way you could land a force that large at Archangel. Two divisions would be about the maximum. Incidentally, that figure has been mentioned in the rumors I've picked up."

"Is there any truth in the report that the Japanese are sending seven divisions to Russia from the Far East?" Reilly asked.

"The main thing is the Allied force at Archangel," Kalamatiano said. He turned to Poole. "Don't you have any information about its size?"

"Xenophon Dmitrievich, as you know, I haven't had any communication with Washington for the past month. I have no information about the Archangel landing or anything else, for that matter. I'm sure the Soviet authorities will let us know one way or the other. We'll be able to judge rather accurately by their treatment of us."

De Vertemont had a rather sour look. "Mr. Poole, if it is left to the French, we'll sweep this Bolshevik regime away as if it had never existed. As to England and the United States—"

The others gathered that de Vertemont did not have a high opinion of France's allies. Poole cut him off, making no effort to hide his displeasure.

"I'm not here to discuss Allied policy. That's a question that has presumably been settled by the Supreme War Council in Paris."

"What *is* the purpose of the meeting?" de Vertemont demanded.

"If you'll be patient, I'm coming to that now." Poole forced a smile. "In the present crisis, the Allied representatives in Moscow must help one another to the maximum extent. You may recall, Colonel de Vertemont, the words of America's ambassador, Benjamin Franklin, who spent some time with the French ministers in Paris. He said, 'We must indeed all hang together or, most assuredly, we shall all hang separately.' He was speaking, to be sure, about the situation of Americans as rebels against the Crown. But our situation is not too different—above all, the situation of our intelligence people. Therefore, Mr. Lockhart, Consul General Grenard, and I are asking you to put aside your normal inhibitions about working with other intelligence services. We request that you cooperate with one another in your activities. First of all, by exchanging information. Second, by ensuring contact through the exchange of addresses in case you can no longer meet openly. Third, by mutual support of operations wherever possible. If there is any objection, we can discuss it right now."

Poole looked at the others, but there was no comment.

"Does anyone have any special problem he would like to bring up?" Poole asked.

"Yes," Kalamatiano said. "I have a problem."

"What is it, Xenophon Dmitrievich?"

"Since our communications have broken down, there's no way to forward my reports. Possibly one of you gentlemen"—Kalamatiano glanced at Reilly and de Vertemont—"can come to my assistance."

"As a matter of fact, I can," Reilly said promptly. "When the Allies landed at Archangel the other day, George Hill's work for Trotsky came to an abrupt end. Not only that—Trotsky ordered his immediate arrest. But Hill went underground and escaped arrest. Although he outranks me, he has generously placed himself under my command."

Reilly went on to say that Hill worked for Military Intelligence, but when he first came to Moscow he had some dealings wtih Trotsky, the newly appointed commissar for war. Hill convinced Trotsky to allow him to help organize a Soviet military counter-espionage apparatus. Hill used this opportunity to build an independent courier system of his own without Soviet knowledge. He recruited former czarist officers to smuggle information out of the country by way of Murmansk. In these activities he had the assistance of several English women who worked in the underground.

"Hill can do the job for you," Reilly said to Kalamatiano. "We'll discuss the details later."

Finally Poole noted that Bruce Lockhart had been raising funds from the Russian opposition in an ingenious way. Through a small British company headed by William Combes Higgs with offices at Number 3 Teatral'ny Proezd, 8.4 million rubles had been raised from wealthy Russians in exchange for notes repayable in pounds sterling in London. Since the Cheka's raid on the British Consulate, this money was being stored for safekeeping in the American Consulate General until Hicks, Lockhart's assistant, picked it up.

"Mr. Reilly has probably received his share of those rubles, if I'm not mistaken," Poole remarked dryly.

Reilly did not seem comfortable with this revelation, shifting uneasily in his seat.

"It's clear that your cooperation is bound to be limited in duration," Poole went on. "I don't know how long it will take to obtain a safe conduct for our nationals to leave via Finland. We'll consult together again when those arrangements have definitely been made. But until then I think we should carry on to the best of our ability."

At the end of the meeting, when they were alone, Kalamatiano and Reilly quickly came to an understanding about Hill's courier system. After Colonel Friede had compiled the intelligence reports, Mariya Friede would deliver the material to Elizabeth Otten at the Sheremetyevsky Pereulok address. Elizabeth would wait for an English woman named Vi, who worked for Hill, to call there. Vi's job was to bring the reports to Hill. He would give them to the women in his employ to copy onto cloth that could be sewn into the clothing worn by the couriers. (According to Reilly, it had been found that sewing paper in the lining of clothing did not effectively conceal the messages, since any probing by inquisitive fingers tended to produce a rustling sound.) At the other end of the line the reports would be forwarded on to Washington.

The euphoria among Allied representatives caused by the military intervention in northern Russia lasted only a short time, and when it ended they were plunged into deep gloom.

Literally dancing for joy, Karakhan of the Soviet Foreign Office informed Lockhart that the Allied forces landed at Archangel amounted to only a few hundred soldiers. (In fact, by February 1919 the Allied combat forces reached a total of about 11,000 men, of whom 4,500 were Americans, 5,000 British, 700 French, and 700 Polish. In addition, 5,000 Russians were integrated into these forces, while the Provisional Government in Archangel had raised another 12,000 men who, because of low morale, proved to be militarily unreliable.)

Bruce Lockhart later described his feelings in these words:

> The consequences of this ill-conceived venture were to be disastrous both to our prestige and to the fortunes of those Russians who supported us. It raised hopes which could not be fulfilled. It intensified the civil war and sent thousands of Russians to their death. Indirectly, it was responsible for the Terror. Its direct effect was to provide the Bolsheviks with a cheap victory, to give them a new confidence, and to galvanize them into a strong and ruthless organism. To have intervened at all was a mistake. To have intervened with hopelessly inadequate forces was an example of spineless half-measures which, in the circumstances, amounted to a crime. . . . The fact remains that, whatever may have been the intentions of the Allied governments, our intervention was regarded by those Russians, who supported it, as an attempt to overthrow Bolshevism. It failed, and, with the failure, our prestige among every class of the Russian population suffered.[3]

A few days later the Latvians Shmidkhen and Spogis showed up at Lockhart's residence at Number 19 Khlebny Pereulok, apartment 24. Shmidkhen delivered Cromie's letter to Lockhart. In the letter Cromie said that he was making his own preparations to leave Russia and hoped to "bang the dore [sic] before he went out."[4] He closed the letter by recommending Shmidkhen as a man who might be able to perform a useful service.

In the course of their conversation, Shmidkhen informed Lockhart that some of the Lettish commanders were wavering in their loyalty to the Soviet regime. They had no wish to fight against the Allies, who were probably going to win the great war and who would soon be in a position to decide Latvia's fate as a nation. After all, President Wilson had come out strongly in favor of national self-determination. Nevertheless, these same commanders would certainly demand definite commitments before they went over to the Allied side.

Lockhart, of course, was fully aware that the Lettish Rifles were responsible for guarding the Kremlin and all important Soviet installations. "I would like to meet one of those men," he said bluntly. "Can you arrange it?"

"I'm not sure. I'll try."

"Do you know anyone you can trust?"

"I hesitate to make any promises. . . ."

"Well?" Lockhart openly showed his impatience. "Do you have anyone in mind?"

"There's one man," Shmidkhen said thoughtfully. "He comes from Riga, as I do. He was an art student before the war. We served in the same regiment as second lieutenants."

"What's his name?"

"Berzin. Eduard Petrovich Berzin."

"What is he doing now?"

"He commands the Lettish Special Section detailed to guard the Kremlin."

"That's very interesting. Can you bring him to see me?"

"As I said, I'll try."

"I'll expect you around noon tomorrow. If you can't come, please let me know."

The next day Shmidkhen came at the appointed time with his friend, Colonel Berzin, whom Lockhart described in his memoirs as a "tall, powerfully built man with clear-cut features and hard steely eyes."

The date of Lockhart's first meeting with Berzin cannot be established with certainty. The *Pravda* story of September 3 as well as other Soviet sources then and later gives the date as August 14. Lockhart himself, writing some thirteen or fourteen years after the event, says that it was August 15. Since there seems to be no reason why the Soviet accounts should have falsified this point, the August 14 date is probably accurate.[5]

Asked by Lockhart about his attitude toward the Allies, Berzin replied without hesitation: "We Latvians have only one desire, to return to our country and live in freedom. As long as Germany remains strong, a tiny nation like Latvia has no chance to be free. Because of the revolution, Russia no longer is a threat to us. But in the event the Allies win the war, as now seems likely, we need their help and sympathy. If we're sent to the Archangel front, we'll surrender to the Allied forces. Is it possible to arrange matters so that we won't be shot down by the Allies?"

"What do you want from me?" Lockhart said.

"Perhaps you could explain our attitude to the Allied commander at Archangel," Berzin said.

Shmidkhen nodded. "I think Colonel Berzin means that a surrender of the Latvian regiments could easily be arranged."

Lockhart explained that he was not in touch with General Sir F. Cuthbert Poole, the British commander of the Allied forces at Archangel. "Nevertheless, I'll give serious consideration to the views you've expressed, colonel," Lockhart said. "Would you be prepared to return to see me tomorrow at the same time?"

When the two Latvians exchanged glances and nodded, Lockhart promptly dismissed them with a friendly look and a handshake.

That same afternoon Lockhart met at his apartment with General Lavergne, chief of the French Military Mission, and French Consul General Grenard. Informed about Berzin's visit, the two Frenchmen agreed that the Latvians probably did not wish to fight against the Allies. They also agreed that it would be a good idea to give Berzin a note that would enable him or his emissary to pass through the Allied lines and make contact with General Poole's headquarters. But they were interested above all in sounding out Berzin on the possibility of the Lettish regiments' participation in a coup d'etat against the Soviet regime.

"It would be worth a considerable amount of money," the vigorous, silver-haired General Lavergne said. He could be counted on to support any aggressive action against the Bolsheviks; two months earlier, in June, while in Vladivostok he had sent a message to his government suggesting the use of the Czechoslovaks along the Trans-Siberian Railway for intervention.

"If money is needed," Lockhart replied, "it will be available."

"That goes without saying."

Lockhart proposed the idea of turning over the contact with Berzin to Reilly, since Reilly planned to go underground and remain behind after the departure of the Allied representatives. The Frenchmen also agreed to this proposal. It would be up to Reilly to stimulate further reluctance on the part of the Latvians to fight against the Allies and to determine whether they could be induced to oppose the Bolsheviks actively.

Once again Shmidkhen and Berzin appeared at the appointed time, and Lockhart introduced Grenard, Lavergne, and Sidney Reilly (under the name Constantine) to the two visitors. Reilly did not bother to tell Lockhart that he had already made the acquaintance of Shmidkhen through Cromie in Petrograd. He was meeting Berzin for the first time, however, and eyed the other man with great curiosity.

Lockhart had said that Berzin was tall and heavily built. Reilly noticed that Berzin had a small black mustache and goatee. The Latvian colonel's hairline was receding, leaving a sharp point in the center, but the most remarkable thing about him was an intense, penetrating gaze—an unfriendly person might have called it a hypnotic stare.

They all shook hands and then sat down, Lockhart, the host, choosing the seating arrangement. Berzin received the seat of honor in a stuffed chair at Lockhart's right, Shmidkhen was seated next to Berzin, and the other three men uncomfortably shared a large sofa facing the rest.

Lockhart spoke first in his usual forthright manner. "I regret that, as I've already said, I'm not in touch with General Poole at Archangel. But I have fully considered your views and conclude that it would be useful for you to contact General Poole directly. I'm prepared to provide you with a pass through the Allied lines for this purpose."

Both Latvians nodded eagerly. "That's very kind of you, sir," Berzin said.

"Allow me to ask you something else," Lockhart said, leaning back in his chair. "Mr. Shmidkhen has informed us that the Lettish Rifles support the Bolsheviks because they are the only faction consistently demanding the dissolution of the Russian empire. Therefore the Bolsheviks thus far offer the sole hope of Latvian independence. Is that correct?"

"Yes, that's true. But the situation has changed."

"In what way?"

Berzin took his time before replying. "As I told you yesterday, the Allies are going to win the war. In that case, the peace settlement will be up to them. The Soviet government will have nothing to say about the final peace treaty because it made a separate peace with Germany. At the same time, we Latvians can't go on endlessly fighting Soviet battles."

Now Consul General Grenard turned to Lockhart and asked him to translate his words into Russian for Berzin. "Judging by your conversation yesterday with the ambassador, you are interested in the fate of Latvia after the war and the overthrow of the Bolsheviks—"

Berzin interrupted Lockhart's interpretation. "The overthrow of the Bolsheviks? I don't know."

Grenard waved a hand, and Lockhart continued on behalf of his French colleague: "I have no directive from my government, but I'm sure that Latvia will receive self-determination for your cooperation, in the full sense of this word."

Reilly spoke for the first time. "Can you Latvians remain neutral? If the Bolsheviks are fighting us, you'll have to decide whether to support them or fight against them. There's no middle way."

"We won't fight against the Allies."

"Will you fight *for* the Allies?"

There was a long pause. Finally Berzin said, "If it comes to a choice between Latvia and Russia, we choose our own country."

"That's the choice you face now."

"Mr. Constantine is right," Lockhart said. He looked solemnly from one face to the other. "You must choose whether you are for Latvia or Russia. If you're for Latvia, then you have to prepare yourself to fight against the Bolsheviks. As Mr. Shmidkhen said yesterday, the Bolsheviks, for better or worse, represent Russia."

Another lengthy silence. "I accept your argument," said Berzin in a low, controlled voice. "What do you expect me to do?"

"If you look at it from another viewpoint, the Soviet government has done its best to help Germany win the war against the Allies. The Bolsheviks, by making peace with them, allowed the Germans to transfer most of their army in the east to the western front. Would a victorious Germany ever agree to an independent Latvia? You yourself have given the answer—*no*. So it's difficult for me to see how you can regard the Bolsheviks as your friends."

Reilly shifted suddenly in his chair, making a loud scraping noise which fastened the gazes of the others on him. "Colonel Berzin," he said softly, "don't you think that a new Russian government—one that hasn't discredited itself by signing a separate peace treaty with Germany—would have more influence on the Allies?" Berzin shrugged. "And if a new Russian government, with the encouragement of the Allies, committed itself to Latvian self-determination, wouldn't that mean much more than Bolshevik propaganda, which so far lacks any substance?"

"I understand what you're suggesting," Berzin said. "Personally I'm more or less in agreement with you. But I'll have to discuss these matters with other commanders."

"Exactly what we would wish," Lockhart said in a sincere tone. "And it's our preference that you regard Mr. Constantine as our representative and conduct future talks with him. Is that agreeable to you?"

"I'll be happy to meet with Mr. Constantine."

Thus Lockhart turned over the principal responsibility for further dealings with Colonel Berzin to Sidney Reilly, whom he later described in these words: "He was a man of great energy and personal charm, very attractive to women and very ambitious. I had not a very high opinion of his intelligence. His knowledge covered many subjects, from politics to art, but it was superficial. On the other hand, his courage and indifference to danger were superb."[6]

After Berzin agreed to conduct future meetings with Reilly, Lockhart said, "Very good. In conclusion, let me just add that to the extent money is needed—"

"I want no money for myself."

"Of course not," Lockhart said soothingly. "I hope you haven't misinterpreted what I was saying. My point is that undertakings of this kind often require money. To the extent that it's needed—"

"I understand."

"How much money do you think you might need to pay in order to ensure the cooperation of your Latvian friends?" Grenard asked. Voluble as always, he went on without waiting for an answer: "Let's say that for their participation senior commanders received a hundred thousand rubles each, company commanders fifty thousand, and rank-and-file soldiers two thousand apiece. How much would that come to?"

"Well, as I've already said, the financial side has little interest for me," said Berzin. He stopped and thought a moment. "I suppose, on the basis of what you've said, that it might come to four or five million rubles."

Lockhart and Grenard quickly agreed that Reilly would be able to supply two million almost immediately and could provide any necessary additional funds within a couple of weeks.

When they parted Reilly arranged with Berzin to meet on Saturday evening, August 17, at the Tramble Café on Tsvetnoy Bul'var,

"Floral Boulevard," the street of flower shops from which it derived its name. They agree that at that meeting Berzin would inform Reilly about his soundings of the other Latvian commanders.

In the meantime Reilly was not idle. One day he and George Hill went to see Patriarch Vasili Belavin Tikhon, the head of the Russian Orthodox Church, whom Paul Dukes, a British spy designated as "S.T. 25," subsequently called "the only . . . man in the whole of Russia whom the Bolsheviks fear from the bottom of their hearts."[7] Reilly and Hill brought with them two suitcases containing five million rubles, which they turned over to the Patriarch.

Patriarch Tikhon and his visitors saw eye to eye on the situation of the Bolsheviks, one they considered extremely precarious. The Soviet regime held only a few industrial cities in addition to Moscow and Petrograd. The Germans or their puppets occupied most of western and southwestern Russia. There were independent regimes in the Transcaucasus and the Cossacks dominated the Don and Kuban regions. Since the arrival of Japanese and American troops at Vladivostok, operating in conjunction with the Czechoslovaks, Bolshevik power had been wiped out in eastern Siberia and was threatened in the Urals. Even within Soviet-held central Russia, strikes and disorders constantly occurred, and the armed resistance of many thousands of Russians seemed ready to break out at any propitious moment. All in all, they concluded, the disunity and demoralization of the anti-Bolshevik opposition were the main elements keeping the Bolsheviks in power. The patriarch added, however, that the Bolsheviks had also gained a measure of popular support with their slogan of "peace, bread, and land"—the second of which, he said, was a mockery, since starvation was rife. Reilly commented that only an Allied victory could bring genuine peace to Russia. The promise of land was as much a mockery as the promise of bread because the Bolsheviks would in due course take away the land seized by the peasants.

They reached an understanding that on the day following a successful coup d'etat services would be held in all churches at which Orthodox priests would explain to their congregations the significance of the coup and justify the actions of the Allies and the Russian opposition.

Reilly's affair with Olga Dmitrievna Starzheskaya, the government typist he had met at the Bolshoi Theater, was also proceeding satisfactorily. Recognizing that Olga was rather naive, he had proposed marriage and been accepted. Thereupon he gave her 20,000 rubles to rent and furnish an apartment where they would live together; from his point of view another safe apartment might become very useful. Olga had also furnished him with some valuable information: on August 28 a plenary session of the Central Executive Committee, including Lenin and Trotsky, and the Moscow Soviet was to take place at the Bolshoi Theater.

At the Tramble Café on Saturday, August 17, Reilly arrived early for his meeting and succeeded in getting a small corner table. Because it was a weekend night, the café was crowded and every table filled up quickly; because the place was crowded, the service was even worse than usual. The service was also bad for another reason: Four waiters, lounging in a corner of the room, deliberately ignored the patrons while they smoked and conversed among themselves. Signs on the walls said "No Tipping" and "Waiters Are Workers, Too. Don't Insult Them with Tips." It appeared that the waiters felt insulted, but no one could tell whether this was because they had been offered tips or because the tips were not forthcoming.

Berzin came into the café, looking furtively around as if he feared that he would be seen by someone who knew him. Then he caught sight of Reilly at the corner table, went over quickly, and sat down. Reilly said, "Well, Eduard Petrovich, how are you?" Berzin merely nodded in reply, and Reilly went on, "With regard to our business, how did things go?"

Berzin averted his gaze. "Not bad," he muttered. "But I am probably going to need a lot of money. Some of my comrades will only be convinced that this is a serious affair if I can show them enough money."

Reilly smiled. From a coat pocket he took out a package and tossed it across the table. Berzin eyed the package with surprise and apprehension. "Don't let it worry you," Reilly said. "That's just a beginning. Seven hundred thousand rubles. Are you satisfied?"

"That will do for now," said Berzin grudgingly, "but I'll need more—much more."

Reilly then explained that the plan for the coup d'etat had been drawn up by General Lavergne, the chief of the French

Military Mission. Since it was now known that the Bolsheviks' Central Executive Committee and the Moscow Soviet would have a plenary session on August 28 at the Bolshoi Theater, the coup had been planned for that date.

The Latvian sharpshooters, who would be guarding the theater, were to arrest the whole Central Executive Committee, including Chairman of the Sovnarkom Lenin and People's Commissar for War Trotsky. At the same time other units would occupy the State Bank, the Central Post and Telegraph, and other key points. As soon as the revolt had taken place, former officers of the czarist army would be assembled for the purpose of maintaining order in Moscow as well as guarding the captured Bolsheviks.

"I hear that Trotsky is thinking of sending two regiments of the Lettish Rifles to the Archangel front," Berzin said.

"We can't prevent that," Reilly answered. "If they are sent to the Archangel front, the regiments should surrender there to the Allies. We'll still have sufficient troops in Moscow to carry out the coup."

Their next meeting took place two days later on Monday, August 19, in a safe apartment at Number 4 Griboyedovsky Pereulok. The street was located within the northerly loop made by the Moscow River just south of the Kremlin. Reilly carefully checked whether he was under surveillance before he entered the apartment house.

The Latvian colonel had arrived before him and was bent over some papers on a table. He gave Reilly a list with the names of the regimental commanders who were prepared to take part in the conspiracy.

On this occasion Reilly asked Berzin to perform a number of assignments. First of all, Berzin was to ascertain whether it was true that at Rogozhskaya Station or in its immediate vicinity there had been stationed nine batteries of five-inch guns and two batteries of eight-inch guns of English construction. Second, he was to determine whether there were several carloads of gold and banknotes guarded by seven hundred Latvians at Mitino Station. Reilly requested that Berzin take steps to prevent this gold from being taken away in case the Soviet regime was overthrown. Finally, Berzin was to establish contact with the Latvian colony in Petrograd and spot Latvians who would undertake to compose and distribute proclamations among the Latvian units.

Reilly's purpose in giving Berzin these assignments was to test him. As he explained to Lockhart, good tradecraft required a case officer to continue testing an agent. "No agent's reliability is certain for all time," he said. In view of the fact that he already knew the correct answers to some of the questions he had raised, the agent's responses would be significant.

"But you consider Berzin reliable," Lockhart said.

"Of course," Reilly replied, "but you can't be too careful."

Two days later, on August 21, Reilly and Berzin met again at the safe apartment. "How are things going?" Reilly asked without delay.

"Very successfully," Berzin said. "I saw the commander of the First Lettish Rifle Regiment and gave him four hundred thousand rubles for his regiment. In the next few days I expect to see the commander of the Fifth Rifle Regiment. I'd also like to give him a large sum of money, but I'm running out of funds."

"It's only money," Reilly said. "Tomorrow I'll bring you another four hundred thousand."

Berzin looked displeased. "If you could bring a million, it would be more helpful."

"I'll see what I can do."

That same evening Reilly attended a meeting in French Consul General Grenard's apartment. Aside from Grenard and Lockhart, General Lavergne, Lockhart's assistant Captain Will Hicks (who survived Russia but died of consumption in Berlin in 1930), and other prominent French and British officials were present.

Reilly, who had, by his own account, called the meeting, outlined his plans for the coup d'etat. He told his attentive audience that the Latvian sharpshooters would guard the Bolshoi Theater as usual on August 28. On a signal from him, Berzin and his men would lock the doors of the theater and Reilly, with a squad of the Latvians, would appear on the stage and arrest the Bolshevik leaders. He assured his listeners that he had no intention of killing Lenin or any of the other Bolsheviks. He suggested that the best way to crush the Bolshevik leaders was to expose them to popular ridicule; he proposed with a smile to march them through the streets of Moscow, Lenin and Trotsky at the head, in their *underwear*.

There were answering smiles and some subdued laughter in the audience.

Other Latvian regiments, Reilly went on, would occupy the Kremlin, the State Bank, the Post and Telegraph, the telephone station, and other important installations. A special detachment would capture the gold reserves at Mitino Station. The Latvian coup would be supported by mobilizing some sixty thousand former officers in Moscow and by carrying out simultaneous uprisings in Petrograd, Nizhni-Novgorod (later renamed Gorky), Tambov, and other cities.

Reilly's listeners were visibly impressed and indicated general agreement with the plan that had been worked out with the help of Lavergne.

On the following day, however, Reilly came to the meeting with Berzin in a less exuberant frame of mind. His change of mood had come about as a result of a brief conversation with Olga Dmitrievna during the night.

> REILLY: Olga, darling, you look so tired. You must be working very hard these days.
> OLGA: Not so hard, Kostya.
> REILLY: But with the plenum of the Central Executive Committee coming next week—
> OLGA: Oh, no. Didn't I tell you? The plenum has been postponed.
> REILLY: Postponed?
> OLGA: Until September sixth.
> REILLY: Indeed? For what reason?
> OLGA: I don't know. Probably they couldn't get ready in time.

At the beginning of their meeting, Reilly informed Berzin about the postponement of the plenum. "Well, perhaps it's all for the best," he said philosophically. "That also gives us more time for our preparations."

"What about the money you promised?" Berzin asked impatiently.

"I could only bring you two hundred thousand today."

"You said it would be *four* hundred thousand."

"I know," Reilly conceded. "In the next four or five days I should be able to give you one million."

Grudgingly, Berzin accepted the money and then went on to tell Reilly about his further negotiations with fellow commanders.

When the meeting ended, they both agreed that the postponement of the plenum would definitely work to their advantage.

On Sunday, August 25, Reilly received an urgent summons to come to the closed Consulate General, which now had the Norwegian flag flying above it. When he arrived he found a group of familiar faces scattered about the room—Grenard, Lavergne, Lockhart, Hicks, de Vertemont, Kalamatiano, and DeWitt Poole himself.

Since the meeting was taking place in the former American Consulate General, Poole by common consent acted as chairman. Everybody looked grim, but each revealed his concern in a different way: Lockhart stared down at his fingertips, with both hands joined together; Grenard tapped a well-shod foot; Lavergne scowled at anyone who met his gaze; Reilly folded his arms and leaned back, looking at the ceiling; and Kalamatiano watched alertly with his green cat's eyes.

"Most of us know why we're here," Poole said, "but I'll go over it again for those who may not be aware of the purpose of the meeting. We've now received notification from the Soviet authorities that Allied nationals resident in Moscow will be permitted to depart. A special train leaves tomorrow night for Finland via Petrograd."

Grenard and Lavergne exchanged glances. Lavergne turned to de Vertemont. "Is there any problem about those bridges?"

"What bridges?" Poole asked sharply.

"Colonel de Vertemont's men are planning to blow up some bridges. Could that interfere with the special train, Colonel?"

"One bridge is over the Volkhov River and another over the Zvanka," de Vertemont replied. "Although both are in the Petrograd area, the blowing up of the bridges couldn't possibly interfere with the train. The timing is different."

"Make sure that it doesn't interfere with the train," Poole said. "I'd like to discuss this later with you gentlemen," he added in an angry aside to Grenard and Lavergne.

"Are *you* planning to leave on the special train?" Kalamatiano asked.

Poole shook his head. "I believe I'm speaking for the principal Allied representatives here. None of us plans to leave—yet. But we probably won't be able to stay much longer. All the others will

83

leave on Monday night. All except Mr. Reilly, Mr. Kalamatiano, and Colonel de Vertemont. They'll go underground to continue with their activities."

Reilly and Kalamatiano left the Consulate General together. "Are you satisfied with the arrangement with Hill?" Reilly asked.

"Everything's fine," Kalamatiano said.

"We'll keep in touch. Let me know if you have any problems."

Reilly's next meeting with Berzin was scheduled for August 27, a Tuesday. In spite of the fact that he still had about two million rubles stored in the safe apartment at Sheremetyevsky Pereulok, Reilly deliberately brought only 300,000 rubles to the meeting.

"But you promised me a million!" Berzin protested.

"I'm sorry," Reilly said, quite unruffled. "I'll bring more next time. But there's something else we need to discuss."

"What's that?"

"I'm planning to go to Petrograd, and I want you to meet me there."

"What do you expect me to do in Petrograd?"

"I need to check on the plans for an uprising there. It would be a good idea for you to familiarize yourself with the organization."

Before they parted, Reilly gave him the address of Yelena Mikhailovna's flat, telling him to say that he had been sent by Mr. Massino. They would meet the next day in Petrograd.

W. Somerset Maugham, who had been sent to Russia by British Intelligence about six months before Reilly, wrote a series of short stories in later years about a fictional British agent named Ashenden. When Ashenden was sent on a mission to revolutionary Russia, the words Maugham wrote about this British agent in the story "Mr. Harrington's Washing" could have been applied to Reilly:

> It was the most important mission he had ever had and he was pleased with the sense of responsibility it gave him. He had no one to give him orders, unlimited funds (he carried in a belt next to his skin bills of exchange for a sum so enormous that he was staggered when he thought of them), and though he had been sent to do something that was beyond human possibility he did not know this and was prepared to set about his task with confidence. He believed in his own astuteness. Though he had

84

both esteem and admiration for the sensibility of the human race he had little respect for their intelligence.[8]

As he set out for Petrograd, perhaps with feelings akin to those of Ashenden, Sidney Reilly projected an image of buoyant confidence in the imminent coup d'etat, which would overthrow the Bolsheviks once and for all.

Chapter 8

THE SPECTACLE of a prize fight is familiar—the two boxers at first warily circling one another in the ring, occasionally jabbing or hooking or launching a single hard punch or a combination of punches. For the most part, the opponents "feel out" one another, probing for strengths and weaknesses. After a few rounds, perhaps, this period of routine sparring comes to an end. One of the boxers throws caution to the wind and attacks with wild ferocity; a series of hammer blows catches the other boxer by surprise; those hammer blows end the fight by felling the unfortunate target and stretching him out full length on the canvas.

It was the Allied agents in Russia who suffered a series of hammer blows at the hands of the Cheka in the last days of August and the beginning of September 1918.

As arranged with Reilly in Moscow, Colonel Berzin went to Petrograd on August 28 and called at the Torgovaya Street safe apartment. He was curious to see Yelena Mikhailovna because Reilly had told him, possibly in jest, that during the war years she had been one of Rasputin's numerous female conquests. But he did not find her at home. When he met Reilly, Berzin learned little about the Petrograd organization. But Reilly allegedly did reveal to him the existence of the Sheremetyevsky Pereulok safe apartment in Moscow.

On the same day Berzin and Reilly were meeting in Petrograd, the special train carrying some ninety-five American evacuees from Moscow stood in the Petrograd railroad yards. George F. Kennan has painted a striking word-picture of the scene:

> The city, famine-stricken, terrorized, deserted now by at least half a million of its former inhabitants, was only the wraith of the great teeming capital that had existed on the banks of the Neva the year before. The cold hand of the Terror was already chilling and laming the place, inflicting upon it that strange species of blight—a lifelessness, a furtive drabness, a sense of the sinister lurking behind a peeling facade, and everywhere a hushed, guarded inscrutability—which seems to be the effect of the communist touch on any great urban area. Dismayed and appalled, the American evacuees, living in their train in the railway yards, wandered through the stricken city, along semi-deserted streets, over pavements already beginning to be grass-grown, among buildings already fading from neglect.[1]

While Reilly was conducting his business in such a changed Petrograd, an event that would have significant repercussions on his future occurred in Moscow, although he remained ignorant of it until he returned to that city. On August 29 the Cheka raided de Vertemont's headquarters at Number 18 Milyutinsky Pereulok, seizing a large cache of explosives as well as money. A number of French agents were captured, but de Vertemont escaped over the rooftops.

Soviet sources have never clarified the background of this raid. The circumstances, nonetheless, can be easily deduced. The Cheka received information about the August 25 meeting of Allied representatives in the American Consulate General shortly after that meeting took place. They knew that the blowing up of bridges over the Volkhov and Zvanka rivers by French agents was discussed at the meeting. In his reminiscences about the period, Jacob Peters observed: "Both of these bridges possessed extraordinarily serious significance because the blowing up of these bridges, cutting off

Leningrad from its food supplies, would have condemned it to death by starvation or capitulation to the Allies." Obviously the Cheka could not postpone action in this case. The raid on de Vertemont's safe apartment with its store of explosives was designed to prevent the French from blowing up the bridges.

Hearing about this raid, George Hill sent off a courier to warn Reilly in Petrograd, but Reilly never received the warning.

The Cheka's hand was forced almost immediately by other events. On August 30 at 11:30 A.M. Moisei Uritsky, the head of the Petrograd Cheka, was shot and killed outside the secret police headquarters at Number 2 Gorokhovaya ("Pea Street"), a few doors away from Rasputin's former house, in the heart of Petrograd by a young Baltic German cadet named Kannegiesser. Lenin telephoned Dzerzhinski as soon as he heard the news and asked the Cheka boss to go to Petrograd and take personal charge of the countermeasures. "In Leningrad there were mass arrests," Peters wrote, "the Red Terror began, and in its course White Guard members among Lockhart's agents were arrested. It became necessary to begin to liquidate this conspiracy in Moscow."[2]

That evening Lenin was leaving a mass meeting at the former Mikhelson plant in Moscow, having delivered a violent attack on the bourgeoisie and its British and French allies, when a woman named Dora Kaplan, a Left SR, critically wounded him with shots in the neck and chest. The attempted assassination of Lenin unleashed the Red Terror in full force.[3]

News of the murder of Uritsky and the wounding of Lenin made Sidney Reilly doubly cautious. He was aware of the Cheka's frenzied activities and could see the mass arrests, which were accompanied by the shuttling back and forth of Cheka automobiles and trucks through the streets of Petrograd by day and night. He soon recognized that his own plans had been disrupted.

On August 31, Reilly made his way through back streets to the British Embassy, where he hoped to see Captain Cromie, the naval attaché, and compare notes with his old ally. Disguised as a workman, unshaven, wearing a cap with the traditional black shirt, he warily approached the embassy, only to discover that he had come too late. There was a cordon of soldiers around the building, and, pretending to be a curious bystander, he learned from one of the soldiers that the Cheka had carried out a raid in the course of which a man answering to Cromie's description had offered resistance, shooting one or more of the intruders, only to be shot and killed himself. Later Reilly saw Cromie's badly battered body being taken away. According to details that he obtained subsequently, the gallant Cromie had stood at the top of the broad double staircase inside the embassy, where the ambassador had received his guests, and defied the Chekists, opening fire when they ignored his warning.

Reilly returned to Moscow by train the same night, although the journey on this occasion proved to be a more arduous one. He used his Cheka identification papers to board the train in Petrograd, but document checks were rigorous and he realized that he would not be able to get through similar checks at the station in Moscow, where the Cheka was more likely to be on the lookout for him. Therefore he left the train at a stop forty miles from Moscow and traveled by horse-drawn cart over primitive back roads to cover the remaining distance.

On August 31, while Reilly was returning from Petrograd, the Cheka struck again in Moscow by raiding Reilly's Sheremetyevsky Pereulok apartment. The Chekists found Dagmara and Yelizaveta Otten in the apartment. Dagmara managed to conceal Reilly's packets of rubles in her undergarments. During the Chekists' search, Hill's courier Vi turned up. Fortunately she remained cool, explaining that she was delivering a handmade blouse (Hill's female couriers always carried with them a package containing a blouse for this very purpose). Discovering nothing incriminating in her possession, the Chekists allowed Vi to depart. Shortly afterward, however, Mariya Friede, who was delivering the reports that Vi had come to pick up, walked into the Cheka trap. She became hysterical and was arrested on the spot. The Chekists also arrested Yelizaveta Otten but allowed Dagmara to go free, possibly hoping that she would lead them to Reilly.

Mariya Friede's arrest with the incriminating material she was carrying led to a search of her mother's apartment, where she lived. Mrs. Friede excused herself to go to the toilet, where she sought to dispose of some papers but was prevented from doing so. A further search of the apartment turned up other secret documents which, the mother admitted, had been entrusted to her by her son, Colonel Aleksandr Friede. He was in turn arrested by the Cheka within the next couple of hours.

The capture of Colonel Friede and his sister Mariya promptly set the Cheka on the trail of Kalamatiano, but the American proved elusive, frustrating all efforts by the Soviet secret police to catch him.

While Reilly was hiding off the Tverskoy Boulevard with a trustworthy Russian who was unlikely to be on the Cheka's list of suspects, Bruce Lockhart was arrested at his apartment in the middle of the night and taken off to the Lubianka, Cheka headquarters in Moscow.

During the night of August 31, Lockhart was conducted along a dark corridor and brought to a room for interrogation. He knew that he was in considerable danger, particularly in the event of Lenin's death. "I was brought into a long, dark room, lit only by a hand-lamp on the writing table," related Lockhart.

> At the table, with a revolver lying beside the writing-pad, was a man, dressed in black trousers and a white Russian shirt. His black hair, long and waving as a poet's, was brushed back over a high forehead. There was a large wrist watch on his left hand. In the dim light his features looked more sallow than ever. His lips were tightly compressed, and, as I entered the room, his eyes fixed me with a steely stare. He looked grim and formidable. It was Peters. . . .[4]

Peters asked Lockhart whether he knew Dora Kaplan. When Lockhart refused to answer, he asked, "Where is Reilly?" Again Lockhart said that Peters had no right to question him. Then Peters produced a paper, which Lockhart recognized as the pass through the Allied lines that he had given to the Latvians. But Lockhart still refused to answer any questions.

At six o'clock in the morning, while Lockhart waited in another room with Hicks, who had also been arrested, the Chekists brought in a woman. "She was dressed in black," Lockhart wrote in his book. "Her hair was black, and her eyes, set in a fixed stare, had great black rings under them. Her face was colorless. Her features, strongly Jewish, were unattractive. She might have been any age between twenty and thirty-five. We guessed it was Kaplan."

In arranging the confrontation, the Cheka expected, of course, that a look of recognition would pass between Lockhart and Kaplan, thus betraying their complicity.

Nevertheless, Dora Kaplan remained silent and withdrawn, ignoring her immediate surroundings while she leaned against the window sill and looked outside into the gathering light of day. Lockhart thought that her composure was unnatural.

Peters described his own confrontation with Kaplan somewhat differently. He said that she refused to identify herself and did not respond to other questions, sobbing uncontrollably the whole time. He wondered whether she was crying because she regretted her deed or because she feared the fate that awaited her.

Dora Kaplan was not left long in doubt about her fate. A short time later Pavel Dmitrievich Mal'kov, the commandant of the Kremlin, who had arrested Lockhart earlier that night, took Kaplan out and killed her with his own hand.

Lockhart was released on that rainy Sunday morning and returned to his apartment, although he was destined to remain at liberty for only a few days. He was worried about his cook and two men servants, who has been arrested at the same time but continued to be confined in prison. But most of all he worried about the Baroness Moura Beckendorff, a Russian woman with whom he had fallen in love. She had also been taken off by the Cheka. An emotional man, Lockhart had a habit of falling in love with pretty women, but at any one time each of these romances was all-consuming.

Lockhart had not seen Reilly since the latter had gone underground and therefore could not have given Peters any information about Reilly's whereabouts even if he had been disposed to do so. Before Reilly went underground, Lockhart asserted, Reilly had come to report on his dealings with Berzin, which were apparently going smoothly. "He put forward a suggestion that after our departure he might be able, with Lettish help, to stage a counterrevolution in Moscow," Lockhart wrote more than a decade later. "This suggestion was categorically turned down by General Lavergne, Grenard, and myself, and Reilly was warned to have nothing to do with so dangerous and doubtful a move."

Considering all the available evidence, Lockhart's statement appears to be self-serving, to say the least. For a man who provided Reilly with millions of rubles (to what end?), who introduced the Latvian commander, Colonel Berzin, to Reilly (merely to arrange a surrender on the Archangel front?), and who was in close touch with two Frenchmen, General Lavergne and Consul General Grenard, who were moving heaven and earth to overthrow the Bolsheviks, Lockhart was asking a great deal when he expected his protestations of innocence to be believed. Lockhart might not have been aware of all the details of Reilly's operations, but he certainly knew in general what Reilly was up to. Finally, Lavergne and Grenard were hardly the ones to reject a proposal to carry out a counterrevolution in Moscow. Lockhart admitted, however, that his policy had been "discredited in the eyes of both the pro-Bolsheviks and of the interventionists"[5] in England; the truth was that he had tried to follow first one course and then another, succeeding with neither.

From his hiding place Sidney Reilly smuggled a message to Dagmara, who was able to shake off her shadows, if any, and keep a rendezvous with him in a house on the Tsvetnoy Bul'var nearly opposite the Tramble Café, where Reilly had met with Berzin. Dagmara told him in detail about the Cheka's raid at the Sheremetyevsky Pereulok apartment.

In writing about this incident in later years, Reilly evidently based his account on Dagmara's story. He claimed that the apartment had been visited in the course of one of the Cheka's routine block searches. Peters, however, said, "First of all, it was necessary to make a search at Reilly's address [Number 8 Sheremetyevsky Pereulok, apartment 85], which had been disclosed to Berzin in Bozozhevskaya's apartment in Leningrad." Here again logic supports the Soviet account, for it would have required an extraordinary coincidence for the Cheka to stumble on this apartment by chance *at that particular moment.*

Because of his contention that the Cheka had been conducting a routine block search, Reilly placed the entire blame on Mariya Friede for the catastrophic consequences.

"And so had the most promising plot ever concocted against the Bolsheviks been broken down by the folly of Mlle. Friede," Reilly wrote. "As absolutely every motor car in Russia had been confiscated by the Bolsheviks, it was understood, not only among my agents, but in general, never to enter a house before which stood a motor car. But poor Mlle. Friede . . . had neglected a most simple and elementary precaution. Our plot had ended in a fiasco."[6]

On the third of September, a Tuesday, the Russian who was sheltering Reilly brought home a copy of *Pravda* of that date. For the first time Reilly learned the full extent of that fiasco from the *Pravda* front-page story.

The headlines said:

Conspiratorial Apartment of Russian Counterrevolution in the English Mission Exposed

Revealed that English Government's Representative Lockhart Spent Millions Organizing Coup in Moscow, Setting Explosions, and Carrying Out Assassinations

"Allies" Wished to Establish Military Dictatorship and Restore Death Penalty. "Allied" Imperialists Wished to Destroy the Workers' Revolution

The accompanying story described how Shmidkhen had approached Lockhart and introduced Berzin to him. Berzin, however, was not identified by name but merely described as the "commander of a Soviet military unit." The newspaper gave Lockhart's correct address, Number 19 Khlebny Pereulok, apartment 24.

Sidney Reilly's subsequent meetings with the "commander" received minute attention. *Pravda* noted that a total of 1.2 million rubles had been paid to Berzin at these meetings.

Pravda said: "The possibility of a revolt was considered for two or three weeks later, i.e., about the tenth of September. The English showed concern about the presence of Lenin and Trotsky, who were to be arrested at a plenary session of the Sovnarkom. They also proposed that the State Bank, the central telephone station, and the telegraph should be simultaneously occupied, establishing martial law with the threat of capital punishment until English military units arrived."

Pravda also reported about a conference at which Allied diplomats discussed measures to worsen Russia's internal situation and weaken the Soviet struggle against the Czechoslovaks and the Anglo-French. "Plans had been worked out by Allied agents situated in all cities of Soviet Russia," the newspaper went on to say, "to interfere with the supply of provisions by blowing up bridges and railroad lines as well as destroying storage warehouses by means of arson and explosions."

It was obvious to Reilly that the Soviet authorities had access to accurate sources of information. They knew about at least one of the meetings he had attended, either the meeting in French Consul General Grenard's apartment on August 21 or the one in the American Consulate General on August 25.

Also clear from the article was the fact that the Cheka had rolled up most if not all of Kalamatiano's network. *Pravda* reported: "The Anglo-French conspirators had established a widespread net of espionage in all commissariats. Searches disclosed secret reports about the eastern front, and officers arrested in this connection (Captain Friede and others) admitted delivering secret reports to the French and English on the movements of Soviet troops and the internal situation in Russia."

Pravda had erroneously given Friede's rank as captain instead of lieutenant colonel (possibly to minimize his importance), but there was no doubt about his identity. In addition, the reference to officers in the plural ("Friede and others") meant that the Cheka had arrested other members of Kalamatiano's group after capturing Friede. Although Dzerzhinski and his associates must have been aware that the Americans stood behind Friede, it appeared to be the strategy of the Soviet government at that moment to avoid attacks on the United States.

The day after the *Pravda* story appeared, Bruce Lockhart was rearrested. His arrest was inevitable in the circumstances, but he precipitated it slightly by going to the Lubianka where he made a personal appeal to Peters on behalf of the baroness, his sweetheart, who was still being held. "You have saved me some trouble," Peters told him. "My men have been looking for you for the last hour. I have a warrant for your arrest."[7]

At first Lockhart remained in the Lubianka under relatively harsh conditions, forced to sleep on the floor and subjected to nightly interrogations. Peters threatened that if he refused to confess he would be turned over to the Revolutionary Tribunal. Eventually, however, Lockhart was transferred to the Kremlin, where he occupied a comfortable suite of rooms in the Kavalariisky Korpus ("Cavalier House"); but he would have been comforted more had he not known that the previous occupant of those rooms, a minister in the Provisional Government, had been executed. Moreover, he knew that few political prisoners left the Kremlin alive. Conditions improved for him after the British government retaliated for his arrest by imprisoning Maksim Litvinov, his Soviet counterpart in England. While Peters still threatened to turn Lockhart over to the Revolutionary Tribunal, the Baroness Beckendorff was released.

By this time Sidney Reilly was moving from hiding place to

hiding place, hardly daring to spend more than one night in any of these places. "At this time I was quite without cover," he wrote later. "I dared reveal myself to no one. I shrank from meeting people of any sort and for a few nights took shelter in an empty room, where I existed without food or cigarettes. It was the latter I missed chiefly."[8] He avoided all of his old safe apartments, assuming that they had been "blown" and that the Cheka would be lying in wait for him.

One person he did see was George Hill, who continued to live underground and had so far avoided becoming the object of a major pursuit. "I sent Vi to one of Reilly's girls," Hill related, "suggesting that he and I should meet and appointing a seat in one of the parks for our rendezvous. I shall never forget my first glimpse of him. He too had grown a beard, and he did look an ugly devil. I told him so and he returned the compliment. By this time we were both completely used to our Russian clothes, and walked up and down the garden at our ease."[9]

Reilly spoke volubly about his plans, clinging to the hope that he could somehow reorganize or regroup his forces and go on with his efforts to overthrow the "Bolshies," as he called them.

"Reilly's bearing, when I met him, was splendid," Hill said. "He was a hunted man; his photograph with a full description and a reward for his capture was placarded throughout the town; he had been through a terrible time in getting away from Petrograd and yet he was absolutely cool, calm, and collected, not in the least downhearted and only concerned in gathering together the broken threads and starting afresh."

As an alternative, Reilly suggested the idea of surrendering himself to the Cheka in the hope that Lockhart would be allowed to go free. Hill said that Reilly's gesture would be useless: The Cheka would hold him as well as Lockhart, and they both would probably be shot. He advised Reilly to return to England as soon as possible in order to report to SIS in person on the whole operation.

Their discussion turned to the question of how the plot had been betrayed. Reilly expressed the opinion that Colonel Berzin could not have been the traitor; if he had talked at all, it would only have come about after he was arrested and perhaps tortured. He also doubted that any of his French colleagues, Grenard or Lavergne or de Vertemont, could have given the plot away. Reilly was more inclined to believe that the traitor was René Marchand, a French journalist employed as the Moscow correspondent of the Paris newspaper *Figaro*.

Marchand's leftist views were well known. But he was by no means the only leftist among the Allied newspapermen in Russia who sympathized with the Soviet regime. There had been Americans like Lincoln Steffens and John Reed who did not profess to be neutral in Russia's internal struggle. Steffens, an incorrigible dissenter, believing in revolution as the only real solution to the problems of mankind and, seeking to formulate its "scientific laws," had been irresistibly drawn to revolutionary Russia. In response to those who called the Bolshevik revolt an adventure, John Reed replied: "Adventure it was, and one of the most marvelous mankind ever embarked upon, sweeping into history at the head of the toiling masses, and staking everything on their vast and simple desires."[10]

Some journalists were outright apologists for the Bolsheviks. They saw "international Socialist revolution" as the solution of all the ills that plagued mankind—war, poverty, hunger, injustice. And, in the name of this grand solution, they were prepared to justify anything. They liked to quote the French proverb attributed to Robespierre, *"On ne fait pas d'omelette sans casser des oeufs"* (You can't make an omelet without breaking eggs).

Philips Price, the correspondent of the *Manchester Guardian*, wrote: "A mighty stream does not cease to be a mighty stream because of the mud it carries along to the sea."[11] The Allied intervention made Price so indignant that he volunteered for service in the Red Army. When this offer was rejected, he wrote a pamphlet, "The Truth About Allied Intervention," for the Bolsheviks, who distributed it to Allied troops.

Nevertheless, Reilly strongly suspected Marchand. He recalled that Marchand had been present on one occasion in Grenard's apartment when he went out of his way to inquire about Reilly's name. Reilly had deliberately mumbled the name when he replied. It was odd, he thought, that the Soviet press, in writing about the so-called Lockhart plot, had said that Reilly used the alias "Reis."

"That was how my name probably sounded to Marchand," Reilly said. "He associated a great deal with people in the French Military Mission. I've heard that his closest friend there is Sadoul, who is practically a Bolshevik, so Marchand must have the same sympathies. I believe Marchand got wind of the plot at the Mission and betrayed it to the Bolos."[12]

Reilly's suspicions about Marchand later appeared to be confirmed when the Soviet press published a letter from Marchand ostensibly addressed to Raymond Poincaré, the president of the French Republic. In it Marchand protested against the "counter-revolutionary" activities of Allied representatives. He reported about the meeting in the American Consulate General (though he had not attended). He complained that the Allies, particularly the French, pledged to assist Russia, were blowing up bridges and setting fire to food warehouses.

On September 6, two days after Lockhart's rearrest, the Cheka issued orders for the arrest of the other Allied officials with the exception of the Americans. The Allied officials happened to be meeting with Poole at the former American Consulate General, now called the Norwegian Legation. When those whom *Pravda* subsequently accused of being participants in the conspiracy—French Consul General Grenard, General Lavergne, Colonel di Castello, and the Englishmen Hicks, Gibson, and Lindner—emerged from the building, the Cheka agents waiting outside attempted to place them under arrest. Poole, seeing what was going on, intervened promptly and dragged the others back inside the gate. He warned the Chekists against violating the extraterritoriality of the Legation. Possibly intimidated as a result of the adverse publicity surrounding the raid on the British Embassy in Petrograd, including the killing of Cromie, the Chekists made no effort to enter the premises. But the building was placed under siege, with a strong guard around the whole property, and water and electricity were cut off. The Cheka settled down to wait, hoping to force the building's occupants into submission sooner or later.

Jacob Peters, who was in charge of the case, found the results thus far unsatisfactory. "In connection with these arrests and searches," he wrote, "there was uncovered a mass of materials of an espionage character which showed that the American, English, and French embassies had developed a broad spy network in Russia. About thirty people were arrested. But, aside from Friede and his sister and several other persons against whom ample data incriminating them for espionage existed, there was no direct evidence against the remaining prisoners. We had not succeeded in catching the three main culprits whom the foreign embassies had appointed to stay in Russia and conduct the spy work after their departure abroad: Reilly, de Vertemont, and Kalamatiano."[13]

Although Peters was not aware of it at the time, de Vertemont was already on his way out of the country. Reilly was preparing to leave. For his part, Kalamatiano felt that the Cheka's net was drawing tighter and tighter around him. Out of desperation, he made up his mind to act before it was too late.

Kalamatiano had weighed the possibility of risking the stringent Cheka controls on the Moscow-Petrograd rail line, changing trains at Petrograd, and travelling another two hours to the town of Byeloostrov, which was then situated on the Soviet-Finnish border. From there, however, he would have to go on foot along a dirt road and through the woods until he reached a point where he could avoid Soviet patrols and wade or swim across the Sestra River, which marked the actual border. Kalamatiano realized that, at his age, he was not up to the perils and hardships of that trip.

Accordingly, Kalamatiano made a fateful resolve: He would go to the Norwegian Legation and find asylum with the other Allied personnel until the Soviet authorities finally granted permission for their evacuation from Russia. He knew, of course, that the Legation was under siege. During the day he joined the crowd that filled the street outside the Legation and watched with amusement as the Allied officials, many of whom Kalamatiano could recognize at a distance, unconcernedly played football in the garden. He also noted the presence of grim-faced Red Guards patrolling the outer limits of the property.

The night was dark and rainy with wisps of mist that seemed to favor his purpose.[14] He approached the former American Consulate General from the side where the little English church stood, slipping through the grounds until he was directly across from the fence, which hemmed in a large house, where the offices were located, a smaller house, where the Allied officials now slept, and the garden. He could see a fire burning outside the front gate where, he assumed, the chilled Red Guards on duty were trying to keep warm. Nothing moved in the darkness close to him; the only sound he heard was the steady patter of rain in the puddles in the road.

Deciding that it was now or never, Kalamatiano trotted across the road to the fence. He thought that the fence would be easy to climb, but his hands slipped and he could not get a firm hold on the wood. He was also hampered by his walking stick, which he attempted to tuck under his arm instead of throwing over the fence, as he had at first intended. Just as he was pulling himself toward the top of the fence, a powerful grip encircled him from behind and at the same time, almost in his ear, there came loud shouts in Russian, calling for help.

He tried to fight off his unseen assailant, struggling in vain. He heard Red Guards splashing through the puddles as they came running to the assistance of their comrade, who was holding on to Kalamatiano's legs with bulldog tenacity. Then he was seized by even stronger arms and dragged roughly away from the fence. It was all over. He had no chance to escape. None at all.

"Precisely at this time," Jacob Peters said in his account, referring to the siege, "Sergey Nikolayevich Serpukhovsky[15] attempted to get through to the Norwegian Legation."

We knew that Serpukhovsky's real name was Kalamatiano, that, under the name Serpukhovsky, Kalamatiano went to the eastern front in order to slip through to the Czechoslovaks, and that the documents with this false name were issued to him by Friede, who worked in the Main Administration of Military Communications. Nothing was found on Kalamatiano. Neither a search of his person nor a search of his apartment produced any materials at all which could help to expose the plot. But I recall that late one night I was called at my apartment by Comrade Kengissep, whom the Estonian government subsequently put to death, and he asked me to come to the Vecheka at once. I found Comrade Kengissep and Kalamatiano in the midst of a conversation. Comrade Kengissep tried to talk Kalamatiano into confessing. Kalamatiano refused to do so. We directed our attention at Kalamatiano's stick (it was a thick stick), began to examine it, and finally opened it to find that it was hollow and contained a bundle of all sorts of notes, enciphered messages, and receipts for money.

Then Kalamatiano saw that he was finished, and finished once and for all. The only remaining question was whose names lay concealed behind the numbers which appeared on the receipts for money. These numbers went up to thirty. The money received by these "numbers" was between 600 and 1,000 rubles. Incidentally, the sum of 1,000 rubles was paid only to Friede, who was also the organizer of the whole business; he had a fund of fifty thousand rubles in his possession. Kalamatiano, however, finally deciphered the names himself, and it turned out that nearly all of them were already in jail, with the exception of some who were located in other cities, where orders were immediately sent for their arrest. . . .[16]

After the siege of the Norwegian Legation had gone on for a week, DeWitt Poole, who, aside from his cook, was the only one permitted to go in and out of the Legation, made a trip to Petrograd to confer with the Norwegians, whose representatives remained in that city. He sought their assistance in negotiating with the Soviet government for the release of Allied officials.

Shortly after his return to Moscow the situation grew worse. The Soviet authorities had learned of American participation in the military intervention and retaliated by arresting a number of American Y.M.C.A. employees. The mood of the Red Guards outside the Legation had also become progressively more ugly as they suffered from the wet, miserable weather. They felt frustrated because the occupants of the Legation showed no signs of giving in (unknown to them, the beseiged Allies had plentiful supplies of food from American Red Cross stores and even one water tap that inexplicably continued to flow). They spoke darkly about going in and finishing off the occupants, who could not take this as an idle threat.

At about this time Poole received a message from the State Department that had been thoughtfully forwarded by Georgi Chicherin. It was actually a radio message intercepted by Soviet monitors. The State Department instructed Poole to leave Russia at once by any available route. Recognizing the hopeless predicament in which he found himself, Poole wasted no time in obeying these instructions. Through neutral diplomats, he requested the Commissariat for Foreign Affairs to issue the papers necessary for his exit from Russia. When he received these papers, he immediately set about leaving.

Poole counted on the lack of accord between the Commissariat for Foreign Affairs and the Cheka in order to make good his departure. The Commissariat wanted to allow all the Allied personnel to leave; the Cheka wanted to imprison them, using them as hostages or shooting them. After receiving the exit papers, Poole had his cook take out a few possessions in a small bag and leave them in a safe place for him. Then he wandered out of the Legation, pretending to the Cheka guards that he was merely going off for a few hours. Instead he reclaimed his bag and headed for the railroad station.

Arriving in Petrograd, Poole contacted the Norwegians, who put him up for the night in the former American Embassy. On the following day he was escorted by two Norwegians to the border at Byeloostrov. The Soviet official at the border procrastinated at first but finally gave way to Poole's protests and allowed him to cross the bridge over the small stream to the Fnnish side of the border. Poole later learned from the Norwegians that an order for Poole's arrest had arrived only ten minutes after he had crossed the border.

Meanwhile, by his own account, Sidney Reilly found himself in an almost untenable position. He could only spend a night here and there. On one occasion he took shelter with a prostitute in a room where the smell of *makhorka*, cheap crude Russian tobacco, was almost too much to bear. Much of the time he went hungry. He could appreciate the daily reports called "Struggle with Hunger" in *Pravda*:

> From the station Kirsanov—20 carloads of potatoes sent to Moscow
> From station Melekhovo—2 carloads of cucumbers
> From station Yasonov—1 carload of cabbage
> From station Pronya—1 carload of cucumbers
> From Astrakhan—20 carloads of herring
> From Ryazyan—36 carloads of hoofed cattle
> Loaded for Moscow:
> At station Petrovsk—loaded 1 car of rye
> From Ekaterinovka—5 cars of rye
> From Balashov—1 car of rye

Reilly was considering various schemes for his departure. But he was not the only one interested in his escape. Someone whom he later identified only as M. told him that pursuers were hot on his trail. "When he approached my agent," Reilly said, "he described me as already surrounded, and his plan for my escape was proportionately expensive. It could not be done, he said, under 100,000 rubles."[17]

George Hill had resolved to rejoin his English friends in the Norwegian Legation. He possessed a passport in the name of Bergmann which he turned over to Reilly; being stronger and more athletic than Kalamatiano, he succeeded in scaling the fence around the Legation and once more donned his British uniform.

With Hill's false passport, Reilly boarded a train for Petrograd. On the train he spotted a German diplomat whom he addressed as an ostensible fellow countryman, and speaking German ceaselessly they journeyed together the rest of the way. With the help of this masquerade, Reilly had no difficulty in passing through the Cheka's document checks.

He was able to find other hiding places in Petrograd until he found a Dutchman who agreed to smuggle him aboard a ship for 60,000 rubles. Reilly believed that the ship would take him directly to Stockholm, but it made a stop at German-occupied Revel, where Reilly had good reason to fear that he might be captured by the Germans. Nevertheless, he did not hesitate to go ashore and took advantage of his brief visit to do some spying on German military installations.

Then he continued his journey to Sweden en route back to England.

Although his mission to Russia had ended in disaster, Reilly retained his confident bearing and his air of optimism. He later told friends that, as he saw the spires and rooftops of Petrograd sink into the purple rim of the horizon, he made a silent vow that he would return one day and bring about the final destruction of the Bolsheviks.

Chapter 9

AS FAR BACK AS JULY the Cheka had become aware that Sidney Reilly was interested in establishing contact with commanding officers of the Latvian sharpshooters. At that time Peters was acting chairman of the Cheka, since Dzerzhinski had been officially, if only temporarily, relieved of his post because, as Dzerzhinski himself said, "I am one of the principal witnesses in the case of the German Ambassador Count Mirbach's assassination." What he really meant was that a great deal of skepticism existed, even in the ranks of the Bolsheviks, about Dzerzhinski's true role in that affair. In actuality, however, Dzerzhinski never ceased to be the head of the Cheka, and every step taken by Peters was based on prior consultation with his chief.

Peters, a Latvian, was the natural choice to handle any Cheka operation involving the Latvian sharpshooters. Some time before, Dzerzhinski had dispatched a number of Chekists to Petrograd with the task of penetrating into counterrevolutionary organizations in that city on the assumption that this could be accomplished more easily there than in the Soviet capital. Two of these Chekists happened to be Latvians, and they were precisely the ones who, under the aliases Sprogis and Shmidkhen, received introductions through contacts in the Russian opposition movement to Naval Attaché Cromie and Sidney Reilly. Once the Allied representatives had taken the bait about the Latvians, it became urgent to decide who in the Cheka would be placed in charge. "After a conference with Comrade Dzerzhinski and Comrade Skrypnik,[1] who even at this time worked in the Vecheka," reported Peters, "we decided that I should handle this matter and direct the work."

Shmidkhen's true name was Jan Buikis. In 1917, when he joined the Communst party, he was serving as a second lieutenant in the 8th Volmar Lettish Rifle Regiment. In March 1918 he was recruited by the Cheka. He was twenty-two years old.

In accordance with Peters's instructions, Buikis encouraged Cromie and Reilly to believe that the commanders of the Latvian sharpshooters could be subverted. After their arrival in Moscow, Buikis and his companion delivered the Cromie letter to the Cheka. After reading its contents, Peters instructed the two men to deliver the letter to Lockhart. Meanwhile Peters looked around for a reliable man among the Latvian commanders to use as an agent in the operation.

Peters already knew Colonel Eduard Petrovich Berzin well. Berzin had carried out other assignments for the Cheka, and there was not the slightest doubt about his devotion to the Bolshevik cause, which had been proved in many trying situations.

When Lockhart showed interest in meeting a Latvian commander, Buikis-Shmidkhen brought Berzin to Lockhart's apartment the next day and introduced the two men. Once Berzin had established direct contact with Lockhart and Reilly, "Shmidkhen" had finished his work and was instructed by Peters to remove himself gradually from the scene.

As it turned out, Buikis-Shmidkhen still had one more task to perform. During Lockhart's confinement in the Kremlin, the Cheka resorted to one of Soviet State Security's favorite tricks, one that has been used against personalities as different as Aleksandr Solzhenitsyn and Greville Wynne. "Unfortunately, too, I was not alone, as Peters had promised I should be," Lockhart related. "I had a companion in misfortune, the Lett, Shmidkhen, who was the cause of all our troubles and who was alleged to be my accomplice and agent. We spent thirty-six hours together, during which I was afraid to exchange a word. Then he was taken away. I never heard what happened to him. To this day I do not know whether he was shot or whether he was handsomely rewarded for the part he had played in unmasking the 'great conspiracy.' "

Lockhart's second alternative—that "Shmidkhen" would be handsomely rewarded—was the correct one. In 1965 KGB Colonel V. Kravchenko wrote an article, "The Secret of Shmidkhen Revealed," which appeared in the magazine *Pogranichnik* (Border Guard).[2] Searching for "Shmidkhen," Colonel Kravchenko tracked him down in "one of the quiet Moscow lanes," where Jan Janovich Buikis, a retired colonel of the NKVD, was still living at the age of seventy in an apartment "whose key F. E. Dzerzhinski personally delivered to him."

Dzerzhinski has been credited with the original idea that brought Berzin into the operation. In his *Pogranichnik* article, Kravchenko wrote: "Dzerzhinski formed a plan: to introduce Lockhart with Shmidkhen's help to one of the Latvian unit commanders loyal to the Soviet state whose position would make him interesting to Lockhart and who, by his capabilities, would be equal to the task." Indeed, Berzin did his job so well that he successfully deceived Lockhart and the other Allied representatives whom he encountered at this time.

While he faded into the background, Buikis-Shmidkhen nevertheless continued to function as Berzin's "cutout" or intermediary in maintaining contact between him and the Cheka. It was assumed that, in the event the Allied intelligence chiefs had Berzin shadowed, his meetings with "Shmidkhen" would arouse no suspicion. The two men met in public places, at Olieny Prudy or in the Sokolniki amusement park, where Berzin passed on his reports.

After receiving, according to Soviet sources, a total of 1.2 million rubles from Sidney Reilly, however, Berzin personally delivered the money to Feliks Dzerzhinski and Yakov Sverdlov. Reilly had boasted of "buying" the Latvian commander for two million rubles, but this may have been Reilly's typical hyperbole, unless someone actually pocketed 800,000 rubles. It is not known whether Reilly obtained from Berzin signed receipts for the money.

Except for military service at the front during the civil war, Colonel Berzin spent his whole subsequent career as a Chekist. He went on intelligence missions to Berlin and London. Later he worked in the NKVD headquarters in Moscow. Then he was assigned to large NKVD construction projects employing tens of thousands of labor camp inmates, in which, presumably, his considerable organizational abilities could be used to the full. One such project was the construction of the paper combine on the Vishera River in the Urals.

Finally, Berzin received the most important assignment of his life: He became the manager of the giant Dal'stroi empire at Magadan in the Kolyma region, where gold, molybdenum, and other metals were mined by labor camp inmates, many of whom died in the arctic cold of fifty degrees below zero. Berzin drew up "simply fantastic plans for the construction of an ocean port, mines, factories, gold excavations, while mapping out future roads and the layout of an enormous city."[3]

Compared with his successors, Berzin had the reputation of being reasonable about the complaints of prisoners. But it is unlikely that he could have headed this project for five years, from 1932 to 1937, if he had not produced results satisfactory to Moscow, and this could only have been achieved by driving the prisoners to the limit of their endurance. Stalin had told him before his departure: "You will answer with your head for the construction in Magadan. With your head!"[4]

In December 1937 Berzin left his post in the Soviet Far East to take leave in Moscow, where his family was waiting for him. At that time Nikolai Yezhov was conducting a purge of the NKVD itself. Berzin traveled home over the Trans-Siberian Railway. When his train reached Aleksandrov, 113 kilometers from Moscow, there was a stop to change locomotives. Berzin descended from the train to stretch his legs on the platform. Snow fell steadily, covering the platform with a smooth white carpet in which his footsteps left clear imprints. Two uniformed men suddenly approached Berzin from opposite sides and informed him that he was under arrest.[5]

Berzin's wife, Elsa, waited in vain for him at the station in Moscow.

Eduard Petrovich Berzin, Soviet hero of the 1918 "ambassadors' plot," as it was sometimes called in the Communist press, recipient of the Order of Lenin for his mining of Magadan gold with forced labor, was shot as an alleged Japanese spy in 1938.

Chapter 10

EARLY IN NOVEMBER 1918, Sidney Reilly returned to England and on arrival in London, with his customary panache, he took a suite at the Savoy Hotel. Vividly describing months of physical hardship while hiding out in Moscow and Petrograd—sleeping in his clothes on the bare floor or anywhere else he could lay his head, unable to wash up or bathe regularly, going hungry much of the time—not to speak of the accompanying mental strain, he declared himself happy now to luxuriate in the Savoy's renowned creature comforts, enjoying the best service, food, and drink then available in England. The great war was just ending. Reilly shaved off the black beard he had grown in Russia and, like a butterfly emerging from its cocoon, made a brilliant reappearance in his Royal Canadian Air Force uniform. He also could display a new order, the Military Cross, awarded to him through the efforts of the Secret Intelligence Service's chief, Sir Mansfield Cumming.

Reilly was seeing a great deal of Cumming in this initial period. Two such flamboyant men inevitably felt a certain kinship. Cumming, a retired navy captain, was a vigorous, square-shouldered, while-haired man of nearly sixty who enjoyed surrounding himself with pretty young women and loved fast cars. His taste for speed had resulted in an automobile crash that cost him a leg. There was a story that he had amputated his leg himself with a penknife in order to free himself from the wreckage. In any case, Cumming got along quite well with an artificial wooden leg and, it was said, sometimes unsettled visitors by taking a knife off his desk and plunging it into the leg. At the same time, he had proved his capacity for intelligence work and earned the respect of his subordinates.

Reilly had been preceded to England by Lockhart, Hicks, and Boyce, all of whom had been released in October under the terms of an exchange for Maksim Litvinov and other Bolsheviks imprisoned by the British government. Boyce, Reilly's SIS superior in Russia, had had the worst experiences of all, he and other Allied personnel being confined with ordinary criminals in a large dungeon where they would have starved had it not been for the help of the American Red Cross. George Hill turned up in London a short time afterward. Although he had left on the same special train guarded by Latvian troops that had conveyed the Englishmen to Finland, he had been sent back into Russia from Finland to carry out a sabotage mission.

Soon after returning to England, Reilly met Cumming and related his adventures during his escape from Russia. That same day, Reilly entertained Lockhart and Boyce at a champagne lunch in the Savoy where he told the same story. Reflecting the euphoria of those days, Reilly thoughtfully presented a gift to Lockhart, a cigar box bearing the inscription:

> To R. H. Bruce Lockhart, HBM's Representative in Russia in 1918 (during the Bolshevik Regime) in remembrance of events in Moscow during August and September of that year, from his faithful Lieutenant, Sidney Reilly.

There was a round of social events that gave Reilly the opportunity to shine, particularly exerting his charm on the ladies, the wives of his colleagues and friends among senior intelligence and diplomatic officials as well as the operations officers with whom he associated at that time. None of this prevented him from simultaneously carrying on an affair with a courtesan who, for a while, met his ever-present need for a woman in his life. (Even now he still had two wives, but he had seen neither of them for years. He had lost track of Margaret, his first wife, who, unknown to him, was living in Brussels, where she had spent most of the war years under the German occupation. Nadine, Reilly's second wife, remained in New York, but he had hardly heard from her since his arrival in England in early 1917.)

On November 12, the day after the Armistice, Reilly gave a little party at the Savoy to which he invited Lockhart, Rex Leeper, then head of the Political Intelligence Department of the Foreign Office, and their wives. "Later, over supper in his suite," wrote Robin Lockhart, Bruce Lockhart's son, in his book about Reilly, "the women were dazzled by Reilly's magnificent claret-colored silk dressing gown and much admired his tortoise-shell hairbrushes, quite unaware of how he had received them from Hill."[1] In Russia, Hill had given the brushes as a parting present to Reilly, who had greatly admired them. In return Reilly promised, after the overthrow of the Bolsheviks, to give Hill Dzerzhinski's Rolls-Royce, the same car in which Peters had once taken Lockhart and Robins to view the destruction wrought on the anarchists' nests in Moscow. (At another supper in his Savoy suite, Reilly reciprocated by giving Hill a pair of silver brushes inscribed "From S.T. 1"— Reilly's designation in the SIS. He apologized at the same time for his inability to present Hill with Dzerzhinski's Rolls-Royce.)

Lockhart and Leeper, both in their early thirties, were close friends. Leeper had arranged the exchange for Litvinov that may have saved Lockhart's life, for there were moments when it seemed that Lockhart would surely be shot by the Bolsheviks. They both agreed that a more massive intervention should be carried out in Russia, cherishing considerably less hope than Reilly that the Soviet regime could be overturned by an internal plot.

In "The Growing Danger of Bolshevism in Russia," a report dated October 14, 1918 (just before Lockhart's arrival in England), Leeper said: "As the military power of Germany is being gradually crushed, Germany ceases to be the greatest danger to European civilization, while a new danger—no less deadly— looms up in the near future. That danger is Bolshevism."[2] He said further: "In the event of the continuation of the war and the intensification of the unrest in Germany, Bolshevism may spread, first to the Russian border provinces and then to the Central Powers, thus becoming a force that would seriously threaten Europe." Leeper recommended that the danger "be dealt with now." In short, he thought that a comparatively small army coming from the Urals might advance on Moscow and put it down by force.

Shortly after his return to England, on the first anniversary of the Bolshevik coup d'etat, Bruce Lockhart delivered a "Memorandum on the Internal Situation in Russia" to the Foreign Office. Lockhart pointed out: "Our victories over Germany have removed the original pretext for intervention."[3] Nevertheless, he advanced various reasons to justify further intervention: the risk of revolution in other countries, the necessity to keep faith with the anti-Bolshevik opposition, humanitarian grounds, and other practical considerations.

"A successful intervention will give the Allies a predominant economic position in Russia," Lockhart wrote. "It will be more than paid for by economic concessions. . . . By restoring order in Russia at once, not only are we preventing the spread of Bolshevism as a political danger but we are also saving for the rest of Europe the rich and fertile grain districts of the Ukraine."

Lockhart proposed a massive intervention involving an Allied army of at least one hundred thousand men, mostly American but with British and French participation. This intervention, mounted on a "proper scale," would strengthen the existing Allied fronts in the north of Russia and in Siberia as well as General Denikin's forces in the south for a coordinated advance on Moscow.

In 1919 Winston Churchill, the new secretary for war and air, would also advocate on the cabinet level a large-scale intervention in Russia to "break up" Bolshevik power. Churchill asserted that the Allies could not fail to intervene "thoroughly, with large forces abundantly supplied with mechanical devices."[4]

At first glance, therefore, it appeared that Reilly would find a favorable climate for his further services, as he proposed to return to Russia without delay and organize a new attempt to rid the country of the Bolsheviks.

Despite the award of the Military Cross arranged by Cumming, Reilly did not receive a totally sympathetic reception from other ranking SIS officers, who felt that, however heroic his behavior, he had *failed* in the operation entrusted to him. Such failures are never taken lightly in the intelligence community: A case officer whose operation is "blown" usually lands in a kind of purgatory where he must suffer until enough time has passed that someone in authority takes pity on him and gives him another chance. Thus it was not surprising that, at least for the time being. Reilly remained out of a job.

But that was not all. The Foreign Office harbored grave doubts about Reilly's reliability after the failure of the "Lockhart plot" (which really deserved to be called the "Reilly plot"). In his memoirs, Lockhart related: "I found that Poole, the American Consul General, took a more serious view of the conspiracy. He was inclined to regard Reilly as an agent provocateur, who had staged this plot for the benefit of the Bolsheviks. . . . I laughed at Poole's fears. . . . Ridiculous as this story was, I found nevertheless that through Poole it had gained some credence in England. When two months later I reached London, I had to go bail with the Foreign Office for Reilly's bona fides. . . . I did so without the slightest hesitation."[5] Even Lockhart's assurances, however, did not wholly eliminate those doubts in the Foreign Office.

In MI5, the British security service, there was also suspicion of Reilly stemming from supposed leftist sympathies, inferred from his close connections with the Social Revolutionaries.

Reilly's difficulties in finding a new job led him to rely more and more on the sympathy and assistance he could expect from Lockhart. In two personal letters to Lockhart written in late November, Reilly discussed his future plans.[6] He expressed the view that it was essential to mobilize popular support against Bolshevism. He proposed the formation of a "League for the Defense of Civilization" to cope with the "great cataclysm relentlessly approaching." He asked Lockhart to help him win the support of prominent people for this idea. He added, "Next year we will have civil war all over the world. You will find me on the side of the 'White Guards' who are bound to lose."

But Reilly also hoped that Lockhart could be of assistance to him in solving his employment problem. Reilly asked Lockhart to "do something" to support his applications to the Secret Service and the Foreign Office to obtain a "halfway decent job" where he could "continue to serve . . . in the question of Russia and Bolshevism." With questionable sincerity, Reilly concluded his appeal to Lockhart with the words "I should like nothing better than to serve under you."

Nevertheless, the hopes that Reilly placed in Lockhart seemed hardly likely to be realized, for Lockhart himself was in trouble. In October and November 1918 the question of Lockhart and his activities in Russia was repeatedly raised in the House of Commons, but only evasive answers could be obtained from government spokesmen. Lockhart could take little comfort from the government's evasiveness. The blame for the fiasco in Russia clearly fell on him, whatever the government did or did not say.

Official secrecy protected Reilly as an intelligence agent from similar public attention, but he could not escape an indirect reference to him in a speech in Parliament about the Lockhart affair. The M.P. Joseph King said: "In recent months we have immensely increased the amount of Secret Service money and there are papers on record which show that one officer alone passed 120,000 pounds in one week in Russia with the purpose of starting a counterrevolution."[7]

Knowledge of this kind doubtless helped to stimulate the rumors that Reilly had misappropriated for his own use a substantial part of the operational funds that had passed through his hands.

Despite his frustrations in obtaining a job, Reilly was still able to entertain many influential people in the intelligence and diplomatic milieu who shared his lively interest in crushing Bolshevism. He had rented a fashionable flat in the Albany, Piccadilly, which could boast of Lord Byron among its famous residents in the course of a century or more, and furnished it lavishly: Louis Seize furniture, Impressionist paintings, handsome Aubusson tapestries and rugs, antique Meissen porcelain clocks, heavy lamps with fringed shades that cast a soft pink glow over everything. The visitors came not only to enjoy his hospitality, personal charm, and good talk but also to see for themselves an apartment that had aroused much curiosity in certain circles in London.

Much of the apartment was filled with memorabilia of Napoleon collected by Reilly over the years and rescued from storage. On one wall of the living room hung an enormous picture, a copy of Jacques Louis David's famous painting *The Coronation* [of Napoleon], whose original was in the Louvre. In the painting, Napoleon, ignoring the pope, placed the crown on his head himself. In the group around the newly crowned emperor stood the fox-faced

Talleyrand, capable of serving so many masters. Reilly had commissioned an indigent French artist to paint a somewhat smaller copy of the original.

A plaster statuette of Napoleon, like one, Reilly said, that Balzac had kept in his study, adorned the top of an inlaid cabinet. There were antique black-and-white prints in dark wooden frames depicting various historic occasions in the great man's life.

Reilly had also collected all the books he could find, some of them rare, about Napoleon. There was a set of volumes bound in gold-stamped morocco that contained Napoleonic recollections and anecdotes; Reilly had taken the trouble to collect them and have them reprinted and bound in this set.

To augment his library, Reilly ordered books by the hundreds from Hatchard's, directly across Piccadilly from the Albany, and placed in them the bookplate with his name that showed Saint George (Reilly?) slaying the dragon (Bolshevism?)—books that today, perhaps, lie obscurely on the dusty shelves of secondhand book stores.

Reilly, witty and effervescent in conversation, discoursed with his friends on many subjects, ever ready to deliver an opinion on history, philosophy, art, religion, or business. He had a particular fascination with the theater and theater people; many of his women friends were actresses or dancers. Nevertheless, his interest in the arts was more visual than aural; music, it seems, left him cold. Some acquaintances, Lockhart among them, considered him superficial. But a man with Reilly's mercurial temperament was not disposed to concentrate on any one area, unless it was his obsession with Russia and hatred of the Bolsheviks. He combined in his nature the qualities of a dreamer and a revolutionary; his ventures, productive of financial and legal worries or scandals throughout his life, were wrapped in secrecy; the path he trod he had to travel alone except for a few fellow ideologists.

Reilly's guests at the Albany included such former colleagues as Bruce Lockhart, George Hill, Paul Dukes, Ernest Boyce, and Major Stephen Alley, Boyce's predecessor as SIS chief in Russia. More imposing figures were Admiral "Blinker" Hall, director of Naval Intelligence, one of Mansfield Cumming's old friends, and Sir Basil Thomson, head of the Home Office's Special Branch. Another visitor was Sir Archibald Sinclair, closely associated with Winston Churchill at the War Ministry, although Reilly had not yet met Churchill himself. Cumming, the chief of SIS, seems to have avoided this sort of social contact with Reilly.

Major Alley organized a luncheon club of Secret Service and MI5 officers in which Reilly was active at this time. Whatever reservations might have existed about him, Reilly was apparently accepted as an equal by British intelligence officers who had either worked in Russia or were exercising Russian desk responsibilities in their respective headquarters. These contacts did not immediately secure an assignment for him, but they kept him *au courant* about Russia.

While a prisoner in the Kremlin, Bruce Lockhart heard some disturbing news. "Krylenko, the Public Prosecutor, had spoken at a meeting," he recalled, "and, amid loud cheers, had announced that the Allied conspirators were to be tried by him and that the criminal Lockhart would not escape his proper punishment."[8] This fate Lockhart was luckily spared through the exchange for Litvinov. Nonetheless, as the end of November approached, word reached London that the Revolutionary Tribunal was about to conduct a trial of the principals in the "Lockhart plot." Sidney Relly himself would have been sitting among the defendants in Moscow had he not made good his escape from Russia.

Chapter 11

THE TRIAL of the alleged partici-
pants in the "Lockhart plot" before the so-called Supreme Tribunal
in Moscow began on November 28 and ended on December 3.
Reilly and his Russian-speaking British colleagues could read
details of the trial in the Soviet All-Russian Central Executive
Committee's newspaper, *Izvestiya*, when the issues of that week
arrived in London.

According to *Izvestiya*, representatives of the Swedish and
Danish legations as well as government officials and relatives of
the twenty persons accused in an "imperialist plot" against the
Soviet Republic attended the opening session.

Those on trial included Lockhart, Grenard, Sidney Reilly, and
Henri de Vertemont (all tried in absentia), Kalamatiano, William
Combes Higgs (who had collected millions of rubles for Lockhart), Jeanne Morans, headmistress of the French girls' school (an
associate of de Vertemont), Aleksandr and Mariya Friede, Yeliza-

veta Otten, Olga Dmitrievna Starzheskaya (Reilly's "fiancée"), a number of Kalamatiano's agents, and four Czechoslovaks.

Inexplicably, General Lavergne was not among the accused.

In view of Kalamatiano's presence as a defendant, it was also noteworthy that DeWitt Poole had not been included among the accused persons. After his escape, Poole had remained for a time in Finland, but when Ambassador Francis, who had returned to Archangel after its capture by Allied troops, fell ill, Poole moved in as chargé d'affaires to replace him. Among the principal defendents, Lockhart, Grenard, Reilly, and de Vertemont had safely left Russia and Poole was on Russian territory controlled by the Allies, while Kalamatiano alone faced a Soviet court.

The prosecutor was Nikolai Vasilievich Krylenko, who had made an extraordinary career with very ordinary talents. Krylenko was ordinary not only mentally but also physically. He was a squat, short-legged man with a flat face, and there were tens of thousands of Russians, perhaps hundreds of thousands, who looked just like him. He had a fixed smile, more like a grimace, or else his face was scowling or twitching. Lockhart called Krylenko an "epileptic degenerate"; he went on to say that Krylenko was the "most repulsive type I came across in all my connections with the Bolsheviks."[1]

A sailor himself, Krylenko had become a Communist and helped the Bolsheviks come to power by delivering speeches on their behalf at meetings of soldiers and sailors. Armed with his credentials of ordinariness, he became very effective at such meetings. During the upheavals of the initial revolutionary period, Krylenko's past military career and Communist affiliation thrust him into unmerited prominence, making him the first Soviet People's Commissar for Military and Naval Affairs and Supreme Commander of the armed forces, since all the czarist generals had been ousted.

Perhaps the task of organizing the Red Army called for qualities of leadership that Krylenko lacked. In any case, that task was undertaken by Trotsky, and Krylenko received a completely different assignment. After taking a couple of legal courses, he assumed a leading role in a newly created Revolutionary Tribunal that would make short shrift of all subversive and counterrevolutionary individuals and groups.

Leaving a man named Karklin, who was cut of the same cloth,

to act as chairman of the court, Krylenko, the public prosecutor, presented the Soviet government's case against the defendants. He stood in the center of the courtroom, posing with hands on hips in a favorite oratorical stance, the peculiar fixed smile on his face. To emphasize his proletarian origin, he wore an unbuttoned jacket and a striped sailor's undershirt that showed through the open collar of his shirt.

The saturnine Jacob Peters, deputy chairman of the Cheka, appeared as the first witness for the prosecution, testifying about the plot hatched by Lockhart and Reilly to overthrow the Soviet government. He described the attempt to subvert the Lettish Rifles by recruiting one of the commanders, Berzin, and giving him 1.2 million rubbles with which to bribe his fellow commanders.

Peters said that René Marchand had reported to the Cheka about the meeting held by American Consul General Poole, which included plans for blowing up bridges and setting fire to food warehouses. Peters believed Marchand's story, he said, because the French officer had almost gone mad with excitement, thinking of the treachery of the Allies in seeking to destroy Russia rather than save her.

Lockhart was allowed to leave Russia, Peters testified, because of an agreement reached by the Commissariat for Foreign Affairs with the English government which permitted representatives of Soviet Russia to leave England.

With regard to M. V. Trestar, chief of the Moscow Military District motor pool, Peters asserted that he had had a very close relationship with the English officer Sidney Reilly and had made it possible for Reilly to use Soviet vehicles. A receipt signed by Reilly for 15,000 rubles was found in Trestar's possession.

Peters also testified about the circumstances of Kalamatiano's arrest, noting that Kalamatiano's walking stick contained a list of thirty-two names enciphered by numbers pertaining to his agents.

Eduard Petrovich Berzin was the next witness.[2] He confirmed Peters's testimony about the planned coup d'etat. Berzin said that first Shmidkhen, a former officer, and then Lockhart tried to persuade him to come over with his sharpshooters to the English side. As Peters had testified, Berzin only pretended to accept this proposal, thereby coming into contact with Grenard, Reilly, and other Anglo-French agents and discovering their plans.

Later in the same session the court took testimony from Kalamatiano. Despite the prosecutor's relentless prodding, Xenophon Dmitrievich was obviously determined to maintain his commercial cover. If he squirmed as he testified, he still maintained a certain consistency in his story.

He said that he had been appointed authorized representative of Pankivel,[3] an American trading firm that opened offices in Moscow and Petrograd in 1916. The firm's business activity concentrated on the sale of automobiles to the Russian government. Trade relations were conducted on behalf of Russia by the Commissariat for Foreign Trade and on behalf of America through the commercial attaché. As a result of the revolution, it became essential to make a factual assessment of the country's political and economic situations in order to gauge the possibilities for further trade relations. Since official sources of information no longer existed, such information had to be gathered by special agents with respect to such particular fields as transportation and banking operations, not to speak of the agrarian, industrial, and general situations in Russia. Some of these reports necessarily treated military matters because the movement of troops via certain stations inevitably interfered with freight.

Kalamatiano explained his encipherment of agent reports by pointing out that the agents were operating at considerable risk to themselves in areas close to the front, such as the Ukraine and Belorussia. He concealed the cipher materials in his walking stick largely owing to the psychological climate prevailing in recent months, when even the most innocent behavior had sometimes been characterized as espionage. He included political reports in his work only for the purpose of determining whether the Soviet authorities could and would fulfill obligations that they assumed in the exchange of trade.

At this point Prosecutor Krylenko asked sarcastically: "What do Agent Number Twelve's reports have to do with trade matters? For example, his reports on the quantity of rifles and machine guns produced by Tula factories, or on formations of the Red Army?"

"As a trader, I was naturally interested in finding out about industry in Tula," Kalamatiano replied. "Information about the Red Army near the front was significant because I needed to know how well the Soviet troops would protect warehouses against the Germans."

Under persistent questioning by the prosecutor, Kalamatiano said that enciphered reports concerning Austrian troops made sense because the advance of forces of the Central Powers into Russia had a direct bearing on the prospects of Russian-American trade relations.

Asked by the court to explain why he was living with a forged passport in the name of Serpukhovsky if his work was completely legal, Kalamatiano answered that the matter had come to a head in July when relations between the United States and Soviet Russia deteriorated. When it was decided that the American representatives should leave, he felt that he should leave, too. Later, however, he decided to remain, since he had lived in Russia for a long time, was married to a Russian woman, and hoped that in due course, when relations settled down again, he would be able to resume his commercial activities. After the arrests of Allied nationals began, he hesitated for some time before deciding to live with a forged passport.

Kalamatiano admitted that he had visited American Consul General Poole. Nevertheless, he denied that he had ever taken part in an official meeting of the kind described in René Marchand's letter. Poole introduced him to Reilly and de Vertemont. Kalamatiano exchanged addresses with the two other men and promised to send them information reports to acquaint them with all trade activity, as they had decided to support one another in view of the unfriendly relations with the Allies. He insisted that his whole conversation with Poole had not lasted more than ten or fifteen minutes. He had heard absolutely nothing about a plot, the blowing up of bridges, or the destruction by arson of food supplies. That was his first and last meeting with Reilly. Neither Lavergne nor Grenard nor Marchand was present at the time in Poole's office.

Kalamatiano further denied that he had ever sent anyone to the Czechoslovakian front, about which espionage reports would have been especially interesting. But confronted with evidence before the court, said *Izvestiya*, he was forced to admit that he had traveled to Samara and Ufa, cities occupied by the Czechoslovaks. Kalamatiano contended, however, that he had gone there to see the American consul.

Subsequently, the court heard evidence presented by Lieutenant Colonel Aleksandr Vladimirovich Friede, identified as a former examining magistrate of the Moscow Military District Court. Friede was solidly built, with an erect soldierly bearing, close-cropped blond hair, and eyes like chips of gray-blue ice in an unsmiling face.

Friede stated that he became acquainted with Kalamatiano, a businessman, at the end of May. After convincing himself of Kalamatiano's reliability and likewise gaining the latter's trust, he became Kalamatiano's closest associate. Friede had no doubt about the purely commercial nature of Kalamatiano's organization and therefore did not hesitate to make two trips to Rzhev, a center of light industry, at Kalamatiano's request, delivering reports to him at the end of these trips. In his capacity as Kalamatiano's principal assistant, he received reports from agents of the organization which he edited and processed in final form. The reports were usually of a political or economic character.

In answer to other questions, Friede acknowledged that he had invited Major General Aleksandr Andreyevich Zagryazhsky, a former colleague who was a judge of the Moscow Military District Court, to work for the Kalamatiano organization. Friede also acknowledged that he had conducted negotiations with P. M. Solyus and Evgeny Mikhailovich Golitsyn about joining Kalamatiano's organization. Friede admitted that he knew about the list that assigned a number to each agent. This numerical system, he said, had first been used for agents operating in occupied areas and later was extended to the other agents carrying out missions on the territory of the Soviet Republic.

"Why did you ask your mother to hide the papers you gave to her?" asked Krylenko.

"I didn't want to involve other people in case the papers came to light."

"Doesn't that mean the papers incriminated people who were mentioned in them?"

"Not necessarily."

"Isn't it true," Krylenko thundered, "that those papers contained military secrets reported by a spy who visited Petrograd, Sestroretsk, Zvanka, and Petrozavodsk?"

Friede did not reply. In further questioning, he confirmed that he had met American Consul General Poole. He also admitted that he had illegally provided Kalamatiano with a certificate bearing his signature from a Soviet institution where he was employed. He conceded that he had not submitted the document for registration but still had assigned a serial number so that Kalamatiano was able to travel with a package to Penza as if on official business. Friede said that 50,000 rubles found in his possession had been entrusted to him for safekeeping. According to *Izvestiya*, he failed to explain, however, why he had hidden the money in a secret compartment behind the mirror of a shaving kit.

He also admitted that he had known about his sister Mariya Friede's trips to Vladikavkaz[4] at the request of American Consul F. Willoughby Smith in Tbilisi. She traveled in the guise of a sister of mercy and received 600 rubles for each trip, bringing a package of reports on her return.

Friede stated that he reworked the reports received from agents, each report in three copies, and gave them to his sister Mariya to deliver to addresses where Reilly was in hiding. He obtained these addresses from Kalamatiano.

"How could you, a former military examining magistrate in wartime, transmit reports of an espionage nature?" asked Krylenko.

"The reports might have been political—or even military," Friede said, "but the information was in the public domain, so it couldn't involve anything criminal."

In conclusion, Krylenko extracted from Friede an admission that he knew Kalamatiano was living under a forged passport.

Mariya Friede, a tall, severe-looking woman, made a brief appearance. She was wearing a long violet-colored dress with a small cross glittering on a gold chain in the open neckline. She testified about her delivery of the packages of reports to the Sheremetyevsky Pereulok address. Then the session of the Revolutionary Tribunal adjourned until the next day.

The November 30 *Izvestiya* reported the continuation of the Revolutionary Tribunal's deliberations when former Major General Zagryazhsky testified. Zagryazhsky was accused of participation in Kalamatiano's espionage activities. According to the indictment, he received payment for information provided to Kalamatiano and also was given 20,000 rubles for payments to agents who supplied other information. This sum of money turned up during a search of his home.

Zagryazhsky conceded that he had worked for Kalamatiano's organization for about a month and a half, from July until the third of September. He was aware that Kalamatiano's colleagues had been identified by numbers. The 20,000 rubles in his possession were to be paid to these colleagues in accordance with A. V. Friede's instructions. Zagryazhsky had a number of conversations with Kalamatiano that were strictly limited to commercial matters. He received for his information the sum of 750 rubles, which he turned over to the Cheka. He denied, however, that there was anything incriminating about his activities.

Izvestiya pointed out that Zagryazhsky's protestations of innocence were contradicted by his knowledge that Kalamatiano was using a forged passport in the name of Serpovsky and that Kalamatiano had gone underground during the period they worked together.

Recalled for additional testimony, Mariya Friede maintained that she traveled to Vladikavkaz not for espionage but for nursing. She made the trip as a sister of mercy for the American Red Cross in order to give aid to Armenian refugees. As a sister of mercy, she received from Consul Smith in Moscow 350 rubles in pay and a like amount for travel expenses. In further testimony, it was established that, at Smith's request, she had delivered a package to the American consul in Vladikavkaz.

She also admitted that, at her brother A. V. Friede's request, she delivered a letter to Elizabeth Otten, an actress of the Moscow Art Theater, and another letter to the headmistress of the Catholic girls' lycée, although she denied that this headmistress was Jeanne Morans. That was the extent, she maintained, of her work for the American organization in which her brother was employed. She had never seen either Morans or de Vertemont.

Called next as a witness was Jeanne Morans, who gave her evidence in French. She stated that she did not know Mariya Friede or any others among the accused, with the exception of de Vertemont. During the period when the school was taking in refugees, de Vertemont had sought refuge there. This was at the beginning of August. She denied, however, that she had ever engaged in any conspiratorial work for de Vertemont.

In subsequent testimony, two other agents of Kalamatiano, Pavel Maksimovich Solyus and Aleksey Vasilievich Potemkin, claimed that they had agreed to supply information to Aleksandr Friede when he told them the information was needed for an American trading firm where he worked.

Z. I. Chesnokovaya, another witness, testified that she and her husband, M. V. Trestar, had first become acquainted with Reilly and his wife in the United States in 1915. Later in Moscow they had known Reilly only by that name, until the last period when Reilly used his wife's name, Massino, explaining that he did so because of the increasingly hostile attitude of Russia toward the United States and England. Chesnokovaya insisted that their relations with Reilly had always been entirely social.

According to *Izvestiya*, the blond actress Elizabeth Otten became hysterical when she was called as a witness. For this reason she had to be removed from the courtroom.

Olga Dmitrievna Starzheskaya, identified as an employee in the administrative section of the Central Executive Committee, testified about her initial meeting with Reilly in the lobby of the Bolshoi Theater during the Fifth All-Russian Congress of Soviets. Reilly had at once made a great impression on her. He called himself by various names such as Constantine, Markovich, and Massino. She did not know that he was English, as he had an excellent command of the Russian language. She had never discussed politics with him and regarded him as a supporter of the Soviet regime, since, by his own statement, he worked in a Soviet organization. In view of the fact that her work was completely mechanical, she could not have provided him with any information for purposes of espionage. Her scruples would not have permitted her to steal any documents. Reilly gave her 20,000 rubles for the purchase of an apartment and furniture, since they shared sincere feelings for each other and had decided to live together.

Ending her testimony, Starzheskaya said that Reilly had spent the night of September 3 with her and had confessed he was not Russian but English. He also told her that he would have to leave Russia. Other details about him she learned only from the newspapers.

Golitsyn, former colonel of the general staff, told the court that he had been placed in the reserve and was unemployed when he first met Kalamatiano. Their meeting took place in the office of William Combes Higgs. When Kalamatiano offered him a job with the American company Pankivel at a salary of 500 rubles a month, he accepted at once because he had to support not only his own family but those of his wife and sister. His task was to collect information about railroad and transport matters. He was also asked to do research on Rzhev, Smolensk, and other provinces.

"As an officer, you considered it possible to give information about the production of weapons in Tula, about the disposition of troops, and so forth?" asked Prosecutor Krylenko.

"I saw no reason why I shouldn't provide the information, since it was subsequently printed in the newspapers," Golitsyn replied.

Having recovered from her attack of hysterics, Yelizaveta Yemelyanovna Otten was recalled as a witness. *Izvestiya* noted that she was a "former" actress of the Moscow Art Theater. This time she remained composed as she denied that she had ever performed any espionage work. Reilly had lived in the same apartment on Sheremetyevsky Pereulok, but she did not know that he was a British officer. Drooping like a wilted flower, she was still able to reply in a steady voice and impart firmness to her denials.

After several Czechs testified, setting forth their dealings with Kalamatiano, which they justified on grounds of Czech patriotism, no more witnesses were called. Prosecutor Krylenko lost no time in demanding sentences for the principals involved in the "imperialist plot."

For Lockhart and Grenard, the highest-ranking Allied representatives on trial who, the prosecutor said, were guilty of arson, espionage, and violations of international law, Krylenko demanded the extreme penalty. First of all, they should be outlawed within the borders of the Soviet Republic. If (presumably as a result of "socialist revolution") they were turned over by workers' deputies in England and France to the Soviet authorities, they should be put to death by shooting.

The prosecutor demanded the same sentences for Reilly and de Vertemont.

He asked for a sentence of death by shooting for Kalamatiano, the central figure in the plot around whom all the counterrevolutionary elements had gathered.

Krylenko repeated his demand for a sentence of death by shooting in regard to Aleksandr Friede, Kalamatiano's right-hand man, and Zagryazhsky, his other principal assistant. *And* for Mariya Friede, who had acted as a courier in transmitting espionage reports, as well as the actress Otten, Reilly's confederate, who had maintained a safe apartment for the conspirators. He asked that lesser sentences be given to the other defendants.

The Revolutionary Tribunal observed a day of rest on Sunday, the first of December.

On Monday the court held a marathon session at which the defense lawyers presented their pleas on behalf of their clients and Prosecutor Krylenko made a final rebuttal. The session did not end until after midnight.

A. S. Tager, speaking in defense of Kalamatiano and Trestar, devoted most of his speech to general questions involved in the case. He attempted to prove that the tasks that Kalamatiano had undertaken were necessary not only from the American point of view but also from the Russian government's point of view. To support this argument, Tager submitted to the court much material from the Soviet press and official publications. This material proved, said the lawyer, that the United States was the only state of the Entente opposed to intervention in Russia's internal affairs and interested in trade with her. A half year before Kalamatiano's arrest, the Russian and American authorities had seriously studied a possible renewal of bilateral trade relations, including areas in which this would be most feasible. The available data thus confirmed the defendant Kalamatiano's explanation as to why the information gathered by him and his colleagues did not have anything to do with military espionage.

Defending Aleksandr Friede and his sister Mariya, the lawyer M. P. Poletika stressed that Aleksandr Friede had joined Kalamatiano's organization only after convincing himself that this organization had no connection with espionage. Moreover, Friede knew nothing about the Lockhart plot and had never met any of the principals.[5] There was even less reason to accuse Mariya Friede of wrongdoing, since she had done no more than carry out the instructions of her brother for the delivery of letters.

Jeanne Morans's lawyer, A. F. Lipskerova, pointed out that Morans had been arrested through an error. The Cheka had carried out a search for de Vertemont and, failing to find him, and arrested Morans mainly because of her past acquaintance with him.

The most dramatic courtroom appearance was that of N. K.

Muraviev, Kalamatiano's lawyer, who made a noble effort to save his client.

"My participation in this case," Muraviev said, "is largely due to the great interest shown by the Norwegian Embassy. Behind Kalamatiano there stands a whole nation that cannot be indifferent to the manner in which the Revolutionary Tribunal behaves toward its representative. The importance of this matter seems even greater in view of the complexity of relations between Soviet Russia and Europe. A favorable clarification of those relations is the work not only of diplomacy but also of the Commissariat for Trade and Industry.

"Taking into account these circumstances, I find it all the more deplorable that there are serious errors in the indictment. Above all, I must take exception on behalf of my client to the fact that the case of the American Consul General Poole has been separated from the case of Lockhart and Grenard. During the trial the existence of a conspiracy between the defendant Kalamatiano and his codefendants Lockhart and Grenard, who attempted to overthrow the Soviet regime, has not been proved. In the absence of proof of such a conspiracy, it is also impossible to speak of a connection between the American Kalamatiano and the Anglo-French plot."

Muraviev then noted an error in the translation of René Marchand's letter that had led to a misinterpretation of the author's statements. An accurate translation showed that Marchand had specifically referred to *isolated* initiatives by different agents which had the effect of creating a plot, and not a plot that involved a number of different actions. Muraviev also asked why the go-between in the attempt to bribe Colonel Berzin, a certain Shmidkhen, had not been arrested and why René Marchand had not been questioned.

"It is obvious," Muraviev went on, "that any foreign mission, in the performance of its political tasks, collects information of a political, economic, and military nature and concerns itself with counterespionage as well. Kalamatiano was an assistant to the commercial attaché of the American mission. How could his interest in the stability of the political regime in Russia be considered criminal? For business relations it does not matter what kind of regime exists; it only matters that there is no anarchy, since no business whatever can be conducted in times of chaos."

Reviewing the evidence presented at the trial, Muraviev said: "There is not a single word about Kalamatiano in Marchand's letter. As for his meeting with Reilly, the court knows about that only because Kalamatiano himself told about it. There were no secrets in Kalamatiano's actions, he behaved openly and used a forged passport only because of his fear of being arrested as a foreigner. The numerical system he used for his agents was based not on secrecy but on well-known business principles. The encipherment of reports from his agents had no other purpose than to withhold the contents from the Germans, since Kalamatiano's agents had to work in the Ukraine.[6]

"The reports from Kalamatiano's agents had nothing to do with espionage. I am speaking now of reports about the mood of the population, about the work of arms factories, and also the movement and disposition of troops. Many reports, like those received from his colleague Golitsyn, for example, were taken directly from the Soviet press.

"In conclusion, I would ask the court," said Muraviev, "to take into account the circumstance that the two most important defendants, Lockhart and Grenard, departed from Russia with the permission of the authorities. The heavy sentence for Kalamatiano recommended to the Supreme Tribunal by Prosecutor Krylenko can only hinder the Soviet government in its accomplishment of those complex tasks requiring the resolution of international relations that at this moment confront the Soviet regime."

Lawyers for the remaining defendants followed Muraviev, presenting their arguments along similar lines. They stressed that Kalamatiano's organization pursued exclusively commercial goals and that its activities had no relationship to the conspiratorial plot of Lockhart and Grenard. In view of these circumstances, it could not be said that there was anything criminal about the actions of the defendants. The Soviet government's official support of trade relations with the United States provided sufficient justification for their work in the Kalamatiano organization. The same positive approach to trade relations was reflected in concrete form by the work of Soviet organizations in April when Kalamatiano and Friede began their activities. It was not until October 25, after the publication of Wilson's note, that the Soviet state decided on a complete rupture of relations with America. The openness and lack of conspiracy in the defendants' actions, the manner in which they took notes, and their unwillingness to flee when they had every opportunity to do so all testified to the fact that they felt no guilt toward the Soviet state.

It was now Prosecutor Krylenko's turn to appear in the limelight, and he took full advantage of the opportunity. Standing as usual with his hands on his hips, his smile now transformed into a glare, he launched into a savage counterattack.

Surveying the defendants, Krylenko said: "I ask the court to take a good look at these defendants. Consider their social composition. They are representatives of groups hostile to the Soviet state and the ideas that it is striving to put into effect. Not a single worker or peasant among them! Former generals, colonels, engineers, businessmen, and representatives of the democratic intelligentsia sharing a certain educational background close to the capitalist class. And," Krylenko went on witheringly, his gaze sweeping the table at which the defense lawyers sat, "who is in court to defend this class hostile to socialism? The representatives of the defense also belong to certain political groupings."[7]

While the defense lawyers shifted uneasily in their seats, Krylenko lowered his voice for a moment. "Let us take the speech made by Defense Attorney Muraviev. In this speech there is an echo of the threat directed at us socialists by the capitalist world. Muraviev asserts that a severe sentence meted out to the American citizen Kalamatiano will sharply reflect on the fates of broad masses of the Russian population. In view of the open war declared on us by international capitalists for the purpose of exerting worldwide pressure on socialism, this threat has a real basis. It must be taken seriously. But we socialists know that it is not such facts that determine complex international relations but facts of enormous economic significance, and the threat that has been pronounced here cannot compel us to forget the basic conflict that exists between the representatives of capitalism and socialism."

The prosecutor disputed the defense contention that the charge of a counterrevolutionary conspiracy had not been proven: The Revolutionary Tribunal gave a broader interpretation to the old concept of counterrevolutionary conspiracy, an interpretation that fully accorded with the deeds of Lockhart, Grenard, Reilly, de Vertemont, and Kalamatiano. Attempting to associate the concept of counterrevolutionary conspiracy with that of military espionage (and confusing the two), the defense sought to divert the court's attention from its basic task. By this means the defense hoped to prove that if there was no military espionage, there could be no crime.

In this part of his rebuttal, Krylenko must have been well aware that the distinction between counterrevolutionary conspiracy and military espionage was germane only in the case of Kalamatiano (as well as Friede, whom he had not mentioned). For neither Kalamatiano nor Friede was in any way involved in the "Lockhart plot" to overthrow the Soviet government. Both were guilty of espionage but had nothing to do with a counterrevolutionary conspiracy.

"The claim of Defender Muraviev that every mission has three sides to its work—political, economic, and military, not to mention counterespionage—is based on the point of view of capitalist Europe's diplomatic representatives," said Krylenko with a scowl. "In our Soviet Republic this phenomenon should not only be exposed and destroyed but also identified as the fraud it is. We builders of a new structure, creators of a new world, will show such activity to the world proletariat as a shameful blot on the records of those responsible for it."

Krylenko paused briefly. "Muraviev has complained about the absence of American Consul General Poole from this trial. Poole's absence is due to concrete factors which made it necessary to renounce an indictment in his case. Kalamatiano's actions were closely linked to the activity of Anglo-American capital. Therefore the defense objection that the Soviet state will offend broad masses of the American proletariat by a terrorist act against Kalamatiano has no foundation. I remain hopeful that this question will be understood in the same way it has been understood by the Soviet state. Exposure of Kalamatiano's activities will clearly prove to them how treacherously American capitalists have behaved in Soviet Russia. Seeking with Kalamatiano's help to bring about the economic domination and conquest of Soviet Russia, American capitalists prepared to lay their hands on the country's political administration. Kalamatiano was an executor of these policies, as proven by the coincidence of his activities with the moves against Russia by the Czechoslovaks, the English landing in the north, and the Japanese in the east.

"As to the other defendants in the case, the evidence produced at this court trial leaves no doubt concerning their complicity in

Kalamatiano's activities. It is impossible to pass by all these greater and lesser 'Solyuses,' as they belong to the type of Judas Iscariots who sell important state secrets to the enemy for a few silver coins.

"In regard to such people, there's no point in debating whether it is admissible to resort to revolutionary terror."

After Prosecutor Krylenko concluded his summation on this grim note, the Revolutionary Tribunal adjourned the trial. On the following day, December 3, the defendants were given an opportunity to speak their "last word" before sentence was passed.

As *Izvestiya* reported in its December 4 issue, Kalamatiano said that he did not consider himself to be guilty of organizing espionage. He appealed to the court to accept his assurance that the activity in which he had been engaged was of a purely commercial character. But if the Tribunal could not bring itself to believe him, he begged that all those sitting here as defendants on his account should be pardoned, since they were innocent of any wrongdoing.

In his "last word," A. V. Friede told the Tribunal that his sister Mariya had not participated in his affairs.

A. A. Zagryazhsky, another defendant, said: "I know well the fate that awaits me, depending on whether or not I am believed. I have led an honorable life up to the time my hair turned gray, and those who know me are accustomed to accept my word of honor. And in such a frightful hour this word of honor is my only real defense. I swear that I am not a conspirator and have remained loyal to the Soviet state."

The actress Otten, looking pale and wan: "I don't feel guilty in any way. I have committed no crime."

Mariya Friede defended her brother and stated that he was the sole support of his old mother.

Potemkin, Solyus, Khvalynsky, and Ishevsky—all agents of Kalamatiano—said in turn that they did not consider themselves guilty of any hostile action against the Soviet state.

Ivanov did not wish to defend himself. "My honorable working life speaks for itself. As a simple peasant, I spent my youth cultivating the earth and feeding myself by working with my hands," he said.

Starzheskaya, her single brown braid behind her head bobbing as she spoke with emphasis, limited herself to a few words: "I have honorably served the Soviet state and committed no crimes against it. In view of all that I have already suffered, I beg the court to set me free."

Other defendants denied any guilt. Golitsyn, among them, said that he had not abused his position and felt himself in no sense guilty.

Combes Higgs, the Englishman, rejected the opportunity to deliver a "last word."

The court pronounced its verdict after the defendants had concluded their "last word" on Tuesday, the third of December, but the full text of the verdict did not appear in *Izvestiya* until December 5.

Freed were Elizabeth Otten, Jeanne Morans, William Combes Higgs, and five other defendants.

Olga Dmitrievna Starzheskaya received a three-month sentence with a reduction for earlier imprisonment. She was denied the right to work for government institutions of the Soviet Republic.

Zagryazhsky, Potemkin, Solyus, Khvalynsky, Golitsyn, Ivanov, Ishevsky, and Mariya Friede were sentenced to five years in prison at hard labor.

Lockhart, Grenard, Sidney Reilly, and Henri de Vertemont were declared enemies of the working class, outlawed in Soviet Russia, and sentenced, if caught, to be shot.

Kalamatiano and Aleksandr Friede were condemned to death before a firing squad.

The verdict of the Revolutionary Tribunal was to go into effect within twenty-four hours.

Chapter 12

THE PRESS OF EUROPE and America paid virtually no attention to the Moscow trial of those involved in the Lockhart case. Western newspapers reported neither the proceedings of the trial nor the sentences that the defendants received.

Strictly in terms of news, it was true, newspaper readers abroad had little interest in Russia, which seemed to be very far away. There was revolution in Germany. Unrest seethed in other defeated countries, such as Austria and Hungary. The people of France and Italy had to bind up their war wounds and think about reconstruction, which, in their minds, involved huge reparations from the Central Powers. In England a General Election—the "Khaki Elections"—was in progress, with Lloyd George seeking reelection on a "Hang the Kaiser" platform. Americans eagerly followed the news of their two million soldiers in Europe (some of whom were cautiously advancing into Germany) and wondered how soon the soldiers would come home. The influenza epidemic was waning. And on the fourth of December, the day after the verdict in the Moscow trial, President Woodrow Wilson sailed from New York on the *George Washington*, anticipating a triumphal tour of France, England, and Italy as well as a still greater triumph at the Paris Peace Conference.

Sidney Reilly, who was ordinarily closely attuned to events in Russia, had other preoccupations at the moment, first and foremost, of course, his problem of lining up a job.

The situation had been complicated by the fact that Mansfield Cumming was having some doubts about Reilly's future usefulness to the Secret Intelligence Service. The Bolshevik propaganda campaign against Allied plots had placed Reilly in the limelight, which hardly enhanced his status as a secret agent. In England there was also unwelcome publicity focusing on Lockhart but not without repercussions on Reilly himself. More significant, however, was the strong opposition to Reilly in the Foreign Office, which regarded his freewheeling, ostentatious ways as a menace to quiet diplomacy. And Cumming could not ignore the negative reactions to Reilly in his own department.

Apart from all of these factors, Cumming had been influenced by some of the questions raised about Reilly's activities in Russia. The manner in which Reilly conducted his operations during that period pointed to serious shortcomings in clandestine techniques. There was also the matter of possible misuse of Secret Service funds entrusted to Reilly. Last but not least, in spite of past services to SIS, too little was known about Reilly to make its chief feel completely comfortable.

As Robin Lockhart wrote: "For all his past achievements, Cumming had to consider the secrecy behind which Reilly hid so much of his real self. His almost megalomaniac personality and grandiose ideas were disturbing. His character seemed so full of contradictions; [he was] ruthless, yet at times highly emotional and sensitive. . . . A gambler, a womanizer, and an exhibitionist who loved luxury, he was quite unlike the average agent whose private life was usually a secluded one in a suburban backwater."[1]

Sidney Reilly chose this unpropitious time to request permanent status on the staff of MI1C. Cumming was both amazed and disturbed by Reilly's request. The amazement came from the fact that over a period of twenty years Reilly had consistently *avoided* closer ties with SIS, preferring to retain his free-lance status.

Reilly's sudden interest in permanent status could not fail to raise Cumming's antennae, particularly in the light of suspicion like that of Dewitt Poole, who viewed Reilly as a Bolshevik *agent provocateur*.

There was one additional factor that must have influenced Cumming's decision. Reilly's obsession with Bolshevism could not strike a responsive chord in Cumming, who was running an intelligence service with world wide interests. Yet, subconsciously, Cumming might have had a still more complex reaction. Joseph Conrad wrote: "A man haunted by a fixed idea is insane. He is dangerous even if that idea is an idea of justice."[2] Perhaps, for this reason if for no other, Cumming felt that Reilly was a dangerous man to have on MI1C's staff.

In a painful interview at the block of flats in Whitehall Court where SIS had its headquarters, Cumming informed Reilly that his request for permanent staff status was out of the question, at least for the time being. He pointed out that Reilly had acquired a notoriety which could not help him to function as an intelligence officer and that, in the circumstances, he could scarcely hope to use Reilly in any capacity. Moreover, the Foreign Office objections made it nearly impossible to use him at a foreign post. The best solution was for Reilly to continue to assist SIS on a free-lance basis, as he had already done for many years.

Reilly appeared to be crushed by Cumming's decision, although he displayed no rancor. He asked Cumming to reconsider and subsequently wrote Bruce Lockhart: "I also venture to think that the state should not lose my services. I would devote the rest of my wicked life to this kind of work. 'C' promised to see the F.O. about this."[3]

Cumming, of course, had no intention of reversing his decision. Nevertheless, he was able to soften the blow by sending Reilly with George Hill, who had transferred from Military Intelligence to SIS, to southern Russia. Their mission was to assess the strength of General Anton Ivanovich Denikin's Volunteer Army, which was fighting against the Red Army.

Hill welcomed this new opportunity to share an assignment with Reilly, whom he liked and respected. "He was a dark, well-groomed, very foreign-looking man," Hill wrote once, "who spoke English, Russian, French, and German perfectly though, curiously enough, with a foreign accent in each case."[4]

The two men departed in the middle of December, making an overnight channel crossing from Southampton to Le Havre on a ship that also had among its passengers the concert pianist Ignace Paderewski, who was returning to Poland to become the new prime minister. To Hill's surprise, Paderewski and Reilly turned out to be old friends and spent much of the time reminiscing about Reilly's mother and sister, whom Paderewski obviously knew well. It was an indirect confirmation of the Polish roots of Reilly's family.

Hill and Reilly followed a roundabout route to their destination, traveling by train from Le Havre to Marseilles and from there aboard British destroyers through the Mediterranean, the Bosporus, and the Black Sea to the south of Russia, where they arrived on Christmas day, 1918. They landed at Novorossisk, the port through which vitally needed French and British military supplies would soon be flowing to General Denikin.

They were posing as British businessmen investigating Anglo-Russian trade prospects. It was a thin cover but sufficed to carry out their mission. They had arrived at a fortunate juncture, as the enemy forces in the area had just been completely destroyed and within a short time the Volunteer Army would conquer the whole of the Northern Caucasus.

Militarily, therefore, Denikin had achieved a sound position from which he could hope to advance rapidly toward Central Russia. He had a base, ample manpower reserves, and an area rich in natural resources—in short, everything he needed in order to build up and expand his army.

The political situation, at least superficially, seemed improved. In the past, there had been constant conflict between the commander-in-chief of the Volunteer Army and the ataman of the Don Cossacks. The ataman insisted on his political authority over the whole area. Up to the Armistice, he had sought good relations with the Germans, whom the Volunteer Army continued to regard as enemies, and tried to remain "neutral" in regard to the Bolsheviks; the Don Cossacks were determined to defend their homeland against the Red Army but had no stomach for fighting that required them to take the offensive into other areas. For this reason, the ataman had resisted all efforts by Denikin and his predecessors to obtain command over the Don Cossack forces. On December 26, however, General Denikin signed an agreement with General Krasnov, ataman of the Don Cossacks, assigning the supreme command to Denikin, who became commander-in-chief not only of the Volunteer Army but also of the Armed Forces of South Russia. At the same time, the Don retained its autonomy.

Nevertheless, friction between Denikin and Krasnov continued until Krasnov was finally replaced by a new ataman. Moreover, Denikin had never succeeded in resolving his problems with the autonomous Kuban Cossacks farther south, and there were also bitter disagreements with the Georgian government, which, in consequence, was stirring up trouble along the Volunteer Army's southern perimeter.

Apart from all these local troubles, Denikin and his advisers had failed to clarify the Volunteer Army's ultimate political objectives, except for their assertion of Great Russian hegemony, "Russia, one and indivisible."

But the worst problem of all, growing out of the political problems, was the chaos and disorganization attending the administration of rear areas. Added to the inefficiency of Denikin's subordinates were material difficulties: Much of the area had been ruined by the severe fighting; rail lines had been torn up or otherwise disrupted; and, to make matters worse, typhus was raging everywhere, taking a heavy toll of both soldiers and civilians.

After sending off their initial rather cautious reports, Reilly and Hill took ship to Odessa, which the French had occupied after the Armistice when the German-sponsored puppet regime in the Ukraine collapsed. At Odessa they touched base with their French colleagues, who proved to be uncooperative.

During this otherwise uneventful visit, Hill related, there occurred a strange incident involving Reilly which remained in his memory for many years, as clear and vivid as if it had taken place yesterday. While walking about the city, the two men passed an impressive house, Number 15, on Alexander III Boulevard. At the sight of this house, Reilly turned white and fell down in a faint. He recovered a few minutes later but, when asked by Hill why he had been affected in this manner, refused to give any explanation. Obviously, however, the house was closely connected with his past life. It could be presumed that this was the home of the family with which he had broken in his youth.

At Odessa, Reilly and Hill separated, Reilly returning to the North Caucasus for another few weeks, Hill making his way back to England. Reilly returned to England and was immediately given a new assignment at the beginning of February. He and Hill were to attend the Paris Peace Conference, which had opened in the middle of January, and keep track of Russian developments there, particularly moves made by the Bolsheviks or the White Russians.

With the help of Admiral Sir Reginald "Blinker" Hall, director of Naval Intelligence, they were accredited as Russian advisers to the British Naval Mission to the Conference. At first they stayed at the Hotel Majestic with the other members of the Naval Mission, but after a short time they moved to a small hotel near the Place de l'Etoile in order to avoid compromising the Naval Mission by their activities.

Reilly learned that, although Russia was not represented at the Paris Peace Conference, "the Russian problem," as one writer put it, "was *the* problem of the peace conference."

From the beginning Woodrow Wilson had been more interested in winning acceptance of his proposal for a League of Nations than in the terms of the peace settlement itself. And it appeared that he wanted to bring Russia into the League of Nations in order to make it a world assembly in the true sense. Lloyd George, the British prime minister, also thought that the League of Nations could not ensure world peace without Russia, a vast country straddling Europe and Asia.

The French thought little of the scheme for a League of Nations and continued to be intransigent in regard to Russia. On the very first day of the conference, Marshal Ferdinand Foch had called for an army, composed mainly of Americans, to be sent to Russia to depose the Bolsheviks. Wilson, however, lost no time in speaking out against Foch's proposal. The president expressed doubt that force could be successfully used in defeating Bolshevism. He also noted that the Allies had yet to determine their political objectives in Russia.

Premier Georges Clemenceau contemptuously rejected the idea that Russia's presence in the League of Nations was essential to the world organization's success. He demanded a *cordon sanitaire* in Eastern Europe to be erected as a barrier against the expansion of Bolshevism. The *cordon sanitaire* would also serve to deny the

Russians access to vital supplies and force them to settle with Europe on Allied terms.

Reilly knew from his conversations with other British officials in Paris that Lloyd George faced strong opposition among his own countrymen. Many influential people agreed with Winston Churchill that Bolshevism should be crushed in its infancy. Needless to say, Reilly shared the same viewpoint. Those who held such views were more in sympathy with the French than with their own prime minister.

Lloyd George, recognizing his weakness, tried to find a compromise. He put forth the suggestion that the Allies invite all factions in Russia to send representatives to Paris for the purpose of conferring with the Allied leaders. This drew a scornful response from Clemenceau, who replied that he refused to sit down with criminals and would not permit a pack of anarchists and murderers to walk the streets of France's beautiful capital.

Wishing to head off any other proposals for intervention, Wilson then suggested that the Allies invite the Russian factions to confer with them at some other place. Clemenceau promptly accepted the suggestion and as presiding officer designated Wilson to send out the invitations. In doing so, he not only hoped to preserve the unity of the Allies but also wanted to please Wilson, who, as he said later, enjoyed nothing more than writing peace notes.

Woodrow Wilson chose Prinkipo Island (later renamed Büyükada Island) in the Sea of Marmara near Constantinople as a site for negotiations involving the Allied Peace Commissioners and the Russian factions, but, much to his discomfiture, only the Bolsheviks accepted. Both persuasion and threats were directed at the White Russians in an effort to bring them to the conference table. In the meantime, Wilson dispatched an American, William C. Bullitt, to Moscow, where he was to ascertain the Bolsheviks' terms for an armistice. If the Bolsheviks responded with reasonable terms, Bullitt could tell them unofficially that the United States would recommend the withdrawal of all foreign troops from Russia.

Clemenceau remained skeptical about all such peace initiatives. He wanted the Allies to consider a war against the Bolsheviks, which he viewed as the only logical solution.

But Lloyd George pointed out that the Germans had been

forced to keep a million men in Russia at a time when they desperately needed reinforcements on the western front, and yet the Germans were occupying only a comparatively small part of Russia. "Is any one of the Western Allies prepared to send a million men into Russia?" he asked rhetorically.

Woodrow Wilson noted that the Allied troops in Russia did not know why they were there. The Allies had not even begun to clarify their objectives in Russia and therefore had no basis on which to act.[5]

This was still the state of affairs when Wilson left Paris for a month to go back to the United States, where he had to sign the bills passed by the Sixty-fifth Congress. Lloyd George had already left the peace conference to deal with the threat of national strikes in England, and at the February 14 session—the last one attended by Wilson before his departure—Winston Churchill, the new secretary of state for war, took Lloyd George's place.

As Wilson was about to leave the session, Churchill took the floor to discuss the Russian item on the agenda. He asserted that the Russian question was an integral part of the war with Germany, and unless the Allies were able to come to the support of the Russians, there was a "possibility of a great combination from Yokohama to Cologne in hostility to France, Britain and America." The Allies had to decide on a policy toward Russia, in particular whether there was to be peace or war.

Wilson turned back to reply to Churchill's speech. He said that he did not know the solution to the problem of Russia. If the Prinkipo conference did not materialize, he would be prepared to accept any military measures that the other Allies considered necessary and feasible.

Wilson's last words were unfortunate, as he thereby encouraged Churchill and others to believe that the United States could be maneuvered into a massive military intervention in Russia. Churchill took advantage of the absence of Lloyd George and Wilson[6] to argue for a program of military action as a means of deposing the Soviet regime. During a stormy debate that was deleted from the minutes (so as to preserve the illusion of unity among the Allies), Churchill urged that the Prinkipo plan be abandoned and that the Allies deliver an ultimatum to the Bolsheviks. Unless the Red Army broke off hostilities and withdrew five miles on all fronts, the Allies would coordinate military operations against the Bolsheviks.

When the reports of Churchill's proposals reached him, Wilson feared that such proposals would embroil the Allies in war with Russia. From the *George Washington* he sent off a wire to his secretary of war with instructions to withdraw American troops from the north of Russia.[7]

On the sidelines, Sidney Reilly found himself with little to do, particularly since it was becoming increasingly apparent that the Russians with whom he maintained contact in Paris would never be given an opportunity to participate in the peace conference. He chafed under this idleness and used the time to become better acquainted with people in the intelligence field who might be helpful to him in the future. One of those he became friendly with at that time was Major W. Field-Robinson, head of the SIS office in Paris.

The most important future connection he made in Paris, however, was with Winston Churchill himself. A British M.P. who happened to be an old friend of Mansfield Cumming introduced Reilly to Churchill at the Hotel Majestic. It was hardly surprising that Reilly and Churchill took to one another at once. The adventurous element in each man appealed to the other. Both were men of action. But the most powerful attraction between them was their agreement on the urgent need to crush Bolshevism. It was to Churchill that Reilly would constantly look for encouragement and support in future years.

Nevertheless, even in this period Reilly could not avoid being reminded of the past, which continued to retain a grip on him. The *New York Times* of February 27 carried a dispatch from Stockholm dated one day earlier. It said: "American Minister Morris has been informed by the Danish Red Cross that an American citizen named Kalamatiano, upon whom the death sentence had been passed by the Bolsheviki, is now detained in the Kremlin, the death sentence having been commuted." The dispatch went on to report that the former Bolshevik financial representative in Norway, who was now in Petrograd, had submitted an official Soviet proposal to Minister Morris for an exchange of Kalamatiano and some other Americans for Soviet representatives held by the Americans in Vladivostok.

But the newspaper contained an even longer dispatch:

Washington, Feb. 26.—An American named Kalamatiano, who as long ago as last December was condemned to death by the Bolsheviki, is being held prisoner in the Kremlin at Moscow, and on several occasions the Bolshevist Government has threatened to execute him unless the United States should make a prompt answer relative to a proposed exchange of prisoners.

Roger Culver Tredwell, former American Consul General at Petrograd, who has, for six months, been held prisoner by the Bolshevist authorities at Tashkent, is still incarcerated. Every time the United States Government has sought to have him released they have come back with a demand for the release of someone in another country. The Bolsheviki first demanded the release of Eugene V. Debs in exchange for that of Consul General Tredwell. Then they demanded the release of [Thomas Joseph] Mooney. They have also insisted upon the release of Bolsheviki in India, where the United States Government has no jurisdiction.

Regarding the release of Kalamatiano, the State Department issued the following late this afternoon:

"The Department of State is in receipt of a statement obtained from a man who was imprisoned with Kalamatiano, in Moscow, to the effect that Kalamatiano was condemned to death by the Bolshevist Government on Dec. 3, 1918, and was incarcerated in the Kremlin at Moscow under particularly rigorous conditions. As late as the 17th of January he was kept in a cellar closely guarded by twelve soldiers of the Red Army whose conversation constantly dwelt on revolutionary politics and particularly the expediency of slaying all foreigners in Russia.

"The representative of the Norwegian Consulate at Moscow obtained with great difficulty authorization to visit Kalamatiano, and between Dec. 3 and Jan. 17 had only succeeded once in seeing the condemned man. On several occasions the Bolshevist Government threatened to execute Kalamatiano should it not receive a prompt answer from the United States Government relative to the proposed exchange of prisoners."

It has never become known why the United States government failed to arrange an exchange of Kalamatiano, as evidently suggested by the Bolsheviks, for Bolshevik leaders who were prisoners of the American forces in Vladivostok. If the exchange was not feasible for some reason, a different exchange could have certainly been arranged through the Norwegian Legation, which represented

American interests in Russia. It is difficult to avoid the suspicion that high American officials preferred to follow one of the traditional rules of espionage—to deny all knowledge of a spy who has been caught.

This tradition, however, has long since been discarded. In more recent times CIA spies have been exchanged for Soviet spies. The CIA has accepted responsibility for its agents imprisoned in China and other countries. Great Britain has also adopted a similar course.

In February 1919, when the *New York Times* carried its dispatches about Kalamatiano, his former colleague Sidney Reilly had no way of knowing that the American would in fact be executed by the Bolsheviks.

George Hill, another former colleague, wrote:

"Kalamatiano, the American secret service agent who had been captured, was taken nightly to the place of execution, but always at the last moment put through another cross-examination in an endeavor to make him give away his own confederates and the whereabouts of Sidney Reilly and the other Allied secret service agents. Kalamatiano lived through it, stood his trial, was condemned to death, and never opened his mouth."[8]

One day, Kalamatiano, forced to watch another execution, was pushed into the line of fire and shot.

Chapter 13

AFTER COMPLETING HIS assignment at the Paris Peace Conference, Sidney Reilly took a short leave to go to New York and see his wife, Nadine, after a separation of two and half years.

The reunion was not a success. He found Nadine waiting on the pier to greet him when his ship docked, and he accompanied her to her apartment on the East Side, where he was to stay during his visit. But from the cool kiss with which she met him on the pier to the restrained atmosphere of their private supper that evening, Reilly could hardly fail to notice that something was seriously wrong.

Nadine, who obviously intended to make his first days in New York as pleasant as possible, recognized that her behavior puzzled him. She broke the news without further delay. Despite his numerous infidelities, Reilly was shocked to learn that Nadine had fallen in love with another man and that they had been living together for some time. She told him that she wanted a divorce.[1]

There seemed to be little more to discuss. Once he had recovered his composure, Reilly agreed to give Nadine the divorce. He visited a few old friends in the city and then departed. Sailing back to England, he avoided other passengers and, unlike his normal sociable self, spent the solitary hours reading the few books he could find in the ship's meager library or sitting in his deck chair, staring at the shifting horizon.

His spirits were not improved by his reception in London. During his absence, Margaret, to whom he was still legally married, had suddenly appeared in England. Having spent the war years in Belgium, she wanted to reestablish contact with her husband. Failing to find him anywhere, she went to the Foreign Office and demanded information about Reilly's whereabouts. When Cumming heard about this visit, he realized that he knew very little about Reilly's past in general or marital status in particular. He asked George Hill to look into the matter and find out how many times Reilly had been married.

Hill disliked the idea of spying on his old colleague. When Reilly returned to England, Hill asked him directly for the information that Cumming had requested. "I have no wife," Reilly replied curtly. "There is nothing to discuss." Then, his face darkly flushed with anger, he called on Cumming. What took place between the two men is unknown, but shortly thereafter Cumming summoned Hill and instructed him to drop his inquiries about Reilly. The inference of blackmail seems highly plausible.

Reilly also had a meeting with Margaret and induced her to leave England almost at once, using a combination of threats and money. Margaret later claimed that Reilly had paid her 100,000 pounds, a huge sum that would appear to have been far beyond his means. Possibly he had acquired the money during the years when he was active in business in St. Petersburg before the war. Or he had earned it in commissions on Russian war purchases before the 1917 revolution. Or, as some people might have suspected, he had misappropriated British Intelligence operational funds in Russia in 1918. Another possibility, however, was that this was simply an effort on Margaret's part to increase her own importance by magnifying the amount of money paid to her by Reilly.

Obediently breaking off his inquiries about Reilly, George Hill went off on another assignment to the Caucasus, where he had to coordinate SIS activities with the Denikin forces. By June, Denikin had made striking military advances in the general direction of Moscow, capturing Kharkov and Tsaritsyn, and the prospects for a march on Moscow looked very favorable. On the other hand, Denikin's military staff and his semigovernment, the Special Conference, still had great difficulty in coping with political and administrative problems in the rear areas.

Meanwhile, Reilly remained in London without any clear-cut assignment. Mansfield Cumming had no idea of how to use Reilly beyond bringing him in as a consultant with regard to the more notable refugees streaming into England during this period. Reilly, a shadowy, enigmatic figure, crouched in the background while Cumming talked to some Russian, later giving the SIS chief his evaluation of the man himself or certain information.

Reilly, frustrated in his career, looked for consolation in his private life, finding it as usual with a woman—in this case, a girl who entered his world in a somewhat circuitous way. Her name was Caryll Houselander and she was only eighteen years old, an impoverished art student with a passionate interest in Russia.

Reilly first heard of Caryll indirectly, through one of her fellow students who met him by chance in the company of some Russian émigrés friendly with Reilly. Caryll's friend told Reilly about the girl, who had had a vision in which she "saw" the death of the czar shortly before the executions in Ekaterinburg and who was strongly attracted to Russia—an attraction reflected in her paintings. Through the friend, Reilly invited Caryll to show him some of those paintings. Caryll allowed her friend to show them to Reilly but, out of shyness, avoided a personal meeting.

Deeply touched by the paintings, Reilly tried to help Caryll financially by buying some of her work, although he pretended that he had only acted as an agent in selling the paintings to other people. Finally, however, Reilly brought about a meeting with Caryll, and their relationship entered a new phase.

He found that she was a mystic for whom painting was only a mode of expression for her deeply religious feelings. She was a Catholic but contemplated joining the Russian Orthodox church. Like Reilly, she was also interested in other religions and had discovered much to admire in the Muslim and Jewish faiths.

Reilly and Caryll spent many hours discussing religion, and in the beginning the spiritual element was dominant in relations between them. With the purity of her face and her long red hair cut in a bang across her forehead, she made him think of a modern Joan of Arc. For her part, Caryll imagined that he was an archangel sent by God to save Russia from the Devil, who had appeared there in the form of Bolshevism.

Inevitably, however, Reilly and Caryll became lovers, and as long as their romance lasted it was very intense, despite the fact that Caryll's feeling for Reilly was stronger than his for her.

Reilly's work for SIS required him to keep in touch with anti-Bolshevik émigrés in both London and Paris, where most of them were concentrated. He always left Caryll at home when he traveled to Paris. The separation from his colleagues in London as well as from Caryll gave him time to think about the future, which, on the basis of his present prospects, must have seemed to offer little hope.

By this time, Boris Savinkov had safely made his way abroad, and he and Reilly met in Paris, where they celebrated their reunion. Both men were in their forties, linked by many common experiences, and they spent a whole night in talk, exchanging information and considering their future plans. Later, responding to Reilly's invitation, Savinkov traveled to London, where Reilly had arranged to introduce him to Winston Churchill, who still strongly believed in a program of action against the Bolsheviks.

The British statesman received Savinkov warmly. Churchill knew that Savinkov had been a terrorist since 1903—"a terrorist for moderate aims," as Churchill put it—fighting against the czarist regime and seeking to replace it with a Western-style democratic government. When the great war began, Savinkov, patriotically supporting Russia's participation in the war on the side of France and Great Britain, gave up his underground activities to go into exile in France. There he wrote a successful novel, *The Pale Horse*, which reflected his experiences as a terrorist. Then he volunteered as an ordinary soldier in the French Army and returned to Russia only after the revolution unseated the czar.

Churchill could appreciate Savinkov's complex nature, which combined the qualities of an intellectual, a writer, an underground fighter, a political leader, and an adventurer. He wrote: "Boris Savinkov's whole life had been spent in conspiracy. Without religion as the churches teach it; without morals as men prescribe them; without home or country; without wife or child, or kith or kin;[2] without friend; without fear; hunter and hunted; implacable, unconquerable, alone."[3]

No little impressed by Savinkov, whom he saw as a statesman of the first rank, Churchill introduced the Russian in turn to Lloyd George at Chequers, the prime minister's residence.

The meeting was disappointing, however, particularly for Savinkov. After the long, debilitating war with Germany, England had only one desire: to bring home her soldiers and forget all the horrors of war. Military intervention in Russia had proved to be a mistake. Therefore Lloyd George was in no mood to listen to exhortations by Churchill and Savinkov to renew the armed struggle against the Bolsheviks.

Savinkov, in his formal black frock coat with its stiff winged collar, his small feet encased in black patent leather shoes, listened with icy politeness while the prime minister expounded one of his pet theories. Revolution, said Lloyd George amiably, was like a disease that had to run its course. In Russia the worst stage of the revolution was already over. Perhaps there would be more convulsions, but the revolution would finally end in the establishment of a more moderate regime that the Russian people as well as the rest of the world could tolerate. How long would this process take? inquired Savinkov. A generation, possibly two generations, Lloyd George replied confidently.

Boris Savinkov, speaking French in a low, emotionless voice, said: "Mr. Prime Minister, you will permit me the honor of observing that after the fall of the Roman Empire there ensued the Dark Ages."[4]

Despite such warnings, the Allies were in the process of withdrawing their troops from Russia. Meanwhile General Denikin had overextended himself in his drive on Moscow, using up all his reserves. The Denikin forces reached their high-water mark on October 14 when they captured Orel, less than 250 miles south of Moscow. But the Red Army launched a devastating counterattack one week later, recapturing Orel and forcing Denikin into a general retreat that was the prelude to his complete defeat.

Reilly continued to take part in Major Alley's luncheon club. On December 3 he attended a "Bolo Liquidation Lunch" with old and new friends such as Dukes, Boyce, Hill, Leeper, and, of course, Alley, the founding father. They came to the Café Royal on Regent Street by taxis, which they dismissed several blocks away, walking the remaining distance to the restaurant in the hope that this would make their arrival less conspicuous. They drank toasts to the liquidation of the Bolos, or Bolsheviks, and ate a luncheon whose menu included ham omelet, filet of sole, and roast pheasant, with "tarte aux pommes à la française" and coffee for dessert.

George Hill, one of the guests, had recently returned from Russia, where the situation of the Denikin forces was going from bad to worse. The Red Army maintained pressure on all fronts and continued its remorseless advance. Within the next two weeks the Reds would occupy Kiev and Kharkov on their way south.

When the members of the Bolo Liquidation Club parted to return to their offices, Reilly went on his way alone.

The lonely road was the one that suited Reilly best. In apparent contradiction to his outwardly gregarious nature, he had always shown a preference for acting independently, confiding neither his ideas nor his plans to others. Even when he did express his thoughts, it was impossible to tell how much of what he said was sincere and how much was calculated.

"I don't believe that the Russians can do anything against the Bolsheviks without our most active support," he had written Bruce Lockhart. "The salvation of Russia has become a most sacred duty which we owe to the untold thousands of Russian men and women who have sacrificed their lives because they trusted in the promise of our support."[5]

Of all the Russians who had fled abroad, Reilly found only Boris Savinkov worthy of this support. The overwhelming majority of Russian politicians did not abandon their petty intrigues and bickering, their continual efforts to pay off old scores, their rejection of any reconciliation with political opponents. Savinkov alone seemed to rise above all that, to have only one thought—the destruction of the Bolsheviks, who, in his view, had betrayed the revolution.

If Churchill's instinct could be trusted, Savinkov had the stature to unite the disparate and contending groups in the emigration and weld them into an effective fighting force that would carry on the struggle by other means, now that the Civil War seemed all but over. Yet it was clear that no one, not even Savinkov, could count on the British government's support.

Reilly's own rejection by SIS told him enough to know that he would have to follow an independent course, with only sporadic help from SIS. Savinkov, on the other hand, had emphasized his need for Reilly's active support and assistance. Reilly had the invaluable foreign connections and political know-how that Savinkov lacked. Moreover, Reilly was able to obtain from Churchill the knowledge of high-level official contacts that was essential in order to win financial and logistical support in Europe (apart from England), where there was greater fear of Bolshevism and hence greater inclination to provide liberal support.

It did not take much urging from Churchill or Savinkov to convince Reilly that he should become Savinkov's "gray eminence," the man who would pull the strings behind the scenes and plot the future strategy of this latest Russian opposition. He communicated his intentions to Churchill, receiving the latter's blessing, and to SIS, which, in the person of Mansfield Cumming, seemed relieved by his departure and at the same time gave him lukewarm encouragement.

Chapter 14

DURING THE NEXT TWO YEARS Reilly was almost constantly traveling from one European capital to another, sometimes in Savinkov's company, sometimes alone, but always on Savinkov's behalf. He was a man with a mission— the holy mission, in Caryll's words, of destroying Bolshevism. The first object was to raise money for Savinkov's Green (peasant) Revolution in Russia, and the money was forthcoming, though never in the amounts that would have relieved the two men and their associates from financial worries. They were, in fact, nearly always painfully short of money.

They went first to France, where Savinkov could be sure of a cordial reception. Savinkov had lived in France during the early war years. He had acquired great popularity at that time, not only because, for Frenchmen, he symbolized France's ally, Russia, but because of their tendency to romanticize him as a terrorist, a republican, and, not least of all, an intellectual. Savinkov had worked closely with the French in 1918 while striving, with his

"Union for the Defense of Fatherland and Freedom," to launch a counterrevolution that would oust the Bolsheviks. He saw himself in a personal duel with Lenin, and the French accepted him at this valuation.

To W. Somerset Maugham, who saw much of him at that time, Savinkov said, "Between me and Lenin it's a war to the death. One of these days, he will put me with my back to the wall and shoot me, or I shall put him with his back to the wall and shoot him. One thing I can tell you is that I shall never run away."[1]

Reilly, using his own contacts, had no trouble interesting French Intelligence in Savinkov's ideas for a peasant revolution. The news of peasant uprisings in central Russia—reflecting growing discontent with the policies of the Bolshevik regime, which discriminated against the countryside in favor of urban, industrialized areas—was evidence that the basis for an extensive, organized rebellion existed. Savinkov also pointed out that the armed forces consisted for the most part of peasants; thus a revolution in the villages was certain to find an echo in the army, which could hardly be disposed to move against its own people. Savinkov's arguments seemed to be confirmed in 1921 by the Kronstadt uprising of Baltic sailors as well as the Bolsheviks' efforts to placate the peasants, among others, when Lenin instituted his New Economic Policy (NEP) in March of that year.

The French government was prepared to provide money, and a suitable theater for Savinkov's operations soon became available in Poland, where there were already large numbers of White Russian émigrés. The decisive event, however, was the outbreak of the Russo-Polish War in April 1920. In such circumstances, Marshal Józef Pilsudski, a friend of Savinkov, was only too happy to allow Savinkov to recruit Russians for a partisan army and to provide additional material support. Within the next year, until the ratification of a peace treaty ending the war in March 1921, Savinkov, aided by Reilly and his SIS colleague Paul Dukes, organized a force of 30,000 partisans to operate in the rear of the Red Army in the forests of Belorussia.

At the same time, using the partisans as cover for the infiltration and exfiltration of his agents, Savinkov began to reactivate the remnants of his old organization inside Russia. In particular, he succeeded in reestablishing contact with Colonel Sergei Pavlovsky, his second-in-command in the League for the Defense of

Fatherland and Freedom, who was still living in hiding in Moscow. Pavlovsky had always used the pseudonym Flegont, the name by which he was known in his conspiratorial work.

Despite these activities, which required much administration and organization, none of the principals stayed long in Poland. Savinkov had established his headquarters in Paris, where he spent most of his time with his secretary, Dickhoff-Daehrenthal, and his secretary's wife, who was also Savinkov's mistress. Savinkov appointed a man named Filosofov as his deputy in charge of Polish operations. Reilly was also spending a great deal of his time in Paris, because of Savinkov's presence there, and traveling to Czechoslovakia, Finland, and Estonia. Since Dukes had moved on to other assignments, Reilly's SIS contact in Poland became a man named Maclaren, a former merchant seaman who wore gold earrings in the style of the old pirates (a flamboyant style that, it would seem, identified him easily for opposition intelligence services like the Vecheka-GPU). Maclaren maintained close contact with Filosofov and passed on the funds supplied by Reilly. This SIS role is all the more remarkable when one considers that the funds originated from the French, Poles, and Czechs and that the British did not furnish a penny.

In Paris, Reilly found time to carry on a romance with a twenty-three-year-old French actress. He was forty-seven but still exercised an undeniable fascination over women of any age, social standing, or ethnic origin. The actress wanted marriage but Reilly, already entangled with Margaret and Nadine, had no interest in taking on another wife. When the actress became pregnant and begged Reilly to marry her, Reilly refused and paid for an abortion.

To his friend Aleksandr Grammatikov, now in Paris, Reilly told the whole story and broke down and cried over the loss of his sweetheart, who, only a few years later, became famous. Grammatikov had arranged for Nadine's divorce from her first husband in St. Petersburg so that she could marry Reilly. At this point Grammatikov put Reilly in touch with a French lawyer who could arrange a divorce between Nadine and Reilly. Although their marriage had been illegal, Reilly was determined to keep this fact a secret from Nadine, even at the expense of a divorce.

Reilly's travels frequently took him to Prague, where he found his former associate Bruce Lockhart in the British Legation. They spent long evenings drinking slivovitz in the night spots around Wenceslaus Square and talking about Russia.

Entertaining several members of the British Legation at lunch, with excellent food and wine, Reilly was in a good humor and, at one point, even broke a rule by referring to his past. He mentioned the fact that he had been born near Odessa.

One of the guests, a young Legation secretary, expressed surprise. He had just obtained a visa for Reilly and looked over Reilly's passport. "How comes it, Mr. Reilly," he said, "that your passport gives your birthplace as Tipperary when you just said you were born near Odessa?"

Reilly laughed heartily. "I came to Britain to work for the British. I had to have a British passport and needed a British place of birth, and, you see, from Odessa it's a long, long way to Tipperary!"[2]

In Prague, Reilly stayed at the Passage Hotel and was a steady patron of the Château Rouge night club, where he renewed his friendship with a singer named Eleanor Toye, an SIS agent under deep cover whom he had first met in Paris during the peace conference.

Despite his frequent attendance at nightclubs run by Russian émigrés, Reilly conducted more serious business in Prague. While Savinkov functioned as a figurehead, Reilly was the de facto leader of the Savinkov organization. It was Reilly who successfully applied for financial support from the Czech government. He also prepared the ground in Czechoslovakia for an eventual move of Savinkov's staff to that country, for there was already reason to fear that their operations out of Poland would no longer be possible once the Polish government had made peace with its Soviet neighbor.

The financial problems of the Savinkov organization remained acute. In June 1921 Maclaren wrote Reilly from Warsaw:

> The position is becoming desperate. The balance in hand today amounts to 700,000 Polish marks, not even sufficient to pay the staff their salaries for the month of July.
>
> Savinkov, who is wanted in Finland urgently in order to bring the Petrograd organization into line and keep them from starting the revolution prematurely, cannot go there, not having the wherewithal to pay for his journey.[3]

That summer Savinkov and Reilly achieved a major goal by holding a secret "Anti-Bolshevik Congress" in Warsaw, bringing together White Russian delegates from all the countries where the struggle against Soviet Russia was being actively pursued. They included delegates who came out of Russia in order to attend the Congress.

While the three-day congress proved to be a success in terms of coordinating the underground struggle, financial problems overshadowed everything else, so much so that Reilly left for Prague before the three days were up in order to see what could be done about raising more money.

Immediately after the Congress, Filosofov reported to Reilly:

> I will tell you frankly that I felt ashamed to associate with people who had come to attend and would return to Russia full of hope and would risk their lives in their work—whereas we are unable to give them help to continue the struggle.
>
> I repeat for the umpteenth time that it all depends on money. The press is ready, the peasants await liberation but without a fully planned organization, it is hopeless. Our chief trouble is that it may not be possible to prevent abortive or premature riots. This applies especially to Petrograd from whence we received detailed intelligence (after your departure). From this we see that riots can be expected at any moment and, if they cannot be supported, it is possible that they will be suppressed. Even Boris Savinkov will not be able to go there owing to insufficient financial aid. In other words—money, money, money!
>
> I am able to say that if the Central Committee issues general marching orders, we can then count on twenty-eight districts including Petrograd, Smolensk, and Gomel. Further, the Ukrainians have joined up and have agreed to act in coordination. We have contacts with about ten other *guberniya* [provinces] in outlying areas.[4]

This financial crisis coincided with something of a personal financial crisis for Reilly. While he continued to live on a lavish scale, maintaining his sumptuous apartment at the Albany in London, staying at only the best hotels, spending freely on food, drink, and entertainment, he had reached the limit of his private resources. He had agreed to make a final settlement with Nadine in connection with their "divorce," and he had also paid a large sum to Margaret as a means of getting her out of England. He had also made numerous loans to friends who were in financial difficulties after the war. Moreover, Reilly was not drawing a regular salary for his work with Savinkov.

Without interrupting his work, Reilly did his best to improve his finances. He gave up his apartment at the Albany and moved into a less expensive place in London. He also engaged in some business ventures, hoping to make some money. He acted as the representative of British business interests abroad. Not content with this, he began to dabble in a pharmaceutical business like the one he had pursued many years earlier. He even toyed with the idea of a pill to cure baldness. Unfortunately, nothing very tangible came of these efforts.

The only seemingly bright spot in his financial picture was a claim he had against the Baldwin Locomotive Company in the United States for commissions amounting to half a million dollars that were allegedly due to him in connection with some of the czarist government's war purchases. Up to this time, however, he had been unable to obtain any satisfaction for his claim. In view of his desperate situation, he decided to place the matter in the hands of lawyers, who, he hoped, would soon achieve a settlement.

The Anti-Bolshevik Congress in Warsaw was the culmination of the Savinkov organization's work in Poland. Soon afterward, just as Reilly had feared, the Polish government let it be known that it no longer wished to allow an anti-Bolshevik organization to maintain its base of operations there.

Reilly's foresight enabled Savinkov to transfer his staff to Czechoslovakia and continue operations from that country. Savinkov received enthusiastic support from General Rudolf Gajda, one of the leaders of the Czechoslovak uprising in Russia in 1918. Gajda, who was strongly anti-Bolshevik,[5] helped Savinkov to organize the so-called Green Guards, who operated in the western Ukraine for some time.

Whatever his personal problems, Reilly never slackened his efforts on behalf of the anti-Bolshevik struggle. His interest extended in many different directions. He did not overlook politics, and he hoped that he could place a spokesman in the House of Commons and even, ultimately, establish an anti-Bolshevik nucleus that would support his objectives.

In October 1922 he urged Paul Dukes, his former SIS colleague, to stand for Parliament. "I need not tell you how important it will be for the accomplishment of all our aims to have a man like you in the British Parliament," he wrote.

He recommended that Dukes should join the Conservative party. "Almost instinctively one evokes the bogey of reaction when one talks of Conservatism," he went on. "It is *reaction*, constructive reaction, which this country and also all the other countries of Europe want after the orgy of destructive radicalism which has been going on since the war."[6]

Paul Dukes had gone to Russia originally to study music at the St. Petersburg Conservatory. A promising career as a conductor seemed to lie ahead of him when the outbreak of World War I interrupted his studies. He volunteered for propaganda work at the British Embassy, where he remained during most of the war. Because of his fluent Russian and knowledge of the country, he was recruited by the SIS, which brought him back to England for training. Then he returned to Soviet Russia with an assignment under deep cover. He soon demonstrated mettle as a secret agent, living as a Soviet citizen under various disguises; he even served for a time in the Red Army. A few years after the war he left SIS to pursue personal interests, such as modern dance, yoga, and the occult. Possibly because of these interests, he did not take Reilly's advice to enter politics, where he could have easily distinguished himself.

In the same letter, Reilly also urged Dukes to visit Boris Savinkov in Paris. "Savinkov was, is, and always will be the only man outside of Russia worth talking to and worth supporting. Everybody else is dead as a doornail," he said. "Notwithstanding the enormous persecution to which he has been subjected, notwithstanding the incredible difficulties he has had to contend with, he has kept his organization both here and in Russia alive, and he is the only man amongst the Russian anti-Bolsheviks who is actually working. It is superfluous to tell you that I am sticking to him through thick and thin and that I shall continue to do so until I find a bigger man. It is not a matter of personal friendship or personal admiration, it is simply a case of what is the best way in which I can serve Russia at the present moment."[7]

Despite Reilly's unqualified expression of confidence in Savinkov, there were stirrings in both the Russian emigration and

Russia proper, pointing in new directions that threatened to pass Savinkov by.

In 1920, General Pëtr Nikolaevich Wrangel, Denikin's successor in command of the Armed Forces of South Russia, had arranged an agreement with the Allied governments providing for the evacuation of all those in the territory under his control who wished to leave. In accordance with this agreement, a total of 145,000 men, women, and children, including most of his troops, were evacuated from the Crimea, where he made his last stand. At first these people found refuge on the Gallipoli Peninsula and the island of Lemnos in installations abandoned after the abortive Dardanelles campaign. In the fall of 1921 they were resettled in Yugoslavia and Bulgaria, where the men worked in coal mines and built roads under military discipline. It was Wrangel's idea to preserve the cadres of his army for a later time when circumstances inside Russia would perhaps make possible a decisive intervention against the Bolsheviks. Wrangel's forces gave their loyalty to the Grand Duke Nikolai Nikolaevich, erstwhile commander-in-chief of the Imperial Army and the czar's uncle, as their titular leader. It remained for Wrangel to provide a framework in which he would function as the active head of the organization.

Wrangel's organization, still amorphous in a political sense, could not be overlooked even in the summer of 1921 when Savinkov and Reilly held their Anti-Bolshevik Congress. They sought to have Wrangel's delegates in attendance at the Congress, but their efforts failed because of the deep distrust and dislike that the Wrangel people felt toward a man who had spent his life in terrorist activities aimed at the czarist regime. In September 1923 Wrangel announced the formation of the Russian Armed Services Union (Russkiy Obshche Voinskiy Soyuz, or ROVS), with branches in a number of countries. The ROVS gradually absorbed veterans of the czarist and White armies in other countries, and its chairman, Wrangel, also hoped that it would prove to be a rallying point for all "nationally minded" Russians. As one writer noted, "The creation of the Russian Armed Services Union, a clearly anti-Communist extraterritorial organization, immediately attracted Moscow's attention."[8]

Meanwhile, it became known in certain restricted circles of the emigration that a Russian opposition organization had emerged inside the Soviet Union. Significant aspects of this organization were, first of all, that it seemed to have come into being without any help or participation from the outside; second, that it was monarchist in character, regarding the monarchy as the only symbol around which all forces inside and outside the country could rally; and third, that the leaders were persons who, it was asserted, held responsible positions in the Soviet government.

First word of this organization, which called itself the Monarchist Organization of Central Russia (MOCR), was brought to the West in the summer of 1921, just about the time that the Anti-Bolshevik Congress was taking place in Warsaw. The bearer of these tidings was a middle-aged, bearded, distinguished-looking man named Aleksandr Aleksandrovich Yakushev, who arrived in Revel (soon to be called Tallinn), the capital of an independent Estonian republic, after a journey from Moscow.

Yakushev, who bore himself with an obvious sense of self-importance, was the type of career bureaucrat who would land on his feet under any regime. He had held a leading post in the Ministry of Communications under the czarist government. When the Bolsheviks took power, he quickly obtained a responsible job as a transportation specialist under the new regime. He was making a private visit in Revel during the course of a business trip to Oslo. He confided to his host the news of creation of the MOCR, in which he had assumed a position of leadership. Yakushev's host immediately passed this information to the Russian monarchist center in Berlin, where it naturally aroused considerable interest.

Early in 1922 a man named Kolesnikov, describing himself as a friend of Yakushev, visited the same individual in Revel. Kolesnikov went into even greater detail about the new organization in Russia. He painted an optimistic picture. Branches of the monarchist organization had already been established in many Russian cities. The main difficulty arose from a situation in which numerous anti-Communist agents were circulating in Russia without any coordination, causing considerable confusion. The only way to deal with this problem was to work out adequate liaison between the MOCR and the émigré organizations on underground activities in order to eliminate this confusion and avoid compromising other operations.

In November 1922, Yakushev himself turned up in Berlin to attend an émigré monarchist congress as the MOCR's representative. Yakushev emphasized that the MOCR was not averse to cooperation with the emigration, since it shared the same aim—the overthrow of the Bolsheviks. The MOCR leaders were convinced, however, that, being on the inside, they could best formulate the strategy and tactics of the anti-Bolshevik movement; what they would welcome from abroad was moral and financial support. His blunt assertion of the MOCR's claim to sole leadership of the anti-Bolshevik movement created consternation among many of his listeners.

It is known that Sidney Reilly visited Berlin in December 1922, only one month later. Whether Reilly and Yakushev met at this time no one can say. But there seems to be little doubt that Reilly must have learned from his contacts in Berlin about Yakushev and the MOCR, even though he may not have been ready to read any special significance into so recent a development. Yet his destiny would bring him together with Yakushev and the MOCR a few years later.

At that moment a more prosaic fate lay in store for him. During his visit to Berlin, Reilly met a woman, Pepita Bobadilla, who was to become his third wife.

Chapter 15

PEPITA BOBADILLA was a blond actress who had made a name for herself in England. She was born in South America and came to London, where as a young girl she started out dancing in the chorus. In due time she progressed to acting roles in West End productions and married Charles Haddon-Chambers, a playwright of some distinction.

Traveling after her husband's death, Pepita visited Berlin and met Sidney Reilly. They were introduced to each other by a mutual acquaintance in the lobby of the Adlon Hotel. The thought of re-marriage had not crossed her mind until then, but when Reilly asked her to marry him, she accepted without hesitation. Within one week they were engaged.

It was to be expected that Reilly would be irresistibly attracted to Pepita. She personified much that he loved and admired. She was a creature of the theater, adept at projecting beauty, glamour, sophistication. At this season of her life Pepita had reached full bloom, a woman of fashion and poise who could walk into any room and be sure of everybody's attention. Of medium height but appearing taller because of her lissome, graceful movements, she was a lovely blonde of the Latin type, with a dusky rose tint to the skin and brown eyes flecked with green.

For her part, Pepita could not be indifferent to the charm that Reilly knew how to direct toward any woman who interested him. The intense expression of his face, especially the eyes, the little attentions, the flowers, and the tender notes that he lavished on her did not fail in their effect.

Perhaps the courtship was accelerated by the fact that Reilly's time in Berlin was limited. As soon as they became engaged, he parted temporarily from Pepita in order to go to Prague and Paris on Savinkov's account.

The wedding took place in London on Friday, May 18, 1923. There was a civil ceremony at the Covent Garden Registry Office on Henrietta Street with Reilly's friends Captain George Hill and Major Stephen Alley as witnesses. Later the newlyweds held a reception at the Savoy, where the small court in front of the hotel was filled with the automobiles of their friends. Among the guests was Mansfield Cumming, who had only a month left to live. Although he knew perfectly well that the marriage was illegal, Cumming attended the reception and congratulated the bride warmly.

The marriage to Pepita ended Reilly's long romance with Caryll Houselander. The red-haired girl, disappointed in love, once again wholeheartedly embraced the Roman Catholic religion. In the years that ensued she achieved renown as a writer of Catholic books. She also devoted much of her strength to caring for the mentally ill and nursing them back to health through her devotion and kindness.

At the time of his marriage, Reilly's financial difficulties came to a head. His problems were so closely related to those of Savinkov that both men confronted a crisis. He could not expect help from his friends in the Secret Intelligence Service. He found that Admiral Sinclair, Cumming's replacement as head of SIS, was, if anything, less well disposed than Cumming toward him, and so he could not hope for a reversal of the latter's decision denying him a permanent staff position.

Reilly did not help to remove doubts about himself by maintaining a confidential relationship with Leonid Krassin, the Soviet trade representative in London. MI5, the British security service, had a strong interest in the nature of their relationship. Yet Reilly refused to divulge any of the details even to his friend Major Alley, who had left SIS and moved over to MI5. Later it was alleged that Reilly had helped Krassin to smuggle funds out of the USSR and had managed to cheat Krassin at the same time, thus obtaining money for anti-Communist activities.

In his present difficult circumstances, Reilly decided to go with Pepita to the United States, where he could press his suit against the Baldwin Locomotive Company in person. If he was successful in court, the half million dollars that he expected to receive would solve his own financial problems and could also help relieve Savinkov's.

Before their departure for America, however, Pepita met Savinkov for the first time. After all she had heard from her new husband, who continued to praise the Russian politician and underground leader in glowing terms, Pepita was terribly disappointed. "A portly little man strutted in with the most amusing air of self-assurance and self-esteem—a little man with a high brow, a beetling forehead, little eyes and an undershot chin [who] posed in front of the mantelpiece," she wrote.

> Now he gave us a view of one side of his profile, now of the other. Now he thrust his hand into his breast in the approved Napoleonic manner, now he flourished it in the air with a theatrical gesture. Every pose was carefully studied and had been studied so long that he had passed beyond the stage of taking even a glance at his audience to gauge the measure of its appreciation. . . . His little court fully shared Savinkov's estimate of his own importance. When he frowned, a cloud settled on the assembly. When he smiled, answering smiles appeared on every face. When he condescended to joke, which was but seldom, it was greeted with discreet and respectful merriment.[1]

So much for the assessment by Pepita Bobadilla, herself an actress, of the acting talents of Boris Savinkov. Her negative reaction did not apparently have any lasting effect on Reilly's attitude toward Savinkov, unless the decision to go to America, separating the two men for some time, partially reflected Pepita's influence.

In July 1923, Sidney Reilly booked passage to New York for himself and Pepita on the liner *Rotterdam*. Lacking money to pay for the tickets because of his desperate financial situation, he borrowed 200 pounds from Field-Robinson, who had been head of the SIS office in Paris but had since returned to London. Reilly explained that he had run out of credit and could only hope to reestablish himself on a sound financial basis by winning his lawsuit in the United States.

According to his own estimates, he was owed approximately $500,000 on orders given the Baldwin Locomotive Company. The British government took over those contracts after the revolution on condition that no commissions involving third parties existed. In view of this stipulation, Mr. Vauclain, head of the Baldwin Locomotive Company, asked Reilly to tear up their written agreement, assuring him that he would personally guarantee Reilly's commissions. On the basis of such a "gentlemen's agreement," Reilly destroyed the paper. When Reilly later sought payment from the other man, Vauclain found various reasons for delaying it, and, after some time, he refused to pay Reilly at all.

While in New York, Reilly stayed at the Gotham Hotel and maintained himself and his wife by selling his memorabilia of Napoleon. He borrowed money wherever he could to pay the lawyers who were handling his case. He watched with frustration as the case dragged through the courts, growing more and more angry with Vauclain, who, it seemed to him, was using every conceivable delaying tactic in order to block a decision. In this way, a year went by without any improvement in Reilly's finances.

Despite his preoccupation with money, Sidney Reilly did not lose sight of his larger interest in the anti-Bolshevik struggle. He kept up a regular correspondence with Savinkov so that he remained fully aware of all developments. He also frequently saw Savinkov supporters in New York and other parts of the United States. Reilly also approached private interests in the United States from which, he was convinced, funds could be raised for Savinkov's operations. He believed, for instance, that Henry Ford, like the financiers Sir Henri Deterding in England and Fritz Thyssen in Germany,[2] woud be only too happy to give financial support to an anti-Communist organization. Certain sources close to the Communist party allege that during this period Reilly established a working relationship with the Ford Foundation and drew up a list of names of persons who were supposedly working secretly for the Bolsheviks in America.

As a cover for his conspiratorial activities in the United States,

Reilly set up an office under the name "Sidney Berns, Importer of Indian Linen." When he went to Washington, where he soon began to move in American intelligence circles, it appears that he called himself Sidney Berns there as well. Reilly, of course, was an old hand at using assumed names; in this case, he might have been motivated to use an alias by his desire to keep British Intelligence in the dark about these contacts.

In his correspondence with Savinkov, Reilly learned about the growing importance of the MOCR, the monarchist group inside the Soviet Union with which Yakushev was connected. This organization had created its own cover under the guise of a commercial firm called the Moscow Municipal Association, which, under Lenin's New Economic Policy, was allowed to engage in legitimate business abroad. Calling itself by the shorthand term "the Trust," the Moscow Municipal Association conducted correspondence with purported foreign firms.

At the same time, there were strong indications that the MOCR had penetrated many Soviet organizations and even had its agents in the secret police. It was due to the role of these agents that the MOCR could arrange for couriers to pass into and out of Soviet Russia with perfect safety.

Yakushev, who functioned as the MOCR's "foreign minister," sent word to his contacts abroad that the organization had been able to recruit Lieutenant General Nikolai Mikhailovich Potapov, a long-time career officer, as its chief of staff. This was exciting news because Potapov was well known to the generals in the emigration, many of whom had served with him in the old Imperial Army. Unlike those generals, Potapov had gone over to the Bolsheviks immediately after their seizure of power. Now, however, it appeared that Potapov had had second thoughts about the Bolsheviks and had joined the opposition within the Soviet regime.

Under false names, Yakushev and Potapov traveled together to Finland and Poland, where they entered into secret negotiations with the intelligence services of the two countries, which were firmly anti-Communist. They proposed an arrangement whereby the Trust would ensure that agents of these two intelligence services could freely cross the Soviet border in exchange for tangible logistical and financial help. Their proposal envisaged so-called windows on the border through which the agents would pass. The intelligence services would control the "windows" on their side of the border; the Trust, using its agents in the Soviet border guards, would control the Russian side of the border. Both the Finns and the Poles found this offer attractive and quickly entered into agreements with the Trust representatives. True to their word, Yakushev and Potapov saw to it that the "windows" were functioning within a short time. Other foreign intelligence services also benefited from this arrangement; soon "liaison officers" were assigned to Western diplomatic installations in Finland, Poland, Latvia, Estonia, etc., along the Soviet borders where the reports of couriers could be handled.

The émigrés also profited by the "windows." By this time the Wrangel organization also had its own underground activities. In March 1924, the Grand Duke Nikolai Nikolaevich summoned General Aleksandr Pavlovich Kutepov to Paris and placed him in charge of the ROVS's Combat Organization, whose mission was to carry out both espionage and sabotage. Kutepov had especially good connections with the Finnish Intelligence Service through a personal friend, General Wallenius, chief of the Finnish General Staff. As a result, Kutepov's agents were assisted in passing through the Finnish "window" as they engaged in their operations.

Direct relations between the Trust and the ROVS were established as early as June 1923, when General Evgeni E. Klimovich, Wrangel's intelligence chief, conferred with Yakushev in Berlin. A year afterward both Yakushev and Potapov were received by the Grand Duke Nikolai Nikolaevich himself.

Boris Savinkov was not left out of the picture. He was in constant touch with Colonel Pavlovsky in Moscow, who vouched for the Trust's reliability. His agents too were going back and forth through the "windows" without the slightest difficulty by the time he made his first tenuous contacts with the Trust, since he also benefited from the help of the Finns and the Poles.

Another important change had taken place in the USSR. In January 1924, following a series of strokes, Lenin died. Savinkov, who had always regarded Lenin as his principal enemy, knew that Lenin's death was certain to bring about a power struggle within the Bolshevik leadership, weakening the stability of the regime. After Lenin's death, Pavlovsky sent a message urging Savinkov to return to Russia to lead a full-scale uprising against the strife-torn Soviet regime. These developments—taken together with a growing awareness of his own impotence in the emigration—made him more and more impatient and dissatisfied.

The marked deterioration in his morale had other causes. Savinkov was deeply disillusioned with Western governments and statesmen, who were guilty, in his eyes, of a complete ignorance of the Russian situation and complacency toward the menace of Communism.

Bruce Lockhart, who met Savinkov for the last time in a night club in Prague in 1923, wrote:

> He was a pathetic figure, for whom one couldn't help feeling the deepest sympathy. He had exhausted all his friends and when later he returned to Moscow . . . I was not surprised. Doubtless, behind that tortured brain there was some grandiose scheme of striking a last blow for Russia and carrying out a spectacular coup d'état. It was a gambler's throw (all his life he had played a lone hand). . . .[3]

A further element in Savinkov's sad state was his morphine habit, to which he yielded still more as he became increasingly depressed. There can be no doubt that Savinkov confided both his unhappiness and his desperate plans in letters to Reilly.

But Reilly revealed his knowledge to only one other person. At this time Paul Dukes was on an American lecture tour. He finally stopped in New York to translate Savinkov's book *The Pale Horse* into English. Reilly assisted Dukes with the translation. One day, without any preliminary, Reilly told Dukes: "I am going to tell you something very, very private. I am not telling anyone else and no one must know. Savinkov is going back to Russia to give himself up. I too am going back, but I shall continue the fight."[4]

It was not resignation, however, but hope that influenced both men in seriously considering a return to Russia. The struggle for the succession to Lenin involved many rivals: Trotsky, Stalin, Kamenev, Zinoviev, Dzerzhinski, and possibly others. Did Reilly, like Savinkov, believe that in the circumstances an internal revolt carried out by the Trust, perhaps within the walls of the Kremlin, was likely to be successful? No one can say. Nevertheless, it seems entirely possible that this was a factor in his thinking.

In June 1924, Savinkov received a visit from an emissary of

the Trust. This man informed Savinkov that the Trust wanted him to come back to Russia in the near future. If Savinkov did return, he would have to go on trial, but the Trust would guarantee that he would be given nothing worse than a jail sentence. Moreover, he would spend his time in prison under privileged conditions. As soon as the time was ripe, the Trust would arrange Savinkov's release so that he could thenceforth take a prominent part in their political activities.

Impressed by the Trust's assurances, Savinkov promised to give serious consideration to this proposal. But he still had not made up his mind a month later when he heard again from his right-hand man, Colonel Pavlovsky. Once more Pavlovsky urged him to return to Russia without delay. Apparently aware of the Trust's proposal, Pavlovsky said that Savinkov had only to take the indispensable first step of returning home and everything else would take care of itself. An uprising was scheduled to occur in Georgia very soon. If Savinkov was on hand in Soviet Russia, he would naturally become the head of the new government.

In New York, Reilly received an urgent request from Savinkov to come to Paris, as important decisions had to be reached as soon as possible. Of course, Reilly understood exactly what Savinkov had in mind, and it would not have been like him if he had failed to respond to the request.

After succeeding by some means in raising the money for the passage, he and Pepita set out for Europe. But he took the precaution of obtaining a life insurance policy, with Pepita as beneficiary, prior to his departure. In all likelihood, he wished to provide some financial security for his wife in the event that he undertook the return to Russia that he had been contemplating for some time.

When Reilly arrived in Paris, Savinkov was away, having gone to Rome for a meeting with Mussolini. Savinkov returned a few days later, but his morale had not improved after seeing Mussolini. It was no new experience for him to be disappointed in a Western statesman. Savinkov reported with disgust to Reilly that the Duce had failed to offer him any financial assistance. The most Mussolini would do was to provide an Italian passport and promise the help of the Italian Legation in Moscow in case of need.

Now Savinkov informed Reilly that he intended to accept the

Trust's offer and return to Russia in a few weeks. He was convinced that he had made the right decision. There would never be a more favorable moment, taking into account the disunity in the Soviet leadership and the confusion in the people created by Lenin's death. He would undergo a trial, recant if necessary his political views in favor of the Bolsheviks, and rely on the Trust's protection to carry on the hidden struggle against the Bolsheviks inside Russia.

No record exists of Reilly's words during his private conversations with Savinkov. Reilly himself stated that he met every day with Savinkov from July 19 to August 10, when Savinkov left for Russia. According to some sources, he tried to dissuade Savinkov from his plan to return. It will be remembered that Reilly had told Paul Dukes some time earlier in New York, "Savinkov is going back to Russia to give himself up," coupling this with the statement that he also planned to return to Russia, "but I shall continue the fight." Obviously, Reilly not only had foreknowledge of Savinkov's intentions but seemed to be in agreement with him on the principle of returning to Soviet Russia. At the same time, Reilly did not tell Dukes that he was *opposed* to Savinkov's decision to give himself up and would seek to dissuade him. In view of the influence over Savinkov that several reliable observers attributed to Reilly, it is improbable that Savinkov would have summoned Reilly to Paris and spent three weeks in discussions with him only to go ahead with the original plan *against* Reilly's advice.

On the other hand, the facts concerning Savinkov's return trip to Russia are abundantly clear. On August 10, 1924, Savinkov set out from Paris in the company of Mr. and Mrs. Dickhoff-Daehrenthal. The Savinkov party traveled to Berlin, where Yakushev of the Trust was waiting. Together they went on to Warsaw. There Yakushev parted from the others, having arranged for them to pass through the Polish "window." Then Yakushev went ahead by another route to ensure that Trust preparations for their reception on the other side of the border had been completed. After Savinkov and his companions crossed the border, Yakushev again was waiting and escorted them to Minsk, where they were to remain for a few days. It was in the house they were staying at in Minsk that Pilar von Pilhau,[5] a short, nearsighted former Baltic baron who had become one of the most feared Chekists, suddenly made an appearance. He entered the room and announced: "I am Pilar, head of the Belorussian OGPU. The house is surrounded by my men. You are under arrest."

Savinkov nodded calmly. "I have been expecting you."

On August 29, *Izvestiya* finally reported the first news of Savinkov to the outside world: "On or about the 20th of the month, our security services arrested on Soviet territory Citizen B. V. Savinkov, the most irreconcilable and persistent foe of Russia's Workers' and Peasants' Government."

Savinkov's trial was already over, having taken place on the two preceding days, August 27 and 28,[6] only about a week after his arrest in Minsk. The events had moved with astonishing speed, largely owing to Savinkov's complete cooperation.

The judge, V. I. Ulrikh, was to make a notorious reputation presiding over "show" trials during Stalin's Great Purge, when he would pronounce death sentences with parrotlike repetitiveness.

The first day's proceedings were conducted behind closed doors. On the second day, after dark, the Soviet authorities rounded up three foreign correspondents—Walter Duranty, Louis Fischer, and a colleague—and conducted them to the court in great secrecy to hear the defendant's concluding statement. The correspondents were not even told the identity of the defendant until they arrived in the courtroom.

Walter Duranty described the scene:

> I had not been two seconds in the room where the trial was to be held before I felt the terrific excitement of everyone present. There were only 200 or so of this "elite first-night audience" but they were the ranking men and women of Soviet Russia. Stalin was not amongst them, nor Dzerzhinski, Zinoviev, or Trotsky, but with these exceptions everyone who was anyone in Moscow was in that hot packed room, all tense and eager as hounds when they sight their laboring quarry and rush forward to the kill. Save myself and two colleagues, no foreigners were present.[7]

Louis Fischer had a slightly different description:

> The courtroom held about 150 people. Among them were Dzerzhinski, first chief of the secret police, Lev Kamenev, assistant prime minister, Chicherin, Karl Radek, Karakhan, and other Soviet celebrities.[8]

Continuing with his account, Duranty wrote:

> The court entered; three youngish men in uniform, with the
> Supreme Judge of the Military Tribunal, Ulrikh, in the center.
> Then came the guards and soldiers and, surprisingly, two sailors;
> and the prisoner, Boris Savinkov.
> A small man, quite bald, about forty-five, who walked with
> rather weak and faltering steps, he wore a cheap, double-breasted
> gray sack suit, with a starched white collar and shirt and a nar-
> row black tie. His face suggested the pictures of young Napoleon,
> but was drawn and white, with deep shadows under the eyes. He
> was quite unafraid, and glanced around with curiosity like a man
> taking his last look at human beings and their petty lies. . . .[9]

Fischer also eyed the defendant with interest:

> Savinkov sat in the witness box between two soldiers with
> fixed bayonets. He was about fifty. The right side of his face
> looked as though a hand had pushed it upward, and in the left
> cheek there was a gash from cheek bone to jowl.[10]

The purpose of this session was to hear Savinkov's final statement and the judge's verdict. In Duranty's words:

> Savinkov was worthy of his audience and his stellar role. His
> final speech, not in his own defense because he did not attempt
> to defend himself, but to explain himself to them and perhaps
> even more to explain himself to himself was the greatest piece
> of oratory I have ever heard. . . .
> Savinkov played no oratorical tricks. Standing alone amongst
> his enemies, he spoke in a low voice in which there was no
> tremor. He told them in substance, "I am more of a revolution-
> ary than you Bolsheviks. When you were hiding underground in
> Russia or talking Marxist ideology in the cafés of Geneva or
> Paris, I carried out the shooting of Tsarist governors and smashed
> Grand Dukes to pieces with bombs." With superb egoism, he
> added, "I was an active revolutionary while you were plotting
> revolution. While you hid or fled I was playing on death's door-
> step." Savinkov concluded: "Here, before your court whose sen-
> tence I know already, surrounded by your soldiers whom I do not
> fear, I say that I recognize without condition your right to govern
> Russia. I do not ask your mercy. I ask only to let your revolu-
> tionary conscience judge a man who has never sought anything

for himself, who has devoted his whole life to the cause of the Russian people. But I add this: before coming here to say that I recognize you, I have gone through worse suffering than the utmost you can do to me!"[11]

"The last words were spoken in the same low voice as the rest," Duranty went on. "Savinkov sat down, opened a box of cigarettes, asked for a light from a guard and began to smoke."

At the end of a trial with no prosecutor, no defense counsel, and no jury, Savinkov was found guilty and sentenced to death. In the aftermath, however, the judge surprised everyone by his leniency. "Imposition of the death penalty," Ulrikh said, "is not required in the interest of preserving revolutionary law and order." Because "motives of vengeance should not influence the sense of justice of the proletarian masses," he commuted the death sentence to ten years' imprisonment.

Sidney Reilly reacted to the news of Savinkov's trial and death sentence, and the later reduction of the sentence to ten years in prison, by writing a letter to London's *Morning Post* which was published on September 8, 1924. Referring to an article about Savinkov in that newspaper, Reilly said, "Your informant, without adducing any proofs whatsoever and basing himself merely on rumors, makes the suggestion that Savinkov's trial was a 'stunt' arranged between him and the Kremlin clique, and that Savinkov had already for some time contemplated a reconciliation with the Bolsheviks. No more ghastly accusation," he added, "could be so carelessly hurled against a man whose whole life has been spent fighting tyranny of whatsoever denomination, Tsarist or Bolshevist. . . ."

It was understandable that, for tactical reasons, Reilly might wish to deny any intention on Savinkov's part of deliberately surrendering himself to the Bolsheviks. Whatever his motivation, the indignation in this letter does not ring true. Moreover, claiming to have been privy to Savinkov's plans—"his last hours in Paris were spent with me"—Reilly did not explain why Savinkov had gone to Russia at all.

Still unaware that foreign correspondents actually had attended the final session of the trial, Reilly put forth a fantastic theory of his own. "Savinkov was killed when attempting to cross the Russian frontier," he suggested, "and a mock trial, with one of their own agents as chief actor, was staged by the Cheka in Moscow behind closed doors."

Reilly privately expressed concern about the effect of the Savinkov affair on Winston Churchill, whom he considered the most influential friend of the anti-Bolshevik movement. Churchill, he said, was the man who could be counted on to back a counter-revolution if given the opportunity. Savinkov's apparent defection had perhaps dealt a fatal blow to such hopes. Therefore, Reilly lost no time in writing directly to Churchill.

> Dear Mr. Churchill,
> The disaster which has overtaken Boris Savinkov has undoubtedly produced the most painful impression upon you. Neither I nor any of his intimate friends and co-workers have so far been able to obtain any reliable news about his fate. Our conviction is that he has fallen a victim to the vilest and most daring intrigue the Cheka has ever attempted. Our opinion is expressed in the letter which I am today sending to the *Morning Post*. Knowing your invariably kind interest I take the liberty of enclosing a copy for your information.
>
> I am, dear Mr. Churchill,
Yours very faithfully,
Sidney Reilly[12]

Churchill unquestionably followed the Savinkov affair with close and continuing interest. He replied promptly to Reilly's letter.

> Chartwell Manor,
Westerham, Kent
September 5, 1924
>
> Dear Mr. Reilly,
> I was deeply grieved to read the news about Savinkov. I do not, however, think that the explanation in your letter to the *Morning Post* is borne out by the facts. The *Morning Post* to-day gives a fuller account of the proces-verbal, and I clearly recognize the points we discussed at Chequers about free Soviet elections, etc. You do not say in your letter what was the reason and purpose with which he entered Soviet Russia. If it is true that he had been pardoned and liberated I should be very glad. I am sure that any influence he could acquire among those men would be powerfully exerted towards bringing about a better

state of affairs. In fact their treatment of him, if it is true, seems to me to be the first decent and sensible thing I have ever heard about them.

I shall be glad to hear anything further you may know on the subject, as I always thought Savinkov was a great man and a great Russian patriot, in spite of the terrible methods with which he has been associated. However it is very difficult to judge the politics in any other country.[13]

Yours very truly,
Winston S. Churchill

After hearing the eyewitness reports of the trial in Moscow, Reilly shifted his ground to accuse Savinkov of having betrayed the anti-Bolshevik cause. He wrote a second letter to the *Morning Post* in which he said:

The detailed and in many instances stenographic press reports of Savinkov's trial, supported by the testimony of reliable and impartial eyewitnesses, have established Savinkov's treachery beyond all possibility of doubt. He has not only betrayed his friends, his organization, and his cause, but he has also deliberately and completely gone over to his former enemies. He has connived with his captors to deal the heaviest possible blow at the anti-Bolshevik movement, and to provide them with an outstanding political triumph both for internal and external use. By this act Savinkov has erased for ever his name from the scroll of honor of the anti-Communist movement.[14]

Thus Reilly detached himself from Savinkov and the latter's dubious actions while once more validating his own credentials as a solid anti-Communist. He still hoped to gain support for his own schemes in influential circles (among such people as Churchill) and seems to have feared that the Savinkov affair would dampen all enthusiasm for a Russian counterrevolution. To some, however, the quickness with which Reilly condemned Savinkov appeared excessive. Winston Churchill, for one, reflected this feeling in another letter to Reilly:

September 15, 1924

Dear Mr. Reilly,

I am very interested in your letter. The event has turned out as I myself expected at the very first. I do not think you should judge Savinkov too harshly. He was placed in a terrible position; and only those who have sustained successfully such an ordeal have a full right to pronounce censure. At any rate I shall wait to hear the end of the story before changing my view about Savinkov.[15]

Yours very truly,
W. S. Churchill

During the same period, Sidney Reilly even received a letter from Savinkov himself, obviously initiated or approved by the OGPU in Moscow. Savinkov wrote his old ally: "Never have I fought for the interests and dubious welfare of Europe, but always for Russia and the Russian people. How many illusions and fairy tales have I buried here in the Lubianka! I have met men in the GPU whom I have known and trusted from my youth up and who are nearer to me than the chatterboxes of the foreign delegation of Social Revolutionaries. . . . What does prison mean here? No one is kept longer than three years and is given leave to visit the town during this time. . . . I cannot deny that Russia is reborn."[13]

If it was Reilly's wish to retaliate for the Bolsheviks' "outstanding political triumph," he did not have long to wait for an opportunity to strike back. Beyond doubt, he was the author of the so-called Zinoviev letter, which caused a sensation in England in October 1924.

Reilly knew that a considerable amount of subversive material from Russian Communist sources was entering England. He conceived the idea that a letter from Grigori Zinoviev, president of the Comintern,[16] directing British Communists to undermine their national government would have an enormous impact on English public opinion. The resultant furor supposedly would have a tonic effect on anti-Communist morale, which had sunk to a new low after Savinkov's much-publicized defection.

For a man like Reilly, the problem of forging such a letter was easily solved. He went to Berlin where one of his former associates in Russia, Orlovsky, who had served as director of the criminal police, was now making his living as one of the operators of a "paper mill," turning out forged Soviet documents that were sold to more gullible intelligence services as genuine official papers smuggled out of Russia by anti-Bolshevik agents. Like ordinary counterfeiters, these fabricators sought to convince their customers by means of format, paper, ink, seals, and the like that their product was authentic. They possessed not only real documents that they could use as models but also special knowledge based on past experience in Soviet organizations, enabling them to make documents that could deceive officials in the same ministry who did not have access to the archives or were not able to check the original serial numbers.

Reilly personally composed the text of the Zinoviev letter. Dated September 15, 1924, it purported to be a "letter of instruction" to the British representative in the Comintern, telling him that British Communists must prepare for armed insurrection and infiltrate into the army and navy so as to paralyze those services when the time came for an uprising. Reilly also arranged for copies of the letter to go to both the Foreign Office and the English press.

At this time a General Election campaign was in full swing, and Prime Minister Ramsay MacDonald boasted in speeches of the Labor government's success in developing cooperation with Moscow. He continued to emphasize this theme even after he became aware of the existence of the Zinoviev letter, which Foreign Office experts considered genuine. When the *Daily Mail* broke the story, the noisy public controversy that followed was a major factor in the downfall of the Labor government in the election.

Reilly did his utmost to keep secret his instigation of the Zinoviev letter, realizing that if it became known, the Secret Intelligence Service would sever all contact with him. Later on, however, he proudly admitted to friends like Major Alley that he was responsible for the forgery.

Reilly's motivation in concocting the forgery remains a mystery. His defenders maintain that he only intended to turn the tables on the Communists in the propaganda war and never dreamed that his letter would help to bring about the defeat of the Labor party. His detractors assert that Reilly was too politically minded to be unaware of the General Election campaign and to fail to see how it might hurt the Labor government. They believe, in fact, that Reilly's main purpose was to bring about a Conservative victory. Perhaps he hoped that the Conservatives would provide massive support to the anti-Bolsheviks.

On the other hand, Moscow also had an interest in defeating the Labor party. The Soviet leaders have always looked upon Western socialists as rivals in courting the favor of the proletariat and, allegedly, traitors to the workers' cause. They prefer to deal with rightist or reactionary governments—Nazi or fascist, Republican or Conservative—where the issues are clear-cut. They prefer an outright enemy to a lukewarm friend.

Reilly's defenders and detractors alike do not seem to have questioned the morality of his behavior in instigating the forgery of the Zinoviev letter. While he sought no personal profit, he was a British subject whose unscrupulous actions affected the outcome of a General Election in his adopted country, and as a long-term SIS agent he had deliberately chosen to deceive various arms of the British government, including the SIS.

Chapter 16

A T THE END OF 1924, not long after the Zinoviev letter scandal, Sidney Reilly and his wife again traveled across the Atlantic to New York.

His case against the Baldwin Locomotive Company had finally come before a court. Mr. Vauclain, the company head, conceded that an agreement had existed, but he stated that he felt no legal obligation to pay anything since Reilly had destroyed the agreement. The judge and jury considering the case rejected Reilly's claim.

Reilly, who had counted on receiving the money, lost all self-control when he saw that the verdict would go against him. The shock of another disappointment was almost more than he could bear. Paul Dukes, who attended the proceedings, said that Reilly "was a very ugly sight indeed," in his rage literally foaming at the mouth, saliva dripping down his chin.

Nevertheless, Reilly did not remain discouraged for long. He was engaged in his own one-man war against the OGPU in America. He lectured and wrote against a proposed American loan to Russia eagerly sought by Moscow. In addition, he made it his business to uncover Bolshevik agents in the United States who were appearing there in increasing numbers; he sometimes carried out surveillance himself in order to track down and identify the Bolshevik agents. Under the name Sidney Berns, he kept in touch with American intelligence officers, providing them with this and other information acquired from émigré sources.

At the same time, Reilly corresponded with his SIS and émigré friends in Europe. He learned from them that the Trust was constantly assuming greater importance in the scheme of things. Even after Savinkov's arrest, the "windows" remained open and the agents of foreign intelligence services as well as those of General Kutepov's Combat Organization were still moving freely over the frontiers. Indeed, in spite of Savinkov's fate—or possibly because of it—the Trust's prestige continued to grow.

The Trust received credit abroad for the fact that Savinkov apparently was not doing badly in jail. He occupied a two-room apartment in the Butyrki, the OGPU's Inner Prison, had the privilege of writing to friends outside the country, such as Reilly, and also gave interviews to foreign journalists.

One of his visitors was William Reswick, an AP correspondent, who described his meeting with Savinkov in these words:

> Savinkov's cell . . . was the biggest surprise of the day. It was a beautifully furnished room with thick carpets on the floor, a large mahogany desk, a blue-silk-upholstered divan, and pictures on the walls. . . . The great conspirator was clean-shaven and smelled of perfume as though a barber had just left him. Most astonishing of all was his state of mind. He behaved like a wealthy and gracious host receiving visitors. Is this mere bravado, I wondered, or absolute courage? . . . We plied Savinkov with questions, to each of which he had a quick, tactful, brilliant answer. He spoke Russian and French with equal ease. Asked why he had returned to Russia, he stepped to the window. Pointing to the Kremlin, he said: "I would rather see those towers from a prison cell than walk freely in the streets of Paris!" . . . In our admiration and pity, for to most of us he was not only a valiant leader but a brilliant writer, we avoided asking any questions that might embarrass him in the presence of his jailers. But there was one exception. Much to our chagrin, a French correspondent asked a question that instantly put Savinkov on the

defensive, compelling a choice between evasion and danger: "Are the OGPU horror stories true or false?" . . . The prisoner replied: "Speaking for myself, they are obviously untrue." I looked at Trilisser.[1] His black eyes flashed with anger. The prisoner, like everybody else in the room, could not help noticing the poor impression "speaking for myself" had made on the Chekist. Yet Savinkov went on talking like a free man until Trilisser put an end to the interview with one word: *"Pora!"* (Time is up!) The effect of that word was instantaneous. Savinkov turned pale and stopped talking. He still smiled as he saw us to the door, but it was a forced smile.[2]

Ernest Boyce, Reilly's old boss in Russia, had become the SIS station commander in Revel, Estonia, where his men were involved in cross-border operations and carried on liaison with the Trust and its emissaries. Boyce personally knew Yakushev, who since 1921 had supplied him with intelligence reports that were highly regarded by SIS. He had also convinced himself of the reliability of two Trust agents, a husband and wife, Georgy Radkevich and Mariya Vladislavovna Zakharchenko (also known as Maria Schultz). They had been on many missions, separately and together, winning Boyce's complete confidence.

Particularly interesting was Maria Schultz, a deceptively carefree and gay young woman of about thirty-five, rather plain, slight of build, with frank gray eyes. Little in her appearance hinted at the hardships and dangers that she had already experienced in her life. Daughter of a general, she had served as a private in a cavalry regiment of the Imperial Army throughout the war and had been widowed twice when her husbands were killed in action. After the revolution she fought with the Whites against the Reds. When the civil war ended, she became one of the most experienced, cool, and daring anti-Communist agents, working abroad with the Combat Organization of General Kutepov, her uncle.

These activities had to be viewed against the background of developments in the Soviet Union, where, as a result of Lenin's death, a struggle was in progress among those who hoped to succeed Lenin as the head of the Soviet state. Trotsky was the one leader whose name had always been linked with that of Lenin at the very summit of power. For that reason, all of Trotsky's rivals joined forces against him, and Stalin, who controlled the party apparatus, knew how to exploit the distrust of Trotsky as a former Menshevik and the dislike of Trotsky's overpowering and arrogant personality to advance his own claim to leadership of the Bolshevik party. As the power struggle between Trotsky and Stalin sharpened, Boyce came to the conclusion that the outcome of the struggle might be determined by the Trust—in fact, if the Bolshevik leadership was sufficiently weakened, the Soviet regime could be taken over by the Trust. In the circumstances, he thought that Sidney Reilly was just the man to make a sound assessment of the Trust's prospects.

Having heard that his former colleague was planning at some point to return to Paris, Boyce wrote in a coded letter dated January 24, 1925, to Reilly in New York:

> There may call to see you in Paris from me two persons named Krasnoshtanov, a man and wife [Georgy Radkevich and Maria Schultz]. They will say they have a communication from California and hand you a note consisting of a verse from Omar Khayyám which you will remember. If the business is of no interest to you, you will say: "Thank you very much. Good day."
>
> Now as to their business. They are representatives of a concern which in all probability will have a big influence in the future on the European and American markets. They do not anticipate that their business will fully develop for two years, but circumstances may arise which will give them the desired impetus in the near future. It is very big business and one which it does not do to talk about. . . . They refuse at present to disclose to anyone the name of the man at the back of the enterprise. I can tell you this much—that some of the chief persons are members of the opposition groups. You can therefore fully understand the necessity for secrecy. . . . I am introducing this scheme to you thinking it might perhaps replace the other big scheme you were working on but which fell through in such a disastrous manner. Incidentally, you would help me considerably by taking the matter up. The only thing I ask is that you keep our connection with this business from the knowledge of my department as, being a Government official, I am not supposed to be connected with any such enterprise. I know your interest in such a business where patience and perseverance against all sorts of intrigues and opposition are required and I know also you will look after my interests without my having to make some special agreement with you.[3]

While Reilly continued to turn his thoughts toward Russia, the United States in which he found himself had completely different interests. In 1924 and early 1925 Americans followed such events as the presidential campaign (which had a dull anticlimax in Calvin Coolidge's victory); the trial of Leopold and Loeb, two rich young men from Chicago, for the "thrill" murder of a school-boy, Bobby Franks; the visit of the Prince of Wales to Long Island, where the press and especially the rotogravure section covered in absorbing detail his polo playing, motorboating, and dancing, also noting that his current reading included *The Life and Letters of Walter Hines Page*; the linking by marriage of Hollywood royalty, in the person of Gloria Swanson, to the nobility of France, represented by the Marquis de la Falaise de la Coudray; and, finally, the exciting story of the Finn Paavo Nurmi, a long-distance runner, who ran with a stopwatch in his hand and defeated the American taxi driver Joey Ray at the Olympic Games, setting a new world record by running two miles in less than nine minutes.

About the same time that Reilly received Boyce's letter, all America—to judge from the front pages of the press—hung in suspense over the fate of an obscure young man from Kentucky, Floyd Collins, who, exploring underground in the hope of finding a new tourist attraction, was trapped by a cave-in. For nearly three weeks, while rescue attempts went on, newsmen gathered outside the cave where Collins was trapped, one of them even crawling down to interview him; and on February 17, 1925, the *New York Times* devoted a three-column headline on page one to announce: "FIND FLOYD COLLINS DEAD IN CAVE TRAP ON 18TH DAY; LIFELESS AT LEAST 24 HOURS; FOOT MUST BE AMPUTATED TO GET BODY OUT."

Throughout 1925 a series of letters in code or in secret writing passed back and forth between Boyce and Reilly, all concerned with the Trust. Was Boyce being honest with Reilly in his express wish to "keep our connection with this business from the knowl-edge of my department" or did the SIS headquarters prefer to remain aloof from the whole operation? Even Boyce made it clear that not only the SIS in general but he personally could accept no official connection with Reilly's project if anything went wrong. It is hard to avoid the conclusion that the SIS had a definite interest in the Trust and wished to use Reilly for a further exploration of the situation, but feared another "Lockhart plot" that could again lead to embarrassing questions in Parliament. If so, Hugh "Quex" Sinclair, the new SIS chief, may have been determined to keep his distance from the operation until its success or failure became clear. In case of a failure, the SIS could disown its station commander in Revel; case officers involved in the affair could be dismissed or transferred.

Reilly was not deterred by the SIS's apparent reservations. He expressed himself enthusiastically about cooperating with the Trust, urging that its representatives be sent to America where financial help was sure to be forthcoming. Moreover, before carrying out a counterrevolution, the Trust should initiate contacts with leaders of the major European powers in order to secure their understanding and moral support. In making this last suggestion, Reilly did not explain how that most indispensable ingredient of a coup d'etat, secrecy, could be maintained while going about Europe and informing foreign leaders of the Trust's plans. Apart from the fact that their discretion could not always be relied on, these leaders sometimes had Communists or OGPU agents in staff positions close to them.

"As regards a closer understanding with the international market," Reilly wrote Boyce in advancing the same proposal, "I think that to start with only one man is really important and that is the irrepressible Marlborough [Winston Churchill]. I have always remained on good terms with him. . . . His ear would always be open to something sound, especially if it emanated from the minority interests.[4] He said as much in one of his very private and confidential letters to me."[5]

Reilly's attempts to obtain more information about the Trust leaders remained unsuccessful. He was aware that the former czarist General Andrei M. Zayonchkovsky supposedly had founded the Monarchist Organization of Central Russia, Yakushev was its "Foreign Minister," and General Potapov had become its Chief of Staff. But he was unable to learn the identities of the other leaders.

Boyce had an agent named Nikolai Nikolaevich Bunakov, who lived in Helsinki and was Boyce's principal liaison man with the Trust. He proposed that Reilly establish direct contact with Bunakov in order to get answers to questions about the Trust, supplying Bunakov with a "letter which he can show to the

Moscow Center or its representatives to the effect that you are interested in the commercial proposition submitted and putting forward any suggestion you may have to make and at the same time if possible give them something which will show that you are in a position to help them."[6]

Bunakov, an émigré, had overcome his initial suspicion to develop growing confidence in the Trust. Like many émigrés, Bunakov still had relatives in Russia. Meeting Yakushev on one occasion, Bunakov said, "My brother Boris is in Moscow. Would it be possible to send greetings to him through you?"

"Of course," Yakushev replied. "But why not see him yourself?"

Bunakov smiled cynically. "Do you want me to deliver myself into the arms of the OGPU in Moscow?"

"There's no need to go to Moscow. He could come to see you here in Helsinki."

"Is that possible?"

"That we can arrange, dear fellow," Yakushev said with a laugh. "We'll deliver your brother whole and unharmed."

Yakushev kept his promise. In due course Boris Bunakov turned up in Helsinki, reporting to his brother that the trip had involved nothing worse than a long walk over a muddy road. One evening a Trust representative appeared at his home, gave him a half-hour to get ready, and took him to the railroad station. The next day he was in Leningrad. From there he went to Sestroretsk and, during the night, with the aid of a frontier guard controlled by the Trust, crossed over through the Finnish "window" and was received by Finnish Intelligence officers and transported to Helsinki.

After his brother's visit and later confirmation of his safe return to Moscow, Nikolai Bunakov became a firm supporter of the Trust and strove in every possible way to increase cooperation between the Trust and the SIS.

Reilly displayed increasing interest and enthusiasm in his correspondence with Bunakov, although he still refused to commit himself to any immediate action. Possibly using his private business affairs as an excuse, he continued to delay a decision. The business he conducted in the United States seems to have had little substance; it did not include aviation, despite the fact that as early as 1910 he had attended an international flying exhibition in Frankfort, Germany, and had become fascinated with the possibilities of aviation. Before the First World War in Russia, Reilly helped to organize a St. Petersburg-to-Moscow air race and, together with some friends, set up a flying club. It is intriguing to think that Reilly, who had all the talents of a promoter, could have been an early entrepreneur of aviation in the United States. His interests during this period, however, were apparently directed elsewhere.

In a letter dated March 25, he wrote to Boyce: "Much as I am concerned about my own personal affairs which, as you know, are in a hellish state, I am at any moment, if I see the right people and prospects of real action, prepared to chuck everything else and devote myself entirely to the Syndicate's [the Trust's] interest. I was fifty-one yesterday and I want to do something worthwhile, whilst I can. All the rest does not matter. I am quite sure that you, although younger, feel likewise."[7]

On April 4 Reilly received a copy of a letter that the Trust had sent to Bunakov. In the letter, it was said that in view of the responsible positions occupied by Trust leaders, they could not all absent themselves from Moscow without attracting unwelcome attention; if Reilly could make a trip to Russia, he would be able to meet the Trust's "shadow cabinet" and make an assessment of its resources on the spot.

This communication inspired Reilly to write Boyce, "I am not only willing but anxious to do so and am prepared to come out as soon as I have arranged my affairs here. Of course, I would arrange this tour of inspection only after very thorough consultation with you and Engineer B. [Bunakov]. Whilst there is no limit to which I am not prepared to go in order to help in putting this new process on the market, I would naturally hate to provide a Roman holiday for the competitors. I think that I am not exaggerating in presuming that a successful inspection of the factory by me and the presentation of a fully substantiated technical report would produce a considerable impression in the interested quarters and generally facilitate the realization of the scheme."[8]

Notwithstanding these statements, an event that occurred shortly thereafter must have given Reilly some cause for reflection. On May 12, 1925, *Pravda* reported that Boris Savinkov had committed suicide by jumping out of a window. The suicide had actually taken place one week earlier (on May 7), some eight months after his capture.

According to the official version of his suicide, Savinkov had become depressed as a result of his ten-year sentence and lack of any prospect for early release. On the day of his death, he sat down after breakfast and wrote a letter to Dzerzhinski: "Either shoot me or give me the opportunity to work. . . . I cannot endure this half-and-half existence of being neither with you, nor against you, of merely lingering in jail and becoming one of its denizens. . . ."[9]

Savinkov's earlier claim that he enjoyed the privilege of going out into the city seemed to be confirmed by further details of this story. After writing the letter to Dzerzhinski, Savinkov called for his car and ordered the chauffeur to drive to Yaroslavl, the city he had seized in July 1918 during his unsuccessful revolt. At Yaroslavl he ate in a tavern and then had the chauffeur drive him at high speed back to Moscow. Inside the prison he mounted the stairs to his fourth-floor apartment. Spotting an open window in the hallway on an upper floor, he threw himself to his death in the courtyard below.

Many émigrés did not believe this story. They suspected that the OGPU, no longer finding Savinkov useful, had killed him and merely invented the suicide story to cover up a murder. Reilly privately expressed the view that the émigrés were wrong: Savinkov could not bear to wait any longer for liberation through the Trust's efforts, he said, and giving way to despair had decided to end his life.

Some years later it became known that the émigrés were right and Reilly was wrong. Savinkov had been thrown out of the window by four Chekists. And the "last letter," which even Savinkov's son in Paris had considered genuine because he recognized some of his father's typical phrases, was a forgery. The true author of the letter was Yakov Blyumkin, one of the murderers of German Ambassador Mirbach, who had been protected by Dzerzhinski and subsequently continued to work for the GPU.[10] In the Lubianka, Blyumkin had frequently engaged in "friendly" conversations with Savinkov while he familiarized himself with the other man's ideas and mode of speech. Thus prepared, he wrote the letter at the time of Savinkov's defenestration.[11]

For all Reilly's daring, he hesitated for some time, even after Boyce notified him that preliminary arrangements had been made for a meeting between Reilly and the Trust representatives. Beset by creditors, Reilly was still trying to straighten out his financial affairs. There could have been other reasons for his caution, such as a lingering doubt about the Trust. It seems more probable, however, that Reilly intended all along, as he had told Dukes, to go back to Russia to "continue the fight" there.

Finally, Reilly and Pepita sailed for Europe; he was leaving the United States for the last time. Reilly, who had a liking for Dutch ships, booked passage on the *Nieuw Amsterdam*. They arrived in Paris on September 3. Waiting for Reilly were General Kutepov, who had just returned from Finland where he had met with the Trust people, and Boyce, the promoter of the whole scheme.

Reilly took part in long discussions with Boyce, Kutepov, Vladimir Lvovich Burtsev, who had once headed the Social Revolutionary intelligence service, and his old and trusted friend Grammatikov. The upshot of these discussions was that Reilly decided to proceed to Helsinki, leaving Pepita in Paris, and meet with the Trust representatives somewhere close to the Soviet border. If he found it advisable, he would even make a trip into Russia to investigate the situation there.

In accordance with these plans, Reilly set out for Helsinki via Berlin, where he met Orlovsky, who had helped him with the forgery of the Zinoviev letter. Orlovsky had also become a strong believer in the Trust and encouraged Reilly to go ahead with the project. On September 21 Reilly arrived in Helsinki to encounter a reception committee composed of Nikolai Bunakov, Maria Schultz, and her husband Georgy Radkevich as well as Boyce's deputy, who was also very positive about the Trust.

Among these new acquaintances, Mariya Vladislavovna or Maria Schultz, impressed Reilly most of all. "She is the head of the concern," he wrote to Pepita, "and her very long skirt cannot disguise the trousers which she is wearing. She is of the American schoolmarm type which, strangely enough, is not uncommon in Russia, very plain and unattractive, but full of character and personality."[12]

Reilly listened to Maria Schultz's passionate and obviously sincere plea on behalf of the Trust and could have hardly avoided being moved. Like the Christian in the catacombs who had unshakable faith in the divinity of Jesus Christ, she believed with all her heart in the Trust as the one true opposition movement.

Reilly wrote: "If only twenty-five percent of what she said is based on facts (and not on self-induced delusion, as is so often the case when the wish is father of the will), then there is really something entirely new, powerful and worthwhile going on in Russia."

There was a radiance about Maria Schultz that affected everyone who knew her. It is impossible to say how she affected Reilly, but the fact that he described her as very plain and unattractive (in a letter to his wife) should not be taken too seriously. Although they spent only a few days together, Reilly could not help trying to conquer any interesting woman who crossed his path, while her admiration for him, stemming from his reputation as the most resourceful and fearless foe of the Bolsheviks, seemed boundless. The almost excessive degree of her grief after Reilly's disappearance in Russia suggests that their brief acquaintance may have been marked by sexual intimacy.

At first there was no word from the Trust representatives, but finally a courier brought a letter with the news that Yakushev and his colleagues would arrive in Vyborg, near the Soviet frontier, on September 24. Reilly, accompanied by all the others except Boyce's deputy, promptly left for Vyborg, where the meeting with Yakushev and two other colleagues took place on September 25 in a safe apartment maintained by Bunakov.

Now, meeting him for the first time, Reilly could see why Yakushev had won the respect of two such different but experienced men as Boris Savinkov and General Kutepov. He was a large man with bushy, sandy hair and disconcertingly bright blue eyes who appeared to be every inch a leader. He moved majestically, with deceptive slowness, an irresistible force. But his personality had the greatest impact on others: He obviously knew what he wanted, he wasted no words and spoke very simply and directly, avoiding vagueness, his understated but concrete formulations proving to be far more persuasive than the seemingly brilliant arguments presented by other people.

Following a general discussion, Yakushev said, "I have been empowered by the Political Council of the MOCR to invite you to come to Moscow for consultations, Sidney Georgievich, I hope you're prepared to accept this invitation. We're convinced that it would be the best way to settle all outstanding problems."

Reilly shook his head. "I regret to say, Aleksandr Aleksandrovich, that I don't have the time. My ship leaves for Stettin [Poland] on September 30. That's only five days from now." Noting Yakushev's disappointment, he went on: "But I plan definitely to return in a couple of months, and the trip can be arranged at that time."

"All the arrangements for your trip have already been made. My colleagues will be very unhappy if you don't come. Unfortunately, I happen to be the only one whose position permits long absences from Moscow."

"I regret exceedingly that I can't go," Reilly repeated.

"Sidney Georgievich, it would be a crime to miss this opportunity," Yakushev said, leaning toward Reilly. "Look, I can guarantee that you won't miss your ship to Stettin. You'll still be able to make the trip to Russia and return in time."

Reilly looked doubtful.

"Today is Friday, the 25th. If you're willing to leave tonight, you can be in Leningrad tomorrow morning. On Saturday night you'll go to Moscow. That gives you all day Sunday to meet with the Political Council. An ideal time, since the members won't have to be in their offices. On Sunday evening you'll return to Leningrad, spend the night and most of the next day there acquainting yourself with some of our people, and leave on Monday night for the border. You'll cross over during the night and be back in Helsinki on Tuesday, the 29th. And your ship leaves from Helsinki on Wednesday, September 30."

"Are you sure this can be done on such short notice?"

"Absolutely."

Reilly thought for a little while. "All right. I'll do it."

Then Reilly changed his clothes, acquiring a rough shirt and trousers, high boots, and a cap, which he wore with an overcoat borrowed from Radkevich.

Carrying a passport in the name of "Nikolai Nikolaevich Steinberg, merchant" that Yakushev had given him, Reilly left for the Soviet border in the company of the two other Trust representatives, a Finnish intelligence officer, Radkevich, and Maria Schultz. He stopped to wet his new boots in a ditch because they were squeaking. At precisely midnight he was ready to cross over into Russia. Maria Schultz, who remained behind, described the border crossing:

For a long while we waited while the Finns listened anxiously for the Red patrol, but everything was quiet. At last one of the Finns lowered himself cautiously into the water and half-swam, half-waded across. Sidney Reilly followed. Then went one of the men out of Russia, until all were across. . . . Peering over the water we could distinctly see them filing obliquely across the field on the further bank. Then they vanished in the gloom. By-and-by we saw their figures faintly outlined one by one against the sky as they crossed the crest. . . . All was silent as the grave.[13]

On the other side the small group was met by their guide, a soldier of the Soviet border patrol. He led them through the forest, partly on foot and partly by cart over muddy roads, to the Pargolovo railroad station seventeen kilometers away. There Reilly parted from Radkevich, who made his way alone back to Finland to report that he had seen Reilly safely aboard the train to Leningrad.

Thus Radkevich was the last of the anti-Communist émigrés to see Reilly. As prearranged, Boyce received a postcard from Reilly mailed to a letter drop; the postmark indicated that the card had been mailed in Moscow on September 27. This was the last communication from Reilly received by anyone abroad.

On the night of September 28, Sidney Reilly failed to cross the border on his return trip to Helsinki, according to the schedule outlined by Yakushev. But during the night Finnish soldiers assigned to border patrol duty heard loud gunfire on the Soviet side of the border. A White Russian attached to the Finnish forces who was supposed to escort Reilly across the frontier never returned. The Finns also received intelligence reports to the effect that Soviet soldiers were seen carrying away bodies.

A few days later *Izvestiya* carried a short news item:

In the night from the 28th to the 29th of September four smugglers attempted to cross the Soviet-Finnish border. . . . They were intercepted by our frontier troops. In the ensuing skirmish two of them were killed, a third—a Finnish soldier— was captured and the fourth mortally wounded.

To Bunakov and Maria Schultz, awaiting Reilly's return in Finland, the deduction from these bits and pieces of information seemed obvious. Somehow the Trust, for once, had slipped up, and Sidney Reilly, attempting to leave Russia on his way back to Helsinki, had had the misfortune to encounter a Soviet border patrol. His White Russian guide, who wore a Finnish uniform, must have been captured. Reilly and his two other companions had been killed.

Chapter 17

AFTER THE SHOOTING incident on the Soviet border, the report in *Izvestiya*, and a long period of silence, Pepita Reilly still did not lose hope. In her heart she felt certain that her husband was not dead. She continued to believe that one day Reilly would reappear without notice and smile at the long faces of his friends who had lacked faith in his remarkable ability to survive the worst.

First of all, Pepita turned to Reilly's former SIS colleagues for information about her husband's fate. She telephoned Lieutenant Colonel Norman G. Thwaites, one of Reilly's closest comrades, but learned nothing from him. Despite intense efforts, she found it difficult to reach Boyce, who had conveniently absented himself from the scene of action and was in London at the time Reilly crossed over into Russia. He wrote Pepita consoling letters from Stockholm and Helsinki but, acting on instructions from his superiors, did not keep his promise to visit her in Paris.

"I have had no later information," Boyce wrote her instead, "and do not now see how I can get any as my only possible source, I hear, has left Helsinki and is now on his way to Paris to see you. You will therefore be advised earlier than I shall. I don't know when I shall hear any more about it as I find urgent business now which takes me abroad again immediately and prevents me coming to Paris."[1]

To discourage her from any further efforts to contact him, Boyce added: "Furthermore, I shall have no permanent address for some time, but will let you know later where I am to be found if you will give instructions for letters to be forwarded from your present address. *Au revoir* and trusting you will soon get more definite and satisfactory information."

Boyce's "best possible source" was of course Bunakov. Nevertheless, Bunakav could tell Pepita little more than she already knew.

"Bunakov arrived in Paris at last," Pepita wrote. "He spoke nothing but Russian, but he handed over to me the letter which, for reasons best known to himself, he had retained till now."[2]

She was referring to Reilly's last letter to her, which he had written just before his departure and entrusted to Bunakov with instructions to deliver it in case he failed to return. The letter read:

My most beloved, my sweetheart,

It is absolutely necessary that I should go for three days to Petrograd and Moscow. I am leaving tonight and will be back here on Tuesday morning. I want you to know that I would not have undertaken this trip unless it was absolutely essential and if I was not convinced that there is practically no risk attached to it. I am writing this letter only for the most improbable case of a mischance befalling me. Should this happen, then you must not take any steps. They will help little but may finally lead to giving the alarm to the Bolshies and to disclosing my identity. If by any chance I should be arrested in Russia, it could only be on some minor, insignificant charge and my new friends are powerful enough to obtain my prompt liberation. I cannot imagine any circumstance under which the Bolshies could tumble to my identity—provided nothing is done from your side. Therefore, if I should have some trouble, it would only mean a very short delay in my return to Europe: I should say a fortnight at the most.

Knowing you, I am certain that you will rise to the occasion. Keep your head and do all that is necessary to keep the fort as regards my business affairs.

Naturally none of these people must get an inkling where I am and what has happened to me. Remember that any noise etc. may give me away to the Bolshies.

My dearest darling, I am doing what I must do and I am doing it with the absolute inner assurance that if you were with me you would approve.

You are in my thoughts always and your love will protect me. God bless you ever and ever. I love you beyond all words.

Sidnushka[3]

Encouraged by Reilly's assurance that he would be safe and obeying his admonition not to make noise that would give him away to the Bolsheviks, Pepita still waited hopefully. She took comfort from the fact that the Soviet press said not a word about Reilly, although it was reasonable to expect that if Moscow had killed or captured him it would have trumpeted the news to the whole world.

But Pepita was not willing to wait forever.

By November it had become clear that the SIS wanted to erase any trace of a relationship, past or present, with Reilly. In London she had tracked down Boyce, who told her that his SIS superiors had forbidden him to have anything to do with her. Boyce asked Pepita to return all of his letters to Reilly as well as any other private papers that could be exploited by the Bolsheviks if such documents came into their possession. Boyce's preventive measures, however, did not save him from demotion in the SIS; he could not escape the onus for his nearly five years of dealing with Yakushev and the Trust or the final fiasco with Reilly. While he managed to avoid outright dismissal from the service, he was sent off with Alley's help to a lesser post in an SIS cover organization, the Societé Française de Tabacs in Paris.

Friends such as George Hill and Stephen Alley also sought information in government circles without success. Hill risked the displeasure of the SIS brass by making informal inquiries at the Foreign Office, where he found that there was no disposition to become involved in the affair. At the War Office as well, officials considered the matter too dangerous to discuss.

In view of the official silence, an edge of despair became more evident in Pepita's actions. Finally she resolved on an extreme step in the forlorn hope that she could force the British government—more specifically, the SIS—to reveal what it knew about Reilly. She placed an obituary notice in the *Times* of London on December 15, 1925:

> Reilly—On the 28th Sept., killed near the village of Allekul, Russia, by GPU troops, Captain Sidney George Reilly, M.C., late R.A.F., beloved husband of Pepita N. Reilly.

The publication of this brief death notice released a flood of publicity in the British press about Reilly's life and exploits, both true and imagined. Nevertheless, the British authorities did not budge from their self-imposed silence, even after questions were asked in the House of Commons.

Robin Lockhart noted: "The Foreign Office, although admitting that Reilly was known to them, said they were unable to make any official statement. They could not state whether or not Reilly was engaged in Foreign Office work."[4]

Pepita received more comfort from Maria Schultz than from anyone else. Maria feared that Reilly had been killed, but she also thought that he might have been wounded in his attempted border crossing and lay somewhere in a Soviet hospital.

"There is a torturing, dark loneliness, full of the unknown," she wrote Yakushev. "I cannot get rid of the feeling that I somehow betrayed Reilly and was responsible for his death myself. I was responsible for the 'window.' For the sake of the movement, I ask to be allowed to work inside Russia."[5]

She made several trips to Russia in an attempt to learn what had happened to Reilly. She turned first of all to Eduard Ottovich Opperput, her immediate superior in the Trust, who was its "Minister of Finance" and who conducted the business affairs abroad that produced most of the Trust's income. Opperput was a tall, redheaded young man with unsteady eyes and a goatee which he fingered constantly. An ethnic German from Latvia, he had served in the Imperial Army. He came from a wealthy landowning family with strong ties to the old regime.

Maria Schultz contacted Opperput in Moscow and inquired about Reilly, but he told her he could supply no additional details. He assured her, however, that there was not the slightest doubt about Reilly's death. The distraught Maria could not believe that this was true. She begged Opperput to help her to obtain further information, but he refused, saying that these inquiries could only endanger the Trust.

On returning to Paris, Maria did her best to comfort Pepita. In long talks that sometimes lasted throughout the night, the two women shared their grief. They also agreed that it might be best for Pepita herself to go to Russia. There Pepita could try to find out more about what had happened to Sidney Reilly and at the same time participate in the Trust's work, helping to achieve the goals for which Reilly had always striven. To this end, Maria persuaded Pepita to take Russian lessons and urged her to join the Orthodox church.

In the meantime there were those who expressed doubts about the Trust, speculating whether, somewhere near the top, there had been an OGPU penetration, a traitor who was giving away the Trust's secrets. Yet many of these doubts seemed to be resolved by another episode that occurred about the same time that Sidney Reilly disappeared in Russia.

Vassily Vitalyevich Shulgin,[6] a former conservative deputy in the Duma, the czarist Parliament, had been active in the anti-Communist movement since the civil war. Shulgin had heard that one of his sons, whom he had not seen since his escape from Russia, was confined in a mental institution in the Ukraine. Having been present at the time of Yakushev's original meeting with General Klimovich, Wrangel's intelligence chief, Shulgin turned to the Trust leader, reminding him of a promise to assist a White Russian political representative in visiting Russia. Yakushev agreed to arrange a tour for Shulgin, who had also obtained General Wrangel's permission to undertake the journey.

For various reasons, a couple of years went by before the trip materialized. In late 1925, then, Shulgin was still waiting in Poland to cross the border into Russia when the local Trust representatives explained to him that his departure had been delayed. An Englishman had been killed crossing the border and therefore new arrangements had to be made for Shulgin's trip.

At last Shulgin, who had grown a beard and acquired a suitably shabby proletarian appearance during his wait, entered Russia through the Polish "window." In the usual manner, he was received by Trust people on the other side. For the next few months he traveled in Russia, using aliases and staying in hiding places provided for him, and there was always a Trust member at his side. In all, nineteen Trust members accompanied him during the journey, and he had the opportunity to convince himself of the existence of a widespread and well-organized anti-Communist underground.

During his journey Shulgin visited such major cities as Kiev, Moscow, and Leningrad, but he never went to the place in the Ukraine where his son supposedly had been confined. A Trust man went there instead, returning with the disappointing news that Shulgin's son had been moved to an unknown place elsewhere in Russia.

While in Moscow, Shulgin was brought to a dacha (villa) outside the capital where he met Yakushev and other Trust leaders, including Eduard Opperput, to whom he took an instant dislike because of the man's catlike, insinuating manner.

Yakushev urged Shulgin to write a book about his trip on his return abroad.[7] Shulgin, surprised, questioned the wisdom of revealing so much information about the Trust, possibly bringing down reprisals on its head. Yakushev dismissed this objection, stating that the Trust had become so powerful that the regime could do nothing against it. "It is more important," said Yakushev, "to let the emigration know that *Russia* has been reborn in the anti-Communist movement here."

Shulgin also encountered Maria Schultz, who was on one of her trips to Russia, and she confided to him that a bitter conflict had broken out between Yakushev and Opperput, the two most active leaders of the Trust. Yakushev opposed the application of terror in Russia, maintaining that it was premature and could only arouse strong resistance on the part of the Trust's enemies, while Opperput demanded that extra measures be taken without further delay in order to accomplish the Trust's goals as soon as possible.

Although the essential findings of Shulgin's trip soon became general knowledge in the anti-Communist emigration, during 1926 distrust of the Monarchist Organization of Central Russia became prevalent in influential circles abroad.

In Poland, Marshal Józef Pilsudski, who had been returned to power as a result of a military takeover, instituted a major review of the Trust. He had long criticized Polish Intelligence's nearly total dependence on the Trust for reporting on the Soviet Union.

One Polish military attaché, it became known, had carefully checked Trust reports against other reports from unimpeachable sources and discovered serious discrepancies. Now Pilsudski decided to test the Trust by asking for a copy of the Soviet mobilization plan in the event of a Soviet-Polish war. Yakushev, who had recently been honored at a private ceremony for his services to Polish Intelligence (he received a gift of a revolver bearing his initials in silver), lost his temper at this supposedly unreasonable request. He pointed out that the Trust had no source in the Red Army General Staff at that particular time and that it would cost $10,000 to obtain the mobilization plan through another source. Nevertheless, the Poles insisted on their requirement, offering to provide whatever funds were necessary. Unable to persist further in his refusal, Yakushev accepted the task, but even then it took several months before a copy of the plan was turned over. Together with his experts, Pilsudski examined the mobilization plan and pronounced it a fraud. Thereupon Pilsudski ordered the termination of all contacts with the Trust.

During this time Maria Schultz had maintained contact with Pepita Reilly, enrolling her as a member of the Trust and continuing to prepare her to participate in its activities. Maria also produced confirmation that the Trust leaders themselves were eager to have Sidney Reilly's wife come to Russia. She delivered a letter to Pepita written in French on unlined paper in a legible and well-schooled handwriting.

Dear Madam,
Mme. Schultz has acquainted us with the contents of your letter and we are very touched by your frankness and by the fact that you are ready to help us in the work to which we have pledged ourselves.

The misfortune that has befallen you appears to us so great that it is impossible for us to find any words of consolation to express our feelings of sorrow. We can only say that hatred of our common enemies binds us to you and compels us to unite our efforts.

Cruel fate has decided that your husband, who was our sincere friend, should perish like many others of our friends, and though we consider ourselves all doomed in advance, we continue to fight in the firm hope that Good will triumph over Evil. Do not think then, dear madam, that you are alone. Be assured that you have friends, friends a little distant perhaps but sincere friends, friends prepared to sacrifice everything for you and to do everything in their power to help you.

Please believe, dear madam, that the death of your husband will be avenged, but to this end your valuable cooperation is indispensable to us. It is with the most lively interest that we have learned of your intentions and the activity which you are employing. We beg you, then, to continue the work for our common cause.

Although we regard you already as a member of our great family, we are happy, madam, to learn of your desire to enter the fold of the Orthodox church, a thing that will unite us even more.

It would be excellent if you would learn our language a little, a thing that would not give you much trouble after what Mme. Schultz has told us of your astounding talents as a linguist. We should then ask you to come to us so that you could take an active part in the work and so that we could introduce you to the members of our group. We would be able at the same time to prove to you our sincere devotion and to work with you to the same final goal. May God come to your aid in your grief and give you consolation in the work that you desire to share with us.

Your distant friends[8]

The letter had four distinct signatures at the bottom, all but one written in the Latin alphabet. The fourth signature was in the Cyrillic alphabet. The first three names were Klein, Levine and King; the fourth, in Cyrillic, was Rabinovich. Evidently the Trust leaders believed that Jewish names were more appropriate for officers of the Moscow Municipal Credit Association. According to Maria Schultz, Yakushev used Klein as a pseudonym and Opperput hid behind the name Levine. She did not know the true identities of King and Rabinovich, but it seems clear that one of them was Potapov.

Once again Maria Schultz sought to persuade Pepita to accept the Trust's proposal and leave for Russia in the near future. Pepita was strongly inclined to go along with the idea, but before she had committed herself, she received a summons from General Kutepov, who asked her to come to the offices of the ROVS at at 29 rue du Colisée.

General Kutepov gave an impression of being taller than the average Russian both because of his erect military bearing and his powerful build—a body like a cannon with a cannonball head protruding from the muzzle. Like many military men, he looked uncomfortable in civilian clothes.

Kutepov offered Pepita a chair and fixed her with his direct gaze, studying her elegant appearance. "I wished to speak with you for one particular reason," Kutepov said, his face unchangingly stern. "I understand Mariya Vladislavovna has been urging you to go to Russia."

Pepita nodded without speaking.

"Well, Mrs. Reilly, I think that would be very unwise." He surveyed her thoughtfully, taking in her fashionably coiffed blond hair and knee-length skirt, which exposed smooth, shapely silken legs. "Very unwise," he repeated.

No one could have mistaken Kutepov for anything but a physically courageous, action-prone officer. He had been known as Kutep Pasha to the men under his command because of his reputation as a stern disciplinarian and his severity in battle. (On Sunday, January 26, 1930, he would be kidnapped by Soviet agents on the street in Paris, driven to the French coast, and placed aboard the *Spartak*, a Soviet ship, his subsequent fate unknown.) He could intimidate people, but on this occasion Pepita Reilly did not allow herself to be intimidated.

"I fail to see why that would be unwise," she replied in a sweet but firm voice.

"Mrs. Reilly, I can tell you that we have grounds for suspecting the Trust. It's entirely possible that the Trust leadership has been penetrated by an OGPU agent. Do you understand what that would mean?"

"Yes," she said, "but—"

"If you go to Russia, there's no telling what might happen to you. Something very unpleasant perhaps. You could be sent to a labor camp."

"From everything Mariya Vladislavovna tells me, I know that the people in the Trust are our true friends."

Kutepov gave her a cold, fleeting smile. "I have ordered Mariya Vladislavovna *not* to take you with her to Russia."

Pepita remained silent.

"I don't expect an answer from you. I only ask you to think about it," Kutepov said, standing up to dismiss her. "Thank you very much for coming."

That was a request Kutepov hardly needed to make. Pepita thought about his remarks night and day for some time but still did not come to a definite decision. Maria Schultz, however, had apparently dropped out of sight. Pepita heard later that Maria had gone back to Russia without even bidding her farewell.

Half a year passed. In the spring of 1927 Maria Schultz reappeared in Finland and, under circumstances that made the whole idea seem to be the height of insanity, wrote a letter to Pepita Reilly in Paris, once again urging Pepita to accompany her to Soviet Russia. Before Pepita even had time to reply, Maria suddenly disappeared forever across the Soviet border.

Chapter 18

IT WAS NONE OTHER than Maria Schultz who had warned General Kutepov about a possible OGPU penetration of the Trust close to the top.

Returning from Russia in November 1926, she informed Kutepov that she had slipped out of the country without the Trust's approval or knowledge. While investigating the circumstances of Sidney Reilly's disappearance, she had become suspicious about the OGPU's involvement. She advised Kutepov to discontinue his use of Trust channels for the time being. She proposed to return to Russia, taking with her three trustworthy agents from Kutepov's organization to help with a further investigation. The passage of the three agents through the "window" had been approved in advance by Yakushev, to whom she had not confided her real intentions.

General Kutepov was understandably alarmed by these revelations, since only a few weeks earlier General Nikolai A. von Monkewitz, his right-hand man and the leading supporter of the

Trust in the ROVS, had disappeared, leaving behind a note saying he planned to commit suicide because of financial difficulties. But Monkewitz's body had never been found, and there were rumors in White Russian circles that Monkewitz, fearing exposure as an OGPU agent, had fled to Russia. In view of this background, Kutepov unhesitatingly approved Maria Schultz's proposals.

Maria Schultz and the three agents reached Moscow without incident, and for a while they encountered no difficulties while they went about their business. Then one of the agents became careless and frankly informed certain Trust members that people abroad had become suspicious of the Trust and that he had come to Russia to find out the truth. Shortly thereafter the agent went out for a walk and never returned. Maria asked her contacts in the Trust to investigate and soon received the reply that the agent had been recognized by a Bulgarian Communist on the street, arrested by OGPU, and shot.

During the winter and onward until spring Maria Schultz became aware that the conflict between Yakushev and Opperput over the Trust's strategy and tactics had sharpened. Yakushev continued to stress political and propaganda "struggle"; on the other hand, Opperput kept pushing for stronger measures involving terror and sabotage.

Early in April 1927, when the conflict seemed about to come to a head, Opperput arranged a secret rendezvous with Maria, warning her not to speak of their appointed meeting to anyone else. While they walked in a park under giant horse-chestnut trees with corkscrew-shaped pink blossoms, Opperput made a devastating confession to Maria Schultz.

Opperput had long been an OGPU agent, he said, but he was not alone. Yakushev, Potapov, and other Trust leaders were also OGPU agents. In reality, the OGPU had controlled the Trust almost from the beginning and placed its men in all the key positions.

It had been different at first when General Zayonchkovsky founded the Monarchist Organization of Central Russia. Zayonchkovsky had brought Yakushev into the organization, and at that time Yakushev sincerely believed in the MOCR's aims and purposes. Then Yakushev made his visit to Revel and incautiously talked about the MOCR to his friend, who immediately sent a letter with the wonderful news to the monarchist center in Berlin.

An OGPU agent at the center secretly obtained a copy of this letter and sent it to Moscow, where Yakushev, who had in the meantime returned from his foreign trip, was arrested at once.

Yakushev sat in jail while the OGPU conducted an interrogation aimed at identifying his accomplices and decided what to do with him. In Yakushev's case, death by shooting was the normal sentence in those days, when *any* organized opposition to the Soviet regime had to be mercilessly eliminated. (Some slight relaxation of this rule, depending on the nature of the organization, did not come until the end of the Stalin era.) But someone in the OGPU conceived a different idea about the tiny monarchist group with which Yakushev was associated, and this idea had a direct bearing on Yakushev's fate.

The "someone" may have been Artur Khristianovich Artuzov, chief of the OGPU Counterespionage Department. Artuzov's true name was Renucci; he was an Italian from Genoa who came to Moscow just before the overthrow of the czar to teach French in a girls' school. Caught up in the excitement of the revolution, Renucci became a Chekist and adopted a Russian name. He was a short, gray-haired man with a small goatee who looked more like a professor than a professional intelligence officer, an ideal father and husband, a lover of music. After joining the Cheka, he rose quickly in its ranks until he had nearly reached the top.

Artuzov discussed Yakushev's case with Dzerzhinski. One of the two men came up with the idea of using the MOCR as a cover for the OGPU's counterespionage operations. The OGPU would place its own men in all the leading positions while the rank-and-file MOCR membership continued to believe that the MOCR was an anti-Communist organization. Under proper discipline, the members could engage in their activities without danger to the Soviet state. They would be permitted to participate in meetings and organize occasional actions, such as writing and distributing anti-Communist leaflets. The MOCR would not only function as a lightning rod that would attract and help to identify elements hostile to the Soviet regime *inside* Russia, but also channel émigré and foreign intelligence activities based *outside* Russia toward the MOCR, where they could be carefully controlled and monitored by the OGPU.

Dzerzhinski approved the plan. As a first step, Artuzov set out to recruit Yakushev as an OGPU agent and use him to facilitate the infiltration of OGPU men into the monarchist organization. While still being subjected to severe physical and mental pressure, Yakushev acquired a cellmate, none other than Eduard Opperput, who told Yakushev that he had been arrested because of his anti-Communist activities.

Obeying Artuzov's instructions, Opperput, who had wormed out of Yakushev the tale of his misadventures, pointed out that the émigrés were all old women who preferred to gab and conduct petty intrigues among themselves rather than to undertake real action. The émigrés were disunited and could agree on nothing, and if they ever returned to power they would restore a regime with all the glaring weaknesses and stupidity of the old regime. They had proved their unreliability in the way they betrayed Yakushev. Despite the obvious faults of the Soviet regime, the Bolshevik program only needed to be properly implemented. Perhaps it was necessary to get rid of the Bolsheviks in order to make the Soviet state live up to its own program: "Soviets without Communists," as the Kronstadt sailors had demanded.[1] The best way to achieve such a goal was to work *within* the Soviet regime toward the required changes.

When Yakushev had been sufficiently softened up, Dzerzhinski talked with him and tried to show him the error of his ways. The Soviet state offered the only hope for Russia. The anti-Communist emigration only served to weaken Russia on behalf of the foreign states that were her irreconcilable enemies and wished to divide Russia, leaving behind only a rump Russian state, as they had done with Austria in the case of the Austro-Hungarian empire. If Yakushev genuinely wished to serve Russia, he should help to nullify the harmful actions of both the émigrés and the foreign intelligence services. In that case, Yakushev would acquire an honored place inside the regime and be able to influence its policies in a positive direction.

This kind of persuasion (not to speak of Yakushev's fears for himself and his family) "brought Yakushev to his senses," as the OGPU might have said. Yakushev agreed to assume the role of the OGPU's principal agent in the MOCR. Since the news of his arrest had been kept secret (his family had been told that he was absent on another *komandirovka*, business trip, for his office), Yakushev soon resumed his normal activity, including his participation in MOCR work. At the same time he was joined by a new colleague, Eduard Opperput, who rapidly made himself indispensable to the monarchist organization.

Everything went well—so well, indeed, that the "capping" of the MOCR with OGPU agents succeeded beyond the most extravagant hopes of Dzerzhinski and Artuzov. The MOCR rank-and-file members went about their work, never suspecting the truth, and when, in due time, they expanded their contacts with the anti-Communist emigration—Savinkov's group, General Kutepov's Combat Organization, and others—their genuine devotion to the anti-Communist cause as well as the vigor and decisiveness of their actions convinced even the most hardened cynics among the émigrés and foreign intelligence officers, with only a few exceptions.

Before long, Yakushev established formal relations with a number of foreign intelligence services and began supplying logistical support for their agents in Russia (whom the OGPU naturally monitored very closely) as well as intelligence reports from alleged Trust sources.

In this manner the OGPU was able to identify its enemies, learn about their plans, and feed them misleading information. But, above all, the OGPU succeeded for several years, from 1923 to 1926, in monopolizing the intelligence channels into and out of Russia.

The foreign intelligence services were so favorably impressed with the Trust's reports and logistical support that they liberally provided funds to the Trust. These funds proved to be sufficient to finance all of the OGPU Counterespionage Department's projects and many operations of the OGPU Foreign Administration, which conducted espionage abroad. One Western intelligence service was so grateful that it rewarded the Trust with eight solid gold watches, which became treasured possessions of Artuzov, Pilar, and other OGPU chiefs.

According to Opperput, the OGPU used the Trust to lure Savinkov and Reilly onto Soviet territory, but in doing so it had finally overreached itself and caused the Trust to fall under strong suspicion abroad.

The Trust's continued existence came into question at a time when Opperput, too, had overplayed his hand. He explained to Maria that the conflict over Trust policies between Yakushev and himself had been a charade, a game played in order to convince the hard-liners in the Trust membership and in the emigration that the Trust was not averse to violence as a method. But Opperput had never ceased to be an anti-Communist; he had cooperated with the OGPU out of expedience but always hoped to use the Trust as a cover for organizing *real* anti-Communist operations against the regime. In his zeal, he had overstepped the limits set on his freedom of action and suddenly reawakened his OGPU bosses' suspicion.

He knew the OGPU and its methods, and he had no doubt that the OGPU would soon take steps to close down the Trust, but it would do so at a time and under circumstances designed to create maximum confusion among its foes. The OGPU would also get rid of those agents who had been compromised, and in all likelihood it would look around for someone on whom to place the blame. Opperput had no doubt that they would make him the scapegoat, accusing him of being a Polish or English spy.

Opperput admitted to Maria Schultz that he had been directly involved in the Reilly case—another reason why the OGPU desired to silence him—but he refused to tell what he knew until he had escaped from Russia. He said that he and Maria could pass through the "window" to Finland as long as the border people were still willing to obey his orders. He also advised Maria to tell her two remaining agents and Georgy Radkevich, her husband, who was in Moscow just then, to find their own way over the border as soon as possible.

Crossing through the "window" into Finland, Maria Schultz and Opperput came into the hands of Captain Rozenström, chief intelligence officer of the Second Finnish Division, which was assigned to that sector of the frontier. Rozenström had received Boris Bunakov, Nikolay Bunakov's brother, when he passed through the "window." Rozenström had also escorted Sidney Reilly to the border on his way into Soviet Russia and listened to the gunfire on the other side of the frontier while awaiting Reilly's return, which never materialized.

Maria Schultz introduced Opperput as an officer of the OGPU's Counterespionage Department who wished to defect in order to reveal to the world that the Trust was completely controlled by the OGPU. This news came as a great shock to the Finns, who had committed themselves unreservedly to the Trust, and General Wallenius, the Finnish chief of staff, ordered a thorough interrogation of the two border-crossers to establish whether or not Opperput was telling the truth. Meanwhile a tight security blanket was dropped over the whole affair.

A week after Maria Schultz and Opperput escaped from Russia, on April 21, the Soviet news agency Tass announced that a "monarchist group operating under the leadership of the former White General Kutepov" had been recently discovered in Moscow and eliminated. There were rumors of many arrests in Leningrad and other cities. On April 24 Kutepov received by courier a letter dated April 16 (a few days after the two Trust members' arrival in Finland). The letter, signed by General Potapov, informed Kutepov that the OGPU had struck at the Trust, arresting many of its people, but that Yakushev and Potapov were safe and the organization continued to function. Potapov said that "all those who had little or no connection with Staunitz [one of Opperput's many aliases] and Zakharchenko-Schultz" were also safe. In the next couple of weeks Kutepov received a number of telegrams signed by Yakushev or Potapov assuring him that the Trust's work had not been interrupted, urging him to stay in touch, and obliquely warning him against Opperput and Maria Schultz.

The first information about Opperput's defection that reached the outside world was disclosed on May 17 in *Sevodnya* (*Today*), a Russian-language daily newspaper in Riga, which published the following letter:

> On the night of April 13th, I, Eduard Opperput, a resident of Moscow under the name of Staunitz since March 1922 and a secret collaborator of the OGPU's Counterespionage Department since that date, escaped from Russia with the purpose of disclosing all the OGPU's secret operations and of thus furthering, to the best of my ability, the Russian national cause.

Now Opperput made public the whole story of the Trust and his own firsthand knowledge of the Reilly affair.

In the beginning, he said, the OGPU had not intended to act against Reilly. Artuzov and his closest colleagues, Styrne and Pilar von Pilhau, agreed that Reilly should be allowed to meet with the ostensible leaders of the Trust in Russia and made to feel that he was really in touch with a powerful and well-disciplined underground. The Trust leaders would try to get Reilly to reveal his plans and come to an understanding with him. Then he would be aided in his return abroad, where he was expected to use all his connections and influence on the Trust's behalf.

Opperput's account coincides in all significant details with a more or less "official" version of the Reilly case published nearly forty years later in Moscow. This version appears in a book entitled *Groundswell* by the Soviet writer Lev V. Nikulin, published in an edition of 100,000 copies in 1965.

In Leningrad, Opperput reported, Reilly was received by Yakushev; Mukalov, an unwitting Trust member; and Shutkin, an OGPU agent, spending the day in the latter's apartment, where another OGPU man named Starov, supposedly a factory worker and deputy of the Supreme Soviet, briefed Reilly on "working conditions."

The same night, Saturday, September 26, 1925, Reilly left for Moscow with Yakushev and Mukalov in a wagon-lit. Starov had already preceded them to Moscow.

On the platform in Moscow Reilly found a welcoming committee composed of Shatkovsky, a former czarist police colonel, Dorojinsky, and Starov—all posing as Trust members but all actually OGPU agents. Reilly later met Artuzov and Styrne (supposedly without learning their true identities) as well as Opperput.

Adhering to the schedule proposed in Vyborg by Yakushev, Reilly was driven on Sunday the 27th to an OGPU dacha at Malakhovka, outside Moscow, for a conference with the Trust's "Political Council." Opperput's account focuses on OGPU maneuvers behind the scenes and ignores the discussions at the Malakhovka dacha. Nikulin's book *Groundswell*, however, describes these discussions in detail.

Among the members of the "Political Council" present on this occasion were Yakushev, Lieutenant General Potapov, and Aleksandr Langovoy, whom Nikulin describes as a "commander of the Red Army." After lunch the guests went into the woods outside the dacha and sat down on the grass in the shade to resume their discussion.

Yakushev brought up the subject of financial assistance.

"No government will give you money," Reilly replied. "Today everyone's house is on fire. Churchill believes, as I do, in the speedy overthrow of Soviet power, but he is not in a position to provide funds. He has been keenly disappointed on a number of occasions. The most important thing for us is to put out the fire in our own house. In the colonies there is unrest. The workers are moving to the left because of the influence of Moscow. Therefore money must be sought inside Russia. My plans to raise money are crude and will probably repel you."

After a pause, Reilly went on:

"In Russia there are treasures of immense value. I am thinking of paintings by old masters, engravings, precious stones, and jewelry. Removing these articles from museums will not be too difficult. Just think of the money—it would amount to many thousands of pounds! Such treasures have an enormous value abroad. It's true that stealing from parts of the museum open to the public would be difficult, but in the cellars, ready and packed, are some marvelous works of art. We must arrange to send them abroad. I myself, without the help of middlemen, can organize their sale. In this way we can obtain substantial sums."

"But this would ruin the reputation of our whole organization," Potapov said, unable to restrain his indignation. "We are not museum robbers!"

Reilly remained unmoved by this protest. "For the sake of the money, a reputation may have to be sacrificed. In any case, it won't be necessary to let more than a few people in on the secret."

He then produced a written list of articles to be stolen: paintings by famous French and Dutch masters, including important Rembrandts; eighteenth-century French and English engravings; miniatures of the eighteenth and nineteenth centuries; antique coins in gold, silver, and bronze; Italian and Flemish primitives; and works of the great masters of the Italian and Spanish schools.

Nikulin wrote: "Potapov and Yakushev, seeking to maintain their composure, listen to these instructions. . . . Is it possible to let this man, to whom nothing was sacred, go free in order to preserve the reputation of the 'Trust'?"[2]

Reilly looked at the others and smiled. "Another method of raising money is by working for English Intelligence. First and foremost, I'm interested in obtaining intelligence about the Comintern. Is this difficult? With determination it should be possible. . . ."

The sun was about to set and dampness settled over the woods.

They returned to the house, but on the way back Reilly took Yakushev aside. "You have the good manners of a gentleman who looks at things more realistically than the other members of the Trust." Swearing Yakushev to secrecy, he said that he had a source who could supply $50,000. He would make that sum available on condition that it was used to organize the theft of valuables from museums and for penetration of the Comintern by the Trust's agents.

"General Potapov is clearly too scrupulous," Reilly told Yakushev. "I must tell you that in an affair of this kind—I'm speaking of counterrevolution—you'll never succeed if you observe moral precepts. Take terrorism, for example. Savinkov told me once that one of his terrorists failed to throw a bomb into a carriage because there were children in it. If you're going to be influenced by principles in your fight with the Soviets, you will achieve nothing. But let's not talk only about terrorism. I look upon my activities from a much broader standpoint—not only from the viewpoint of politics, but also as a businessman. I want to interest you in this deal. You won't overthrow Soviet power in three months. We must prepare a thorough plan for the 'export' of art treasures. I have personal influence with the press. When I return from Moscow, I'll offer the *Times* a series of articles under the title of *The Great Bluff*. Of course, this will mean another visit to Russia—and not only one. We must collect documents, facts, and figures, or else we shall not be believed."

The indignation on the part of hardened OGPU operators at Reilly's plan for stealing art treasures represents hyprocrisy of a high order. The OGPU itself was involved in selling valuables abroad—jewelry, rare coins, works of art, including priceless Russian icons—in exchange for hard currency. Nevertheless, this aspect of the story is plausible enough if one can accept the story as a whole. It appeared plausible to Reilly's friends. Robin Lockhart related:

> There may be some truth in the claim that Reilly planned to raise funds by looting Russian museums. Certainly General Spears, who knew little of Reilly's secret activities, recalls that Reilly had a plan to bring out of Russia valuable old coins and other antiques. To Lieutenant Colonel Thwaites, who by 1925 was no longer in the SIS, Reilly had spoken of recovering Napoleonic treasures cached in Moscow.[3]

In Opperput's account, there was much scurrying of OGPU officers to and fro, arousing Opperput's suspicions. At the Malakhovka dacha Opperput noticed many security people surrounding the villa; later he became aware that the security cordon around the villa had been drawn even tighter. When he demanded an explanation from Styrne, Artuzov's deputy, the latter admitted that Reilly was about to be arrested. At this point a car pulled up, and Puzinsky, Artuzov's second deputy, and several Chekists, evidently assigned to carry out Reilly's arrest, got out. Opperput argued with Styrne and Puzinsky against the arrest, and Styrne finally agreed to raise the matter once more with Artuzov. Puzinsky and his men were to remain with Reilly, however, until a final decision was made.

If Opperput could be believed, the assumption was that there had been second thoughts about letting Reilly leave Russia as originally planned. One might theorize that the Counterespionage Department headed by Artuzov had made these plans but that other top OGPU officials had questioned the whole idea and brought about an urgent reappraisal of the situation.

Counterespionage (CE) people have always been disliked and distrusted by other intelligence officers (and the feelings are mutual). CE specialists are pessimists; the other officers are optimists. CE people see the world as one great interwoven conspiracy and regard everything without exception with dark suspicion bordering on paranoia. In the eyes of "normal" intelligence officers engaged in espionage, the CE practitioners are devoted to esoteric, intricate games involving the doubling and redoubling of agents and playing them back against the CE specialists on the opposing side in a bewildering manner.

The CE specialists are seen as spoilsports who persist in introducing complications into perfectly straightforward operations and casting suspicion on entirely reliable agents whose loyalty cannot or should not be doubted. Still, no one has figured out a way to dispense entirely with CE officers without running the risk that one's own agent may turn out to be a double agent, as in the so-called Lockhart plot.

The OGPU's CE practitioners had achieved an enormous success with the Trust, but other OGPU chiefs, possibly jealous of this success, argued that the resources employed in the Trust operation could be more productively directed into foreign intelligence operations. The assumption, then, is that the plans of the Counterespionage Department were crossed by other influential elements in the OGPU that demanded the elimination of a dangerous enemy in the person of Sidney Reilly and the liquidation of the Trust, supposedly because it had outlived its usefulness.

Dzerzhinski, who evidently experienced similar doubts, submitted the question to the Politburo. It should be remembered that the Trust had been an OGPU extension of Lenin's New Economic Policy. Thus the NEP encouraged development not only of the private sector of the economy but also of economic ties with the capitalist world, and the Trust's business activities abroad fitted well into this concept. Now, however, there was already some thinking on the Politburo level about the eventual termination of NEP, which could not help but affect the Trust as well. Moreover, the cunning Stalin saw that the Trust was a two-edged sword that might be turned against the regime. Therefore the Politburo decided that Reilly could not under any circumstances be allowed to leave Soviet Russia; he was to be arrested without delay, even at the risk of damaging the Trust's reputation abroad. In any case, the Trust was to be gradually phased out. These are conclusions that can be drawn from Opperput's description of the OGPU maneuvers that occurred during Reilly's stay in Moscow.

At the Malakhovka dacha Reilly glanced at his watch and observed that it was time to return to Moscow in order to catch the evening train to Leningrad. According to Opperput, Reilly rode with Puzinsky, driving to Opperput's apartment in the city. At the apartment Shatkovsky gave Reilly a railroad ticket and told him that they would proceed separately to the station and meet there.

Nikulin wrote that it had been planned to arrest Reilly in the car on the way to Moscow, but Reilly said he wanted to mail a postcard to his friends abroad as proof that he had visited Moscow. In order to find out to whom the card was addressed, they took Reilly to the "flat of one of the GPU agents."

Opperput stated that he received a telephone call from Pilar von Pilhau at the apartment. Pilar asked him to pass on a message to Puzinsky: He (Puzinsky) was to act in accordance with his orders, i.e., to arrest Reilly. Nikulin wrote that Starov called the OGPU headquarters to report the delay while Reilly was writing his postcard (addressed to Boyce's letter drop) and received instructions to arrest Reilly as soon as he had mailed the postcard.

Both Opperput and Nikulin agree that Reilly was arrested in the car (while presumably riding to the railroad station) and taken to the Lubianka. Opperput, however, reported that Puzinsky made the arrest, and not Starov, as the Nikulin book implies. Nikulin indicates that Reilly remained in the Lubianka for slightly more than a month.

Groundswell also describes how the OGPU tried to cover up the Trust's connection with the Reilly arrest by arranging a "shooting incident" on the night of September 28 on the Soviet-Finnish border. This staged incident, which involved a good deal of shooting and noise, made it appear that the Reilly party had been ambushed and Reilly himself had been killed. This was the same incident that *Izvestiya* subsequently reported. The OGPU kept unwitting Trust members in the dark; the first news of Reilly's "death" that reached them filtered in from Finland.

The lengths to which the OGPU was prepared to go in order to cover up the affair is shown by the interesting case of Toivo Vyakhi, which did not become known until many years later. Toivo Vyakhi was the commander of a Soviet frontier detachment. In September he received a summons from the plenipotentiary representative of the OGPU in the Leningrad Military District, Stanislav Adamovich Messing, who entrusted him with the task of safely conducting across the border a man identified to him as Reilly. Later, in order to hide the truth, Toivo Vyakhi was "exposed" as a Trust agent, arrested, convicted, sentenced to be shot —and apparently shot.

But Toivo Vyakhi did not die. He was secretly transferred to the USSR's Pacific coast and given a new name, and he continued to serve in the border forces. He eagerly desired to inform his closest friends that he was no traitor, but the powers-that-be did not allow him to communicate with anyone he had previously known. In 1968, in an anthology called *Special Mission*, Colonel of State Security Ivan Mikhailovich Petrov, formerly Toivo Vyakhi, told his true story.[4]

Opperput said that Reilly was at first treated decently. He received the same apartment that Savinkov had occupied in the "Inner Prison" of the Butyrki and, like Savinkov, enjoyed the privilege of going for drives in the country. He was even furnished with his favorite brand of whiskey (Robin Lockhart calls this an obvious flaw in the story since Reilly never drank whiskey).

When Reilly kept insisting that he knew nothing about British Intelligence and had come to Russia only to gather material for his book, *The Great Bluff*, the OGPU tightened the screws. He was thrown into a cell, lost all his privileges, and found himself under interrogation at all hours of the day and night. Finally, after being forced to watch a number of gruesome executions, Reilly broke and agreed to cooperate.

Nikulin's book gives the text of a statement that Reilly allegedly wrote after being told that his death sentence pronounced in absentia in December 1918 was to be carried out. The statement read:

> To the President of the GPU
> F. E. Dzerzhinski
> After prolonged deliberation, I express willingness to give you complete and open acknowledgement and information on matters of interest to the GPU concerning the organization and personnel of the British Intelligence Service and, so far as I know it, similar information on American Intelligence and likewise about Russian émigrés with whom I have had business.
>
> Moscow, The Inner Prison
> 30th October 1925
> Sidney Reilly

Opperput asserted that the OGPU, no longer having any use for Reilly, carried out the execution; but instead of killing him in the Lubianka cellar where ordinary criminals were executed, they arranged for him to be shot by Ibrahim, one of the OGPU's top executioners, while out for his daily walk in the Vorobyovy Hills (now called the Lenin Hills).

The Nikulin book is more specific about dates, reporting that Reilly's execution was carried out on November 5, 1925.

After Opperput's defection, there were many people in the emigration who distrusted him and refused to accept him as a legitimate defector. Maria Schultz, however, believed in his sincerity. She remembered how Opperput had made sure that her agents had a chance to escape before he sought to escape himself. When Opperput offered to accompany her and other agents on a terrorist mission into Soviet Russia in June 1927, Maria gladly accepted his help.

General Kutepov visited Maria Schultz in Finland and was highly alarmed by the changes that he saw in her. Recognizing that she was a sick woman, apparently on the verge of a nervous breakdown, he ordered her not to return to Russia. But Maria Schultz disobeyed his orders. Hysterically seeking revenge, she had two teams ready to carry out bombings: One team, which included her and Opperput, would attack an OGPU billet in Moscow, the other, led by a man named Larionov, would act against a Communist party club in Leningrad. Larionov had been told to wait until the Moscow operation was carried out before proceeding with the bombing in Leningrad. Distrusting Opperput, Larionov ignored this instruction. His team carried out the mission and returned safely to Finland, but Maria Schultz and Opperput never came back.

Nothing more was heard of Opperput, who had betrayed Maria and the third member of the team to the OGPU, until the Second World War. Then he reportedly turned up in Berlin under the alias Baron Alexander von Manteuffel, posing as an antique dealer from German-occupied Kiev, and was arrested by the Gestapo and executed as a Soviet spy.

It is obvious today that Opperput was one of the first in a long line of *fake* Soviet defectors. There have always been genuine Soviet defectors, of course, but Soviet Intelligence periodically sends carefully briefed "defectors" to the West. They are prepared to offer a few tidbits of intelligence so that they appear to be both legitimate and valuable sources. Their task includes the identification of personnel, handling methods, and types of information sought by Western intelligence sources; if possible, they are to make themselves useful to these services and penetrate their operations.

Seven months after Reilly's disappearance, the OGPU decided to abandon the original story of the "shooting incident" on the Soviet-Finnish border and Reilly's death as a presumed smuggler. The new version of the Reilly affair fit in neatly with the OGPU's plan to abandon the Trust, creating as much disarray as possible in the ranks of their enemies.

Opperput successfully carried out his mission as a defector, putting out the OGPU's prepared story which largely destroyed the Trust. Once he had done his job, he returned with anti-Communist agents to the USSR, betrayed them, and vanished back into the hidden world of Soviet Intelligence.

Opperput's account about the Trust was substantially accurate because it suited the OGPU to expose the Trust as an OGPU front. Nevertheless, Opperput may not have told the whole truth. His tale about the beginnings of the Monarchist Organization of Central Russia, Yakushev's activities as an anti-Communist, his arrest, and his recruitment under the Chekists' relentless pressure could have been an invention. It is entirely possible that, from its very inception, the MOCR was a creation of Soviet State Security.

At the same time, the Opperput version of the Reilly case cannot be considered reliable. The Nikulin book is equally suspect, even though it appeared forty years later. The two versions offer mutual corroboration in the same way that two persons who have their heads together support one another with perjured stories. Both stories break down on the same point: Reilly's execution shortly after the OGPU had allegedly broken him. The Nikulin book makes the point even clearer, reporting that Reilly offered to reveal all his knowledge on October 30, yet was executed on November 5. The detailed interrogation of an important spy could never be completed in the space of *six days*. Such an interrogation, if properly conducted, takes months. There was certainly no need for haste in Reilly's case.

Throughout its sordid history, Soviet State Security has made a practice of sentencing its victims to death—but, if the victims are important enough, they are kept alive for indefinite periods of time, since there is no way of foreseeing when an individual may be able to provide some valuable piece of information overlooked in the course of earlier interrogations.

The case of Colonel Oleg Penkovsky, who betrayed Soviet nuclear arms secrets to the CIA and MI6, affords an instructive example. Penkovsky had had many contacts with American and British intelligence officers; he knew many of them by sight, if not by name. He had been debriefed in depth by American and British Intelligence and had not only supplied these services with numerous written reports but also turned over many secret documents. Penkovsky was sentenced to be shot by the Soviets on May 11, 1963, but the KGB continued to interrogate him after the trial. Lieutenant General Gorny, the military prosecutor, took the unusual step of holding a press conference a week after the trial to insist that the sentence had been carried out on May 16.

Greville Wynne, who was convicted of espionage together with Penkovsky, later wrote that Penkovsky "was sentenced to death, but the sentence was not carried out. It was nearly two years later that I learnt how Penkovsky, imprisoned for further interrogation in a remote village, had taken his own life."[5]

There are other reasons to disbelieve the Opperput and Nikulin versions of Reilly's death.

After the assassination of Pyotr Lazarevich Voikov, the Soviet minister to Poland, the Soviet government released a statement on June 8, 1927, claiming that this killing was the work of British agents. The statement accused the British government of a series of actions hostile to the USSR—from the rupture of diplomatic relations to attacks on Soviet institutions abroad—culminating in Voikov's murder. The statement went on to say that the British government was also guilty of offenses committed on Soviet territory, referring in this connection to Sidney Reilly:

> In the summer of 1925, a certain merchant carrying a Soviet passport with the name of Steinberg was wounded and arrested by the Frontier Guard while illegally crossing the Finnish border.
>
> During the inquiry a witness declared that his name was actually Sidney George Riley [sic], and that he was an English spy, a captain of the Royal Air Force, one of the chief organizers of "Lockhart's plot," who by sentence of the Tribunal of December 3, 1918, had been declared an outlaw.
>
> Riley declared that he came to Russia for the special purpose of organizing terroristic acts, arson and revolts, and that when coming from America, he had seen Mr. Churchill, Chancellor of the Exchequer, who personally instructed him as to the reorganization of terroristic and other acts calculated to create a diversion.
>
> His written testimony is in the possession of the government. Riley's evidence was entirely corroborated by material seized during further arrests.[6]

This passage of the official statement implies that the original report of a "shooting incident" on the Soviet-Finnish border during the night of September 28, 1925, was correct and, moreover, that Reilly was wounded and captured alive on that occasion. The statement, however, is completely at variance with both the Opperput and Nikulin versions of Reilly's capture.

Curiously enough, several months later the Soviet press again mentioned Reilly, this time in connection with the trial of terrorists charged with bombing the Communist party club in Leningrad in July 1927. (In reality, Captain Larionov's team of three men escaped to safety in Finland after the bombing.) The terrorists on trial were accused of being "in close contact with the Secret Intelligence Service of England."[7] The press further referred to Reilly as the "British chief directing terrorist acts in Soviet Russia" and as a "confidential agent of Churchill."

It is far more curious to read certain passages in a book published in Moscow in 1940 under the title *Subversive Activity of Foreign Espionage Services in the USSR*, Part I (Part II was never published). The author was Vladislav Nikolaevich Minayev, a Soviet writer with close ties to the State Security apparatus, who frequently wrote on themes connected with foreign espionage and subversion. One cannot help assuming that Minayev had access to secret police sources while working on this book.

What did Minayev write about Sidney Reilly? First of all, one is struck by this passage:

> In the fall of 1925 the English spy Sidney Reilly, who is already known to us, was dispatched over the Finnish frontier into Soviet territory. He carried a passport in the name of a merchant, Steinberg. Arrested by the OGPU in 1927, Reilly testified that "he came to the USSR in 1925 with the special mission of organizing terroristic acts, arson, uprisings, etc."[8]

Thus in this book Minayev clearly states that Reilly was arrested by the OGPU in *1927*—not in 1925, as stated by other sources. Could this be a typographical error? Hardly, since no professional writer would write: "Arrested by the OGPU in 1925, Reilly testified that 'he came to the USSR in 1925. . . .' " Had Minayev simply made a mistake about the year of Reilly's arrest? Such a possibility cannot be excluded but seems improbable in view of the confidential sources at Minayev's disposal.

Continuing his account, Minayev writes:

> Finding himself in the USSR, Reilly carried out his abominable work. Pretending to be a native of Russia, "Comrade Rellinsky," he succeeded in penetrating into the Leningrad criminal investigation department and creeping in as a candidate party member. Here he was struck down by the OGPU's avenging hand.

If Minayev can be taken at his word, Reilly must have been at liberty for some time in the USSR or he could not have "carried out his abominable work." None of the versions of Reilly's activities ending in his death in 1925 gave him any such opportunity.

Such considerations have led various sources to hypothesize that Reilly was free in Soviet Russia as late as 1927. Robin Lockhart, for example, wrote: "If the Russians had executed Reilly in 1925, he could hardly be directing terrorism in 1927. Or was he? Had the Russians let him slip through their fingers?" And again:

> There was also the possibility that Reilly had faked his own death at the Finnish frontier just as he had staged a "suicide" in his youth at Odessa. He might have realized that "The Trust" was not genuine and that all his years of struggling against the Bolsheviks had been in vain and so vanished to assume a new identity—perhaps in South America again. This theory would also account for the initial silence of the Russians. Later, when the GPU were satisfied that the British knew as little as they did about Reilly's whereabouts they issued a deliberately vague propaganda story that they had captured Reilly and that he had "confessed." The GPU's intention might have been to ensure that if Reilly did turn up in Britain again, whatever story he told would be disbelieved by the British Intelligence Services. He would be permanently discredited. This theory may sound implausible but Dzerzhinski, who was still alive at the time, was quite capable of producing a scheme as devious as this.[9]

Another source suggested a similar theory. Let us assume, he said, that Reilly did not trust his wife and purposely misinformed her when he said he was going into the USSR for only three days. He had prepared himself long and carefully for the crossing and the subsequent espionage and diversionary activity. In order to prevent anyone from searching for him, he wished to convince everyone that he was dead. For this purpose, he faked an unsuccessful border crossing and left behind the body of a person who was to be falsely identified as himself, Sidney Reilly. Such an identification was made easier by the behavior of his unsuspecting wife. The Chekists fell for the deception, believing that the man killed on the border really was Sidney Reilly. And on Russian territory Reilly then outsmarted the Chekists and eluded their surveillance. Therefore (speculates this source) Reilly was not killed on September 28, 1925, at the border. He was not shot on November 5, 1925, in Moscow. He lived until 1927.

Nevertheless, for many people the mystery of Sidney Reilly did not end there. As frequently happens in such cases, for a long time there was no end to the rumors and unsubstantiated reports that had Reilly appearing at widely separated times and places.

In 1926 rumors circulated among the inmates in Moscow's Butyrki prison that an important prisoner, an English spy, was being held there in solitary confinement. This information came from a Pole, a former inmate of the Butyrki, who also reported that by "water-pipe communication," when the prisoners tapped out messages in Morse code, one inmate had identified himself as S.T.1 (Reilly's old designation in SIS). This was some months after Reilly supposedly had been executed. Later, the Pole said, the messages from S.T.1 ceased and he heard that the prisoner had lost his mind and was occasionally taken out for walks by his jailors.

A White Russian who escaped from a Soviet prison traversed Siberia to reach safety in China in October 1927, reporting at that time that Reilly was in a Soviet prison but had become insane.

In 1931 a British representative in the Middle East who visited a Soviet freighter was approached by a sailor who told him in perfect English that he had to save his life by jumping ship. That same night the sailor came to the Englishman's home and identified himself as Reilly. He related that he had been in prison in Moscow and had been brought under guard to Odessa for further interrogation, where he obtained a gun from one of his guards and shot his way out, thereafter stowing away on a ship. He asked for money and clothes, spent one night with the Englishman, and vanished the next day.

Up to the end of the Second World War, SIS continued to receive reports that Reilly had turned up in various parts of the world—in Russia, in the Middle East, in North or South America.

During the war George Hill, Reilly's old comrade, was assigned as a liaison officer with the NKVD in Moscow. Although he learned nothing about Reilly from his NKVD contacts, another British officer was told by an NKVD man in 1944 that Reilly was alive but still kept under surveillance.

In 1956, when Great Britain and the Soviet Union were temporarily on good terms, an approach was made to Khrushchev and Bulganin for information about Reilly, without success.

Reilly's tangled web also enmeshed the women who had been closest to him. When in 1931 Pepita published an account of Sidney Reilly's life, "written by himself, edited and completed by his wife," the publicity brought Reilly's legal wife, Margaret, out of hiding in Brussels. Margaret came to England and promptly sued the publishers for damages, and as a result only 2,000 copies of the book appeared. Nevertheless, the serialized story in the *Evening Standard* had the effect of stimulating questions in the House of Commons and demands on the Foreign Office to press the Soviet government for information about Reilly's fate. Finally, in 1935, Reilly's former sweetheart Caryll Houselander had a mystical experience in which she found herself sharing the confinement of "someone" and bearing the same torments. If such experiences are significant, it may be that Reilly was still alive ten years after his reported death.

Presumably no one could have appreciated the mystery surrounding Reilly's ultimate fate better than Reilly himself, who had always tried to preserve the mystery of his origins and personal life. Since Reilly would have passed his one-hundredth birthday in 1974, however, there is little chance that he is still alive and well and hiding in South America in the company of those other improbable refugees, Hitler and Bormann.

Epilogue

S IDNEY GEORGE REILLY was to
many people a hero—sinister and somewhat flawed—but a hero
nonetheless. In a world that was more concerned with ends than
means, he represented the forces of good locked in an inexor-
able struggle with the forces of evil. As a spy, Reilly had positive
qualities that included courage of a high order, nerve, guile, re-
sourcefulness, and organizational talent. If, in his seven years of
conspiratorial work against the Bolsheviks, he had had an almost
unbroken string of failures, it appeared to be more a matter of
bad luck than any fault of his own.

Still, one precept that should never be forgotten in espionage,
as in life in general, is that appearances are deceptive.

How did it come about that Reilly, an experienced and clever
spy who had been successful in all his missions up to that time,
suddenly lost his touch and met with one setback after the other
from 1918 on? Despite his Russian birth, native command of the
Russian language, and long experience in prerevolutionary Russia,

222

had he failed to understand the inner dynamics of the Russian Revolution and the psychology of the masses? Did he underestimate the Bolsheviks?

The key to Reilly's true attitude can be found in his visit to the Kremlin immediately on his arrival in Moscow in May 1918. Reilly went straight to the Kremlin and asked to see Lenin, but was received instead by Bonch-Bruyevich, head of Chancery of the Sovnarkom and a close personal friend of Lenin.

Years later Reilly wrote that his friend Grammatikov, who knew Bonch-Bruyevich personally, brought about the meeting with the Soviet leader. "Bonch-Bruyevich received Grammatikov and myself very graciously," Reilly recorded. "Grammatikov introduced me by my own name, informing him that, though English by nationality, I had been born in Russia and lived there all my life, and was in fact to all intents and purposes Russian. I corroborated this story and added that I was very interested in Bolshevism, the triumph of which had brought me back to Russia."[1]

Reilly's account of the *circumstances* of his meeting with Bonch-Bruyevich is totally contradicted by the known facts, which were related by Bruce Lockhart in considerable detail. Most significant, however, is the description of Reilly, his Russianness, and his interest in Bolshevism. Reilly puts these words partly in Grammatikov's mouth, but they probably came from Reilly himself during the meeting with Bonch-Bruyevich in the Kremlin, which certainly did not include Grammatikov.

The loyalty that Reilly felt toward Russia runs like a scarlet thread through his life. He invariably refused to spy on Russia and was known to cooperate with the Russian secret police, the Okhrana. In the years just before World War I in St. Petersburg Reilly spied on the Germans, *not* the Russians. With the outbreak of war he went to the United States and represented Russia in purchasing arms and other war material that Russia desperately needed. It was only when the Russian outlook in the war became hopeless that he rejoined the SIS and spent the final two years on the British side. After returning from Russia in late 1918, he concentrated nearly entirely on Russian affairs during his last seven years in the West.

Reilly's political orientation was not what it appeared to be on the surface. His arrest as a student by the Okhrana when he became involved with a Marxist revolutionary group might be considered a youthful indiscretion. But despite the fact that Reilly portrayed himself as a Conservative sympathizer in England, he maintained over the years close contacts in socialist circles abroad (even though many of these contacts were clearly anti-Bolshevik) and had certain discreet contacts with Bolsheviks. In consequence, MI5 —an institution perhaps inclined toward suspicions of this kind— regarded him as a leftist.

One observer has written: "Reilly was not himself a Tsarist; he was well to the left of Kerenski, much closer to a man like Savinkov and the Social Revolutionaries. . . . Even his fanatical abhorrence of Bolshevism was somewhat too loud, too flamboyant."[2]

Reginald Orlando Bridgeman, an openly pro-Soviet officer of the British Diplomatic Service, from which he retired in 1923, said he never seriously believed that Reilly was "so strongly anti-Bolshevik as he made out. To me he always admitted that in the long run it might be better to join them than to fight them. . . ."[3]

The problem is not to be deceived by appearances. The British agent Kim Philby, who joined the Anglo-German Fellowship, a Nazi front, and became a correspondent friendly to the Franco side in the Spanish Civil War, was an early convert to Communism without formally joining the party and accepted recruitment as an agent of Soviet Civilian Intelligence (then the NKVD). In World War II in Japan, Richard Sorge, a German correspondent with "reliable" Nazi sympathies and close ties to Nazi Germany's embassy in Tokyo, was a long-time Communist and agent of Soviet Military Intelligence (the GRU). Sidney George Reilly, the Conservative supporter and friend of Churchill, the most noted Bolshevik-eater of all, engaged in capitalist enterprises such as business and finance but was most at home with Russian socialists and left-wing politics and worked as a double agent for the Cheka.

Some people in the SIS suspected that Reilly had gone over to the Bolsheviks when he disappeared into Russia in 1925. Although they may have been right in one sense, the date of his real defection could be more properly placed in 1918.

What we know about Reilly's activities in Russia in the second half of that year strongly suggests that Reilly went to the Kremlin and revealed to Bonch-Bruyevich that he had been sent by the British government to bring about the fall of the Soviet regime. At his request, Reilly was probably put in touch with Dzerzhinski and the two men arrived at an agreement for secret cooperation. In order to conceal the real purpose of this visit, which possibly could be reported to the Allies, Karakhan of the Soviet Foreign Office informed Lockhart about Reilly's call at the Kremlin and made it appear that Reilly was guilty of nothing worse than a diplomatic lapse.

There arises the question of motivation. Unlike Kim Philby, Sidney Reilly was not attracted to Communism as the solution to the world's ills, nor did he share Philby's smug attitude, "One does not look twice at an offer of enrollment in an elite force." (The Cheka in any case was far from an elite force in 1918, although it had already become formidable enough.) In all probability, Reilly remembered first of all how an obscure Corsican lieutenant had ridden the wave of the French Revolution and exploded to the top. Why should not another lieutenant ride the wave of the Russian Revolution and reach the crest?

Looking at the Russia of 1918, Reilly could see only the Bolsheviks as an organized, disciplined force with real leaders. The Left Social Revolutionaries were hotheads, lacking not only self-control but foresight as well. Boris Savinkov was a talented leader and organizer but incapable of governing. The democratic parties had discredited themselves and lost popular support during the period of the Provisional Government. The monarchists and the military were equally antediluvian. All in all, it was only with and through the Bolsheviks, despite their precarious situation, that a man with overweening ambitions like Reilly could hope to reach power. And the very precariousness of their position made the Bolsheviks still more disposed to place a high value on the cooperation Reilly had to offer.

American Consul General DeWitt C. Poole sized up the situation correctly when he accused Reilly of being an *agent provocateur* in his association with the Allied Intelligence Services. That was precisely the role that Reilly must have worked out for himself with Dzerzhinski's approval.

He started with Savinkov and the latter's Union for the Defense of Fatherland and Freedom, funneling English money in that direction and plotting with Savinkov a revolt against the Soviet regime.

At the same time Reilly developed his first tenuous contacts with the Left Social Revolutionaries, who at this point were preparing a coup d'etat of their own against the Soviet regime in Moscow.

Since the French were also involved with the Savinkov organization and the Left SRs, Reilly established a close working relationship with de Vertemont, the French Intelligence Service chief in Russia. He got on well with his French counterpart despite an unwillingness to be drawn into de Vertemont's favorite bombing and arson actions, and together they planned the separate but coordinated uprisings by Savinkov and the Left SRs.

Fully informed by Reilly about the Left SR Central Committee's plan to murder German Ambassador Mirbach as the signal for the coup in Moscow, Dzerzhinski deliberately did not interfere because this plan fitted in with his own hope to torpedo the Brest-Litovsk Treaty, which he had strongly opposed, and force the Germans to reopen hostilities. He covered up his involvement by going to the Left SR headquarters during the revolt, supposedly to confront the rebels. With Reilly's help, he saw to it that none of the top Bolshevik leaders showed up at the Bolshoi Theater on the day of the armed revolt, thus aborting the Left SRs' plan to capture the entire Bolshevik leadership at one stroke. Alerted to the danger, the Latvian sharpshooters moved in and suppressed the revolt. The whole affair resulted in the destruction of the Left Social Revolutionary party and its elimination as a power factor within the Soviet state. The Left SR (and Dzerzhinski) plan to provoke the Germans into a reopening of the war failed, however, when Germany did not allow herself to be provoked. Reilly himself overacted somewhat when he rushed to the Bolshoi Theater, announced the failure of the revolt to his friends, and in plain sight of everyone ostentatiously went through his pockets for allegedly compromising documents, which he tore up, stuffing the pieces inside seat cushions or swallowing them.

It had been planned to coordinate Savinkov's seizure of Yaroslavl and other cities with the Allied landing at Archangel. Reilly encouraged Savinkov to begin the revolt prematurely by informing him that the landing would take place much earlier than it actually did. The French, overeager as always, assisted Reilly in his efforts by also telling Savinkov that the landing would take place "soon." Meanwhile Dzerzhinski spread rumors with false information that the Allies had already seized various points on the rail line south from Archangel to Vologda. Later Savinkov blamed the French, claiming that they had misled him. It took a few weeks to crush Savinkov's revolt, but in the end he and his organization were also eliminated as a threat to the Soviet regime.

Nevertheless, Allied plotting continued to be a danger to the Bolsheviks, particularly after the expected Allied landings had taken place. There was also the worrisome involvement of the Czechoslovaks, who had seized most of the Trans-Siberian Railway and seemed about to link up with the Allied intervention forces.

It is impossible to say whether the final provocation—the idea of subverting the Latvian regiments—was the idea of Reilly or Dzerzhinski. Certainly the Soviet leaders were at all times sensitive to any possible approach to the Latvians, who constituted those leaders' Praetorian Guard. In any event, the matter was soon taken in hand by the Cheka, which might well have been proud of its triple play: the *double agent Shmidkhen* attracting the attention of the Allies (with Reilly's assistance) and bringing in the *double agent Berzin,* who was turned over by Bruce Lockhart to the *double agent Reilly.*

It was Reilly who betrayed the substance of what had been discussed at the American Consulate General on August 25. Dzerzhinski's hand was forced at last by the urgent necessity to take action not only against de Vertemont's plan to blow up bridges in the Petrograd area, which would have cut off the city's supplies, but also against the assassination of Uritsky and the near-fatal shooting of Lenin.

The countermeasures adopted by Dzerzhinski inevitably revealed the extent of the Cheka's knowledge about Allied plotting, information that could only have been obtained from a traitor. Fortunately, there was already a traitor in the picture, René Marchand, who had his own sources in the French Military Mission and, indignant that France should try to harm rather than help her erstwhile ally, told all he knew about Allied plans to the Cheka. Reilly thus was able to point to Marchand as the informer, drawing on reports in the Soviet press, and divert suspicion from himself.

Dzerzhinski evidently felt that it would still be useful to have an agent in the enemy camp. After the collapse of the "Lockhart plot," Sidney Reilly, sought everywhere, with his picture on posters and a price on his head, "escaped" to England, where he was received as a hero and decorated for his exploits.

A penetration of the SIS headquarters at this point would undoubtedly have been a remarkable achievement for the Cheka, which was barely a year old. But Reilly's application for permanent status in the SIS raised some eyebrows in view of his long insistence on a free-lance relationship and his absences extending on occasion to years at a time. The application seemed particularly ill-timed because Mansfield Cumming, the SIS chief, was beginning to have doubts about Reilly personally as well as his future usefulness. Without pressure from his Cheka bosses, Reilly probably would not have chosen such an unfavorable moment to raise the question of his future status.

Soviet Intelligence had to wait roughly two decades before finding the right man in Kim Philby to penetrate MI6 and, eventually, almost become its chief. Philby, however, had certain advantages that Reilly unfortunately lacked: He was a native Englishman, had come from a distinguished family, and had attended the schools of Britain's upper class, including Trinity College, Cambridge. (Interestingly enough, certain Soviet authors—V. N. Minayev, for example—tried to invent a similar background for Reilly, claiming that he was born in Ireland and had graduated from Oxford.) There was another important difference between Kim Philby and Sidney Reilly. While Philby was an intelligence bureaucrat *par excellence*, an ideal headquarters man, Reilly was far more happy in the field, where he could be independent and go his own way, than he would ever have been at headquarters surrounded by bureaucrats. Yet headquarters was the place to be if one hoped to advance into SIS's upper echelons.

Balked in his efforts to obtain permanent status in the SIS or to enter government service in some other department, Reilly accepted a couple of temporary assignments.

First of all, he went to the south of Russia to assess the prospects of General Denikin's Volunteer Army on behalf of the SIS. It was not an assignment that could bring in much for the Cheka, since Dzerzhinski already had numerous agents on the spot to report about Denikin, and even the British and French plans for supporting the Volunteer Army were known to Dzerzhinski. Reilly's next assignment took him to the Paris Peace Conference, where he followed Allied diplomatic maneuvers on the Russian question inside the conference and the intrigues of Russian politicians outside the conference. No doubt his encoded reports to the Cheka in Moscow on these aspects of the peace conference proved to be of value to Lenin and other Bolshevik leaders.

In the years that followed, however, Reilly must have been a disappointment to Moscow, for he did not have the kind of access that is indispensable for a top agent. As Savinkov's chief adviser and strategist, he saw Churchill from time to time, and he also accompanied Savinkov to meetings with other European leaders. Some of what he saw and heard must have found its way into his reports.[4] But Savinkov gradually lost any influence in those quarters. Reilly, acting for Savinkov, had his own contacts with various East European intelligence services which doubtless yielded information of interest to Moscow. Savinkov's activities were of minor interest.

Finally the time came when Savinkov was sufficiently disillusioned with the West to make him receptive to suggestions for a return to the USSR. At the proper time, Reilly played his assigned part by bringing his influence to bear and making certain that Savinkov's resolve to go back did not weaken at the last moment. Moreover, the letters that he wrote afterward in condemnation of Savinkov, and the subsequent public controversy over the future of anti-Communist activities, served to demoralize anti-Communists everywhere and weaken their morale. None of this prevented Reilly from continuing to involve himself as an *agent provocateur* in the secret work of Western defense and intelligence agencies, which was, as a result, doomed to failure.

The forgery of the Zinoviev letter, about which Reilly boasted to his friends, portraying it as a great anti-Communist propaganda coup, neatly coincided with Moscow's policies by helping to turn out a Labor government that the Bolsheviks strongly disliked for both ideological and tactical reasons. It was one of the last useful actions that Reilly could perform for the Cheka abroad.

It was clear to Dzerzhinski that Reilly had reached the limit of his usefulness and should be recalled. Reilly had failed to accomplish his principal mission of making a deep penetration of the SIS. The threat of the anti-Bolshevik crusade had long since faded in most of the capitalist countries, where people had lost faith in the anti-Bolsheviks and tired of squandering financial and logistical resources on an apparently hopeless undertaking. This could be regarded as one of Reilly's accomplishments, since he had provided Moscow with inside information that helped to frustrate these schemes. The OGPU already had many agents in the Russian emigration and could get along without Reilly's direct participation. All things considered, Dzerzhinski concluded, Reilly was now likely to be more valuable in Russia, where his knowledge and experience would be available to new agents dispatched abroad who would not suffer from Reilly's disadvantages: being too well known and possessing a history that inhibited future usefulness.

Dzerzhinski had occupied himself more and more with economic questions during the preceding two years, but he still was very much in charge of the OGPU, and he wanted to bring Reilly back to the USSR. Nevertheless, this had to be done in such a manner as to avoid the appearance that, like Savinkov, he was changing sides. Reilly's contributions to the work of the Cheka could be of supreme value if Soviet Russia's enemies did not dream that Reilly was still alive and might be cooperating with the Cheka.

Reilly was growing restless himself as the struggle over the succession to Lenin continued to intensify and public speculation abroad focused on the relative chances of Stalin, Trotsky, Kamenev, Zinoviev, Dzerzhinski, and others. He feared that he was missing a unique opportunity to move up in the Soviet hierarchy at a time of great change. After all, he probably reasoned, his services to the new Russia, by preserving and protecting the Soviet regime, had been considerable. Yet as long as he stayed abroad, far from the center of power, he could only observe events and take no part in them. Moreover, if Dzerzhinski took over the leadership of the Soviet regime, Reilly's place was more than ever in Moscow, in close proximity to the secret police chief with whom he had had a lengthy professional connection and, in addition, shared a Polish background. Could anyone be more useful to Dzerzhinski than the man who had personally known so many Western statesmen, known their strengths, weaknesses, and vices, their behavior and speech, their idiosyncrasies, even their thoughts?

In consequence, the OGPU and the SIS had developed a parallel interest regarding Reilly. While the OGPU desired Reilly's return to the USSR, the SIS counted on Reilly to meet the Trust people even if it became necessary to make a trip into the USSR. From the OGPU's point of view, the SIS plan afforded an ideal cover for Reilly's return.

At their meeting in Vyborg, one can conjecture that Yakushev transmitted to Reilly an order from Dzerzhinski to go to Moscow to report personally to him. Reilly was already prepared for such an order, and the plan for this contingency, which had been worked out sometime earlier went into effect. He wrote the final letter to Pepita, which he left with Bunakov, telling the British agent to deliver it only if he failed to return on time. After he arrived in Moscow, Reilly received the order from Dzerzhinski himself to terminate his activities abroad. In order to cover up the circumstances of Reilly's return, the OGPU staged the "shooting incident" on the Soviet-Finnish border and, just to make sure that none of the interested parties outside the country missed it, inserted an item about the imaginary smugglers in *Izvestiya*.

We know of course that the "shooting incident" on the border was a sham, and we can be sure that Reilly was not executed on or about November 5, 1925, as asserted by some Soviet sources. There is only one Soviet source that provides a plausible explanation of what *did* happen to Reilly. We should recall Minayev's words: "Arrested by the OGPU in 1927, Reilly testified that 'he came to the USSR in 1925. . . .' Pretending to be a native of Russia, 'Comrade Rellinsky,' he succeeded in penetrating into the Leningrad criminal investigation department and creeping in as a candidate party member. Here he was struck down by the OGPU's avenging hand." This laconic statement appears to contain all the relevant information. The rest can be inferred from the basic facts given by Minayev.

Sidney Reilly must have spent the first year after his return at the OGPU headquarters in Moscow. It can be assumed that during the same period the OGPU wanted to do everything possible to please Reilly. One way in which the OGPU sought to please Reilly was by trying to induce Pepita, whom he still loved, to come to Russia. The same observation that was made about Kim Philby's women applied to Reilly's women as well: "They were an assorted collection . . . with apparently little in common, except that they all, in turn, mattered to him, and that they were ultimately sacrificed—together with his own feelings and peace of mind—to the harsh demands of his secret life. . . ."[5] The OGPU, however, was handicapped by the fact that it could not tell Pepita that Reilly was still alive; on the contrary, the pretense had to be maintained that he was dead. The Trust's clumsy efforts during 1926 to bring

Pepita to Russia were reflected in later years by the clandestine operations of Soviet Intelligence, which at different times brought to Moscow the wives of two other defectors, Eleanor Philby and Melinda Maclean. Unfortunately for Reilly, Pepita allowed herself to be dissuaded and never went to Russia. Nevertheless, Reilly being Reilly, he perhaps consoled himself before long by acquiring a Russian wife.

The critical date in this period of Reilly's life was July 20, 1926, when Feliks Edmundovich Dzerzhinski died. It was reported that Dzerzhinski suffered a fatal heart attack in the midst of a stormy session of the Central Committee, but rumors circulated in Moscow at the time that Dzerzhinski had been poisoned. In that Byzantine atmosphere such suspicions were not unusual, and among the rivals for power the arch-plotter Stalin seemed fully capable of almost any crime.

In any case, Dzerzhinski's sudden death was bound to have a negative effect on all those in the OGPU who had been closely associated with him in one way or another. In the course of the next year Stalin disposed of his rivals in the party and consolidated his hold on the OGPU. V. R. Menzhinski, who succeeded Dzerzhinski as head of the OGPU, came like his predecessor from the Polish nobility, but he had little interest in secret police work. He was neutral in his attitude toward Stalin but obedient to Stalin, the general secretary of the Communist party. He left most of the work to Yagoda, his deputy, who was Stalin's man, and Yagoda proceeded to get rid of Dzerzhinski's men.

One by one, all of Dzerzhinski's closest colleagues disappeared from the scene—Peters (accused, among other charges, of helping Reilly's old SIS friend, Paul Dukes, in 1919), Artuzov, Styrne. Pilar, and others. Reilly, who had again assumed his old name of Rellinsky, was at first exiled from Moscow and sent off, possibly with a touch of irony, to the criminal investigation department in Leningrad, where he had once been active. According to Minayev, he had also become a candidate member of the party. Finally, in 1927 (one year later), the OGPU "discovered" Reilly, who had slipped into these privileged positions under his assumed name, and, in Minayev's words, struck him down with its avenging hand.

In all likelihood, since a death sentence already hung over his head, Reilly would have been executed after his arrest in 1927. Perhaps he was brought to Moscow before the end and became one of those prisoners dragged toward the Lubianka's execution cellar across the inner courtyard where they could hear the OGPU chief Menzhinski, a gifted pianist, playing music of his favorite composers, Grieg and Chopin, on the grand piano that he kept behind a screen in his office.

There exists a remote possibility, however, that the OGPU, instead of killing Reilly, sent him off to some distant island of the Gulag Archipelago. Relly's survival in the labor camps would then account for the reports about him that surfaced from time to time up to the end of the Second World War.

In a certain sense, Sidney Reilly was a godfather to such Soviet agents as Kim Philby, Donald Maclean, and Guy Burgess. But Reilly differed from these godchildren in that he cared nothing for the future of Communism or the world historical "balance of forces." If he cared for anything, it was for *Russia*: to build a strong Russia that happened to be ruled by Bolsheviks.

Reilly played an important part in perpetuating the hostility that had been deliberately created and fostered by the Soviet leaders from the moment they seized power.

Within Soviet Russia, Reilly helped to eliminate the Bolsheviks' foes by engaging in counterrevolutionary activities that provoked them into foolhardy actions. If anyone doubts that the Bolsheviks would consider having an agent like Sidney Reilly take part in planning a counterrevolution against them, there are convincing parallels in Russian history at the beginning of the twentieth century. For example, Sergei Vasilievich Zubatov, head of the Moscow Okhrana, succeeded in placing Yevno Azev, one of his agents, as director of the "Fighting Section" of the Social Revolutionary party. Azev planned and carried out a number of assassinations of high czarist officials, including the murder of Minister of the Interior Wenzel von Plehwe, Zubatov's superior, who had actually *approved* Azev's recruitment. The Okhrana's strategy was aimed at penetrating and controlling the revolutionary groups, sometimes disposing of individual members. In Reilly's case, the Bolsheviks' aim was to provoke action on the part of the counterrevolutionaries in order to destroy them as a group.

When world revolution failed to materialize in the first years of the Soviet regime, the Bolshevik leaders found it to their advantage to follow a "no war, no peace" policy marked by the same basic hostility between Communism and the West—alternating for tactical reasons with brief intervals of thaw—and to wait for the moment when they could exploit some adversary's weakness, primarily to expand their territory.

Why have Sidney Reilly's services never been acknowledged or recognized by the Soviet regime?

In 1958 a book was published in Riga (in Soviet Latvia) under the title *Latvian Revolutionary Workers*, with a contribution by V. Rayevsky. He wrote as follows about the 1918 events: "At the beginning of August in Moscow there arrived as subordinates to the English envoy Lockhart the best agents of English Intelligence: the experienced provocateur Shmidkhen and the pride of the British secret service Captain Reilly." The author indignantly went on to say that a book by two foreign authors (Kahn and Sayers) had "entirely unjustly blackened a true son of the Latvian people, the steadfast Bolshevik E. Berzin." Within the next decade, another author published a book in Riga about Eduard Petrovich Berzin's life, relating his true role in the "Lockhart plot" and rehabilitating him (after his execution as a Japanese spy) for the loyal and devoted Chekist he was in reality.

In 1965 the agent Shmidkhen was rehabilitated in Soviet press articles that identified him, as we have seen, as the retired NKVD colonel Jan Buikis.

Nevertheless, Sidney Reilly is unlikely to receive the same treatment. The last service he can perform for the Bolsheviks is to remain forever the incorrigible British officer and representative of the wicked imperialist forces who was sent to Russia to head the whole spy network directed against the people's government of the first socialist state.

It seems improbable, therefore, that any monument will be erected in the vast Dzerzhinski (formerly Lubianka) Square near the statue of Feliks Dzerzhinski, the founder of the Soviet state security—secret police—apparatus. As one Soviet citizen has ironically suggested,[6] if such a monument were to be erected it ought to bear the inscription:

> To heroes of espionage
> RELLINSKY, BERZIN, SHMIDKHEN-BUIKIS,
> AND SPROGIS
> From a grateful people

The monument would be a graceful addition to the square, facing the massive reddish facade of a seven-story building, with bars and screens over the lower windows, which once belonged to an insurance company and now is the headquarters of the KGB. On the left side of Dzerzhinski Square stands the Children's World (*Detsky Mir*) department store specializing in children's goods. Perhaps the existence of a monument to Sidney Reilly in that location would be appropriate compensation to the bogeyman about whom Soviet children have read in their schoolbooks for so many years.

Notes

CHAPTER 1

1. R. H. Bruce Lockhart, *Memoirs of a British Agent* (London: Putnam, 1932), p. 277.
2. Russia's second-largest city. In 1914 its name was changed from St. Petersburg to Petrograd, reflecting the war with Germany and Russian patriotism. In 1924, after Lenin's death, it was named Leningrad.
3. Lockhart, *Memoirs,* p. 277.
4. Reilly's romantic nature, revealed by his interest in collecting books about Napoleon, receives further confirmation in the book-plate he invented for himself: a picture of Saint George slaying the dragon, with a young girl gazing rapturously at the knight rescuing her.
5. Richard Deacon, *A History of the Russian Secret Service* (New York: Taplinger Publishing Co., 1972), p. 143.
6. SIS received the designation MI6 (in place of MI1C) some years after World War I.

CHAPTER 2

1. Lockhart, *Memoirs*, p. 222.
2. General Judson's views are illustrated at various points in George F. Kennan's *Soviet-American Relations, 1917–1920,* vol. I: *Russia Leaves the War* (Princeton: Princeton University Press, 1956). On page 42 Kennan notes: "General Judson became, shortly after the Revolution, a strong advocate of the policy of working through, rather than against, the Soviet leaders in the effort to prevent the removal of German forces from the eastern to the western front. . . ." Kennan also notes (page 100) that Judson suggested to Washington that he offer his collaboration to the Soviet government in the technical drafting of the armistice, hoping thereby to influence the wording so as to bind the Germans not to transfer troops from the eastern to the western front. Judson is quoted (on pp. 107–8) to the effect that "it became apparent to me . . . that the Bolsheviks were in to stay . . . and . . . whatever we might think of them, were in a position to determine many questions that would perhaps vitally affect the outcome of the war. . . . The facts could not be altered. . . . The inevitable had to be faced and the best made of it. . . ." A communication from Ambassador Francis is cited (on page 123): "Judson has insisted for some time that Soviet is de facto government and relations therewith should be established. . . ." Finally (page 193), Kennan writes that "the General's hopes were placed on the possibility of what he called a 'failure' of the armistice agreement. He had recommended . . . that he be authorized in advance, for the event of such a 'failure,' to express 'friendly appreciation for the Soviet position and to promise to the Soviet authorities 'all the U.S. troops the Trans-Siberian Railroad could transport,' plus . . . 'assistance on a large scale of every other character.' "
3. Lockhart, *Memoirs,* p. 225.
4. *Ibid.,* p. 282. The Social Revolutionary party, the revolutionary party of the peasants, became split after the Bolsheviks' seizure of power. The Left Social Revolutionaries, favoring a dictatorship of workers and peasants, broke away from the main party in 1917 and joined the Bolsheviks after the coup in forming the Soviet government.
5. Lockhart, *Memoirs,* pp. 225–26.
6. Robins must have shared a dramatic flair with his sister Elizabeth, an American actress. When Raymond, her favorite brother, gave up his law practice in 1897 and joined the Klondike gold rush,

she also went to Alaska and helped to work the claims, which
brought him a fortune by the turn of the century. As an actress,
she toured in plays all over America. She had an unhappy marriage to an actor, who kept a suit of armor in his dressing room
and donned the armor to drown himself in the Charles River at
Boston. Elizabeth later became a great success on the London
stage playing Ibsen heroines and secured the patronage of many
famous theatrical and literary people, including Oscar Wilde,
Henry James, and George Bernard Shaw.
7. Lockhart, *Memoirs,* pp. 258–59.

CHAPTER 3

1. Pepita N. Reilly and Sidney Reilly, *Britain's Master Spy* (London:
    Elkin, Mathews and Marriot, 1931), p. 22.
2. Lockhart, *Memoirs,* p. 257.
3. Reilly and Reilly, *Britain's Master Spy,* p. 14.
4. G. A. Hill, *Go Spy the Land* (London: Cassell, 1932), p. 196.
5. *Ibid.,* pp. 222–23.
6. During World War II, Poole headed the Foreign Nationalities
    Branch of the Office of Strategic Services, a predecessor of the
    CIA. The Foreign Nationalities Branch overtly collected intel-
    ligence on foreign areas from U.S. citizens and foreigners.

CHAPTER 4

1. Lockhart, *Memoirs,* pp. 181–82.
2. Winston S. Churchill, *Great Contemporaries* (New York: Putnam,
    1937), p. 103.
3. Dimitry V. Lehovich, *White Against Red* (New York: W. W.
    Norton & Co., 1974), pp. 140–41.
4. Yakov Khristoforovich Peters, *"Vospominanii o rabote v Vecheka
    v pervy god revolyutsii"* [*Reminiscences of work in the Vecheka
    in the first year of the Revolution*], *Proletarskaya Revolyutsiya*
    [*Proletarian Revolution*] No. 10 (33), 1924, pp. 16–17.
5. Lockhart's neighbor in an adjoining room at the Elite was Yakov
    Blyumkin, Cheka chief of counterespionage, destined to play a
    key role in the Mirbach assassination. Blyumkin's presence in the
    next room raises the possibility that the Cheka had Lockhart
    under audiosurveillance.
6. *Pravda,* Moscow, July 3, 1918.

CHAPTER 5

1. Tsaritsyn was renamed Stalingrad in 1925. After Denikin held the
    city for several months in 1919, Red Army troops under Stalin's

command succeeded in recapturing Tsaritsyn, on perhaps the only occasion when Stalin commanded troops during the Civil War. The Soviet victory in the battle of Stalingrad in February 1943 marked a turning point in World War II, but despite its historical eminence the city's name was changed to Volgograd in November 1961, after Nikita Khrushchev's further revelations about Stalin's crimes at the 22nd Party Congress.

2. G. Kurpnek, *Povest' o nepodkupnom soldate* [*Tale of the incorruptible soldier*] (Riga: "Liesta" Publishing House, 1966), p. 96. Dzerzhinski later maintained that his signature had been forged and that the seal validating the signature was in the hands of the SR leader Aleksandrovich (true name: Pyotr Aleksandrovich Dmitrievsky), a deputy chairman of the Cheka. Dzerzhinski's role in the affair was, however, decidedly murky, as he had bitterly opposed the Brest-Litovsk Treaty and was one of three members of the Bolshevik Central Committee who openly declared their opposition but abstained from voting because of Lenin's threat to quit if the treaty was rejected (a walkout by Lenin would have split the party). It is interesting that, after Mirbach's assassination, Dzerzhinski not only protected but reinstated Blyumkin, one of the murderers. Dzerzhinski's claim that his signature had been forged on the letter to Mirbach could not be confirmed because Aleksandrovich was shot on the evening of July 7 immediately after his capture.

3. Lockhart, *Memoirs,* pp. 300–301.

4. The battalion commander was Colonel Eduard Petrovich Berzin, with whom Reilly would later be associated in a new plot.

5. Later renamed Gorky Street.

6. Béla Kun led an abortive communist revolution in Hungary in 1919 and fled to the Soviet Union, where he was executed in 1937.

CHAPTER 6

1. Kennan, *Soviet-American Relations,* vol. II, *The Decision to Intervene* (Princeton, 1958), p. 379.

2. Renamed Sverdlovsk in honor of Yakov Sverdlov, who died of typhus in 1919.

3. Kennan, vol. II, p. 349.

4. Peters, *Reminiscences,* p. 21.

5. Kennan, vol. II, p. 455.

CHAPTER 7

1. Peters, *Reminiscences,* p. 26.

2. Lockhart, *Memoirs,* p. 309.

3. *Ibid.*, pp. 311–12.
4. *Ibid.*, p. 315.
5. Lockhart also asserted that Shmidkhen had been accompanied by Berzin at their first meeting. Shmidkhen claimed in his own account (published in 1966) that he and his comrade Sprogis, who had originally met Cromie and Reilly in Petrograd, together made the *first* visit to Lockhart, delivering Cromie's letter; Shmidkhen introduced Berzin to Lockhart at a second meeting. Shmidkhen's account appears more plausible.
6. Lockhart, *Memoirs,* p. 323.
7. Robin Bruce Lockhart, *Ace of Spies* (London: Hodder Paperbacks Ltd., 1969), p. 73.
8. W. Somerset Maugham, *Complete Short Stories,* vol. I, *East and West* (Garden City, New York: Doubleday & Co., 1934), p. 604.

CHAPTER 8

1. Kennan, vol. II, p. 461.
2. Peters, *Reminiscences,* p. 25.
3. In *Stranitsy iz zhizni F. E. Dzerzhinskovo* [*Pages from the life of F. E. Dzerzhinski*] (Moscow: 1956), p. 71, the Soviet writer Pavel Georgievich Sofinov states that, according to official Vecheka statistics, 31,489 persons were "repressed" on territory controlled by the Soviet government in 1918. Of this total, 6,185 were shot, 14,829 imprisoned, 6,407 placed in concentration camps, and 4,068 held as hostages.
4. R. H. Lockhart, *Memoirs,* p. 318.
5. *Ibid.*, p. 347.
6. Reilly and Reilly, *Britain's Master Spy,* pp. 62–63.
7. R. H. Lockhart, *Memoirs,* p. 325. Lockhart's account is confirmed by Peters (*Reminiscences*, p. 28), who adds the unsubstantiated charge that the Baroness Beckendorff was a German spy, although he says that this information is based on evidence from another prisoner as well as documents on hand. Such charges were not uncommon during those war years. U.S. Ambassador Francis suffered both official and unofficial criticism because of his friendship with a Russian woman, Matilda deCram, who was suspected of being a German agent.
8. Reilly and Reilly, *Britain's Master Spy,* p. 73.
9. Hill, *Go Spy the Land,* p. 225.
10. John Reed, *Ten Days That Shook the World* (New York: Vintage Books, Random House, 1960), p. lii.
11. M. Philips Price, *Die Russische Revolution* (Hamburg: Verlagsbuchhandlung Carl Hoym Nachf. Louis Cahnbley, 1921), p. 5.

12. See George F. Kennan, *Russia and the West Under Lenin and Stalin* (Boston: Atlantic Monthly Press; Little, Brown, 1961), p. 51. Referring to Sadoul's position on the French Military Mission, Kennan wrote: "Sadoul was a Socialist. . . . His sympathies for the Soviet regime grew steadily as his disgust mounted for the Russian policy of his own government. He eventually became a full-fledged member of the French Communist Party and a stout Stalinist."
13. Peters, *Reminiscences,* p. 26.
14. The exact date is unknown. Kalamatiano was probably captured on or about September 15.
15. Peters was mistaken. Kalamatiano actually used the surname Serpovsky.
16. Peters, *Reminiscences,* pp. 26–27.
17. Reilly and Reilly, *Britain's Master Spy,* p. 72.

CHAPTER 9
1. N. A. Skrypnik, an Old Bolshevik whom Stalin persecuted for his Ukrainian leanings, killed himself on July 7, 1933.
2. *Pogranichnik [Border guard]* no. 233, 1965, pp. 12–14.
3. *Latyshskiye revolyutsionnye deyateli [Latvian revolutionary workers]* (Riga: 1958), p. 66.
4. Kurpnek, *Tale,* p. 238.
5. *Ibid.,* pp. 12–13. Marshal Mikhail N. Tukhachevski, later accused with other military leaders of committing treason on behalf of Nazi Germany, seems to have been similarly arrested in 1937. This method guaranteed a minimum of outside attention and resistance.

   Kurpnek's account of Berzin's arrest is almost certainly the authentic one. Other accounts are contradictory, although all agree that Berzin was homeward bound on leave at the time of his arrest. In *The Great Terror* (New York: Macmillan, 1968), Robert Conquest writes that Berzin was arrested at the airfield. An unofficial Soviet source claims that Berzin was taken off the ship at Aleksandrovsk while traveling to Vladivostok from Kolyma. The confusion here is probably between Aleksandrov (near Moscow) and Aleksandrovsk (a Pacific port).

CHAPTER 10
1. Robin Lockhart, *Ace of Spies,* p. 81.
2. Available in Great Britain's Public Record Office, File FO 371/3344.
3. *Ibid.,* File FO 371/3337.

4. Richard H. Ullman, *Anglo-Soviet Relations, 1917–1921,* vol. II, *Britain and the Russian Civil War* (Princeton: Princeton University Press, 1968), pp. 90–98. These pages cover Churchill's as well as other proposals for intervention, and the opposition they encountered, principally on the part of Lloyd George.
5. R. H. Lockhart, *Memoirs,* pp. 322–23.
6. Lord Alfred Milner MSS (Box 110, File C-2) include two personal letters to Lockhart from Reilly dated November 23 and 25, 1918.
7. Robin Lockhart, *Ace of Spies,* p. 83.
8. R. H. Lockhart, *Memoirs,* p. 331.

CHAPTER 11

1. R. H. Lockhart, *Memoirs,* p. 257.
2. It remains unclear whether E. P. Berzin had an active duty assignment in the period leading up to the trial and, if so, what that assignment would have been. The problem is compounded by the confusion that exists about Berzin, perhaps because various writers have not realized that Berzin is a common Latvian name and that there were a number of Berzins active in the revolutionary era. As a result, E. P. Berzin has been confused with other Berzins.

   For example, in a generally excellent book, *Black Night, White Snow* (New York: Doubleday, 1978, pp. 581–82), Harrison E. Salisbury writes that the commission sent from Moscow to investigate the situation of the Czar and his family in Ekaterinburg was headed by Ye. [sic] P. Berzin, "later to become Dzerzhinski's secretary." In *Let History Judge* (New York: Alfred Knopf, 1971, p. 216), Roy E. Medvedev also refers to E. P. Berzin as "former secretary to Dzerzhinski." Nevertheless, G. Kurpnek, the Soviet author of E. P. Berzin's biography, makes no such claim, although this author writes at length about Berzin as a Chekist and lavishes much praise on Dzerzhinski; one might expect that if Berzin had been Dzerzhinski's secretary, the author would have mentioned this in addition to Berzin's other Cheka assignments. Possibly it is a case of mistaken identity. There was another Berzin in the top ranks of the Cheka: Jan Karlovich Berzin, who left the Cheka in 1920 and headed Soviet Military Intelligence (also known as the GRU); he was destined like the other Berzin to be arrested in 1937 and shot.

   Salisbury went on to state that Ye. P. (i.e., E. P.) Berzin "was acting as commander of the North Urals Siberian Front" at the time he headed the commission that went to Ekaterinburg. Salisbury's source was Sergei P. Melgunov's *Sudba Imperator Nikolaya*

II posle otrecheniya [*The fate of Czar Nicholas II after abdica-tion*], pp. 377–78. But Melgunov wrote only that "in accordance with a directive of the Center, the commander of the North Urals Siberian Front Berzin" was assigned to lead the commission. It would have been difficult, though perhaps within the realm of possibility, for E. P. Berzin to carry out this assignment, since the commission's formal report was delivered to the Sovnarkom in Moscow on June 27, 1918. (It will be remembered that E. P. Berzin commanded an artillery battalion in the crushing of the Left SR revolt on July 6–7, 1918.)

Further light is shed on the subject by the Intelligence Section File of Headquarters, American Expeditionary Forces Siberia (1918–19), Two Volumes (Unclassified), U.S. Army Russian Institute Library, Garmisch, Germany. By the time of the Moscow trial, Vatsetis, who commanded the division of Lettish Rifles in which E. P. Berzin served, had become commander-in-chief of the Forces of the Soviet Republic. An intelligence report on Soviet Order of Battle dated November 16, 1918 (nearly two weeks before the trial), lists the "3rd Red Army, headquarters at Perm, Berzin, Commander." A similar report issued on December 20, 1918, lists "Lashevich, Temporary Commander" of the 3rd Army. Thus it is possible that, if E. P. Berzin *had* actually commanded the 3rd Army, he could have absented himself sometime between November 16 and December 20 to go to Moscow and testify at the trial.

The question of who commanded the 3rd Army, however, appears to have been settled by the Large Soviet Encyclopedia. A biographical listing for Reinhold Iosifovich Berzin (1970 edition) describes him as "commanding from June, 1918 the North Urals Siberian Front on whose basis the 3rd Army was created." Hence there seems to be little doubt that it was R. I. Berzin (rather than E. P. Berzin) who headed the commission that went to Ekaterin-burg in June and who subsequently commanded the 3rd Army.

3. This is an exact transliteration from the Cyrillic alphabet of the name given in *Izvestiya*. It has not been possible to identify this firm or to establish its precise name in English.

4. Vladikavkaz was subsequently renamed Ordzhonikidze. The Bolshevik leader Grigori Ordzhonikidze quarreled with Stalin and died by "suicide" in 1937.

5. Although some foreign sources have asserted, without corroboration, that Friede was associated with Reilly, all the evidence indicates that Friede's statement was true. He had never met Reilly and knew of him only through Kalamatiano.

6. At that time the Ukraine was occupied by German forces.
7. As early as June 1918, the Vecheka issued a notice clearly seeking to intimidate defense attorneys: "If any citizen of the city of Moscow undertakes . . . to accept money or agrees on a specific fee for intercession or defense, this will constitute in itself a crime equivalent to extortion or blackmail. . . ." This was a privilege supposedly reserved for relatives or friends acting free of charge.

CHAPTER 12

1. Robin Lockhart, *Ace of Spies,* p. 94.
2. Joseph Conrad, *Nostromo* (New York: Random House Modern Library, 1951), p. 422.
3. Milner MSS.
4. Hill, *Go Spy the Land,* p. 201.
5. See Richard Goldhurst, *The Midnight War* (New York: McGraw-Hill Book Co., 1978), p. 182, for a discussion of this.
6. Clemenceau was also absent during the same period, having been wounded in an attempted assassination, but he and Churchill essentially agreed on the Russian question.
7. The last American troops were withdrawn from Archangel in June 1919.
8. Hill, *Go Spy the Land,* pp. 257–58.

CHAPTER 13

1. Nadine remained ignorant of the fact that Reilly had committed bigamy in marrying her.
2. In reality, both Savinkov's mother and his son had joined him in European exile.
3. Churchill, *Great Contemporaries,* p. 104.
4. *Ibid.,* p. 109.
5. Milner MSS.

CHAPTER 14

1. W. Somerset Maugham, "The Terrorist," *Redbook* (New York), October 1943.
2. Robin Lockhart, *Ace of Spies,* p. 102. This jocular reference to the famous World War I song does not explain Reilly's choice of birthplace, which probably dates back to his assumption of an Irish surname around the turn of the century. The alleged protocol of his OGPU interrogation in 1925 gives Connemara, Ireland, as his birthplace.
3. Robin Lockhart, *Ace of Spies,* p. 104.
4. *Ibid.,* pp. 99–100.
5. Gajda, notorious as an adventurer and a troublemaker, was ac-

cused in 1926 of cooperating with Soviet Military Intelligence while chief of the Czech General Staff. During the Hitler period he led a small Czech fascist party.
6. Robin Lockhart, *Ace of Spies*, p. 107.
7. *Ibid.*, p. 108.
8. Dimitry V. Lehovich, *White Against Red*, p. 423.

CHAPTER 15

1. Reilly and Reilly, *Britain's Master Spy*, p. 113.
2. Thyssen in later years helped to finance the Nazis.
3. R. H. Lockhart, *Memoirs*, p. 182.
4. Robin Lockhart, *Ace of Spies*, p. 113.
5. Pilar von Pilhau, one of Dzerzhinski's most feared lieutenants, was executed during the Great Purge.
6. The Soviet press reported an uprising in Georgia on August 28 that had been quickly suppressed after the rebels seized one town and resorted to arms at various points. Since Pavlovsky had been captured many months earlier and was being used by the OGPU in his correspondence with Savinkov, the reported "uprising" was probably engineered by the OGPU to flush out Savinkov agents just before the announcement of Savinkov's arrest.
7. Walter Duranty, *The Curious Lottery* (New York: Coward-McCann, 1929), p. 128.
8. Louis Fischer, *Men and Politics* (New York: Duell, Sloan and Pearce, 1941), p. 118.
9. Duranty, *Curious Lottery*.
10. Fischer, *Men and Politics*, pp. 118–19.
11. Duranty, *Curious Lottery*.
12. Robin Lockhart, *op. cit.*, p. 118. Reilly's letter to Churchill is undated but must have been written some time between September 1, when the *Morning Post* published its article about Savinkov, and September 5, when Churchill replied to this letter, which obviously contained a copy of Reilly's response to the *Morning Post*, subsequently published on September 8.
13. *Ibid.*, pp. 118–19.
14. *Ibid.*, p. 120.
15. *Ibid.*, p. 119.
16. The Comintern was the international Communist organization under Moscow control that engaged in worldwide subversion. It was abolished by Stalin in 1943 as a tactical concession to the USSR's wartime allies.

CHAPTER 16

1. Mikhail Trilisser was a senior official long in charge of the

OGPU's Foreign Administration, which conducted espionage abroad. Trilisser, a fanatical Communist, was disposed to violent methods in his operations but lost his position around 1930. He was also independent and abrasive, finally incurring Stalin's displeasure and being purged in the thirties.

2. William Reswick, *I Dreamt Revolution* (Chicago: Regnery, 1952), pp. 8–11.
3. Reilly and Reilly, *Britain's Master Spy*, p. 169.
4. This reference is to the anti-Communists.
5. Robin Lockhart, *Ace of Spies*, p. 131.
6. *Ibid.*, p. 131.
7. *Ibid.*, p. 132.
8. *Ibid.*, pp. 132–33.
9. *Pravda*, Moscow, May 12, 1925.
10. Blyumkin, a GPU assassin, was himself executed as an alleged Trotskyite agent in 1929.
11. A similar fate overtook Czech Foreign Minister Jan Masaryk, who committed "suicide" when Soviet Chekists threw him from a window in Prague in 1948.
12. Reilly and Reilly, *Britain's Master Spy*, p. 190.
13. *Ibid.*, p. 213.

CHAPTER 17

1. Robin Lockhart, *Ace of Spies*, p. 144.
2. Reilly and Reilly, *Britain's Master Spy*, p. 199.
3. *Ibid.*, pp. 194–95.
4. Robin Lockhart, *Ace of Spies*, p. 145.
5. Lev Veniaminovich Nikulin, *Mertvaya zyb'* [*Groundswell*] (Moscow: 1965).
6. In 1917 Shulgin had gone with Aleksandr Guchkov to the Czar to ask for his abdication.
7. The book, titled *Tri stolitsy* [*Three Capitals*], was published in Berlin in 1927 after the manuscript had been sent to Yakushev in Moscow for final approval.
8. Reilly and Reilly, *Britain's Master Spy*, pp. 250–52.

CHAPTER 18

1. Early in 1921 a revolt broke out in the Soviet Baltic Fleet. The mutinous sailors—early supporters of the Soviet regime—seized control of the Kronstadt naval base, situated on an island near Petrograd ten miles from the mainland. The Bolsheviks refused to negotiate with the sailors and finally succeeded in putting down the revolt by attacking across the ice.

2. Nikulin, *Groundswell*.
3. Robin Lockhart, *Ace of Spies*, p. 185.
4. Petrov was lucky. A decade later (in the thirties) he would have become merely another victim of the Great Purge, eliminated as a matter of convenience.
5. Greville Wynne, *Contact on Gorky Street* (New York: Atheneum, 1968), p. 9.
6. Robin Lockhart, *Ace of Spies*, pp. 148–49.
7. Such charges meant no more then, of course, than charges in more recent times that seek to make the CIA responsible for anything and everything to which the Soviet regime objects.
8. Vladislav Nikolaevich Minayev, *Podryvnaya deyatel'nost' inostrannykh razvedok v SSSR* [*Subversive activity of foreign espionage services in the USSR*], Part I (Moscow: 1940), p. 87.
9. Robin Lockhart, *Ace of Spies*, pp. 151–52.

EPILOGUE

1. Reilly and Reilly, *Britain's Master Spy*, p. 15.
2. Deacon, *History of Russian Secret Service*. See pp. 264–68 for his evaluation of Reilly.
3. *Ibid.*, pp. 302–3.
4. For a time Reilly probably found an easier solution to his problem of communicating with Moscow and could dispense with Soviet contacts outside England: He was in a position to pass his reports through Leonid Krassin, the Soviet trade representative in London, with whom he pretended to be engaged in private business dealings.
5. Patrick Seale and Maureen McConville, *Philby: The Long Road to Moscow* (New York: Simon and Schuster, 1973), p. 244.
6. Revolt I. Pimenov, *Kak ya iskal shpiona Reili* [*How I Searched for the Spy Reilly*] (Leningrad: 1968), reproduced in Radio Liberty Samizdat Archive AS 1089 (Munich: 1972), p. 27.

Sources

Bailey, Geoffrey. *The Conspirators.* New York: Harper & Brothers, 1960.

Carr, Edward Hallett. *A History of Soviet Russia, The Bolshevik Revolution 1917–1923,* 4 vols. New York: Macmillan, 1950 (vol. 1), 1953 (vol. 3).

Chamberlin, William Henry. *The Russian Revolution,* 2 vols. New York: Macmillan, 1935.

Churchill, Winston S. *Great Contemporaries.* New York: Putnam, 1937.

Cline, Ray S. *Secrets, Spies, and Scholars.* Washington: Acropolis Books, 1976.

Conquest, Robert. *The Great Terror.* New York: Macmillan, 1968.

Dallin, David. *Soviet Espionage.* New Haven: Yale University Press, 1955.

Deacon, Richard. *A History of the Russian Secret Service.* New York: Taplinger, 1972.

Deutscher, Isaac. *Stalin: A Political Biography.* New York and London: Oxford, 1949.

Dukes, Sir Paul. *Red Dawn and the Morrow: Adventures and Investigations in the Red Russia*. Garden City, N.Y.: Doubleday, Page & Co., 1922.

—. *The Story of "ST 25": Adventure and Romance in the Secret Intelligence Service in Red Russia*. London: Cassell, 1938.

Duranty, Walter. *The Curious Lottery*. New York: Coward-McCann, 1929.

An Englishwoman. *From a Russian Diary, 1917–1920*. London, 1921.

Fischer, Louis. *Men and Politics: An Autobiography*. New York: Duell, Sloan and Pearce, 1941.

Footman, David. *Civil War in Russia*. New York: Frederick A. Praeger, 1962.

Francis, David R. *Russia from the American Embassy*. New York: Charles Scribner's Sons, 1921.

Freud, Sigmund, and William C. Bullitt. *Thomas Woodrow Wilson, Twenty-eighth President of the United States: A Psychological Study*. Boston: Houghton Mifflin, 1967.

Goldhurst, Richard. *The Midnight War: The American Intervention in Russia, 1918–1920*. New York: McGraw-Hill, 1978.

Haupt, Georges. *Makers of the Russian Revolution: Biographies of Bolshevik Leaders*. Ithaca, N.Y.: Cornell University Press, 1974.

Hilger, Gustav, and Alfred G. Meyer. *The Incompatible Allies: A Memoir-History of German-Soviet Relations, 1918–1941*. New York: Macmillan, 1953.

Hill, G. A. *Go Spy the Land: Being the Adventures of IK8 of the British Secret Service*. London: Cassell, 1932.

Hyde, H. Montgomery. *Stalin: The History of a Dictator*. New York: Farrar, Straus & Giroux, 1971.

Ironside, Lord. *Archangel, 1918–19*. London: Constable & Co., 1953.

Jones, Rhodi Jeffreys. *American Espionage: From Secret Service to CIA*. New York: Free Press, 1977.

Kedrov, Mikhail Sergeyevich. *Za sovetskiy sever* (The Struggle for a Soviet North). Leningrad, 1927.

Kennan, George F. *Soviet-American Relations, 1917–1920*, vol. 1, *Russia Leaves the War*, vol. 2, *The Decision to Intervene*. Princeton, N.J.: Princeton University Press, 1956, 1958.

Kravchenko, V. *Chekisti o svoem trude: Pod imenem Shmidkhena* (Chekists Discuss Their Work: Under the Alias Shmidkhen). *Nedelya* 11 (March 6–12, 1966).

—. *Taina Shmidkhena raskryta* (The Secret of Shmidkhen Revealed). *Pogranichnik* (Border Guard) 23 (1965): 12–14.

Kurpnek, G. *Povest' o nepodkupnom soldate* (Tale of the Incorruptible Soldier). Riga: "Liesta" Publishing House, 1966.

Lehovich, Dimitry V. *White Against Red.* New York: W. W. Norton, 1974.

Lockhart, R. H. Bruce. *British Agent.* London and New York: G. P. Putnam's Sons, 1933.

———. *My Europe.* London: Putnam, 1952.

Lockhart, Robin Bruce. *Ace of Spies.* London: Hodder Paperbacks Ltd., 1969.

Medvedev, Roy E. *Let History Judge.* New York: Alfred A. Knopf, 1971.

Minayev, Vladislav Nikolaevich. *Podryvnaya deyatel'nost' inostrannykh razvedok v SSSR* (Subversive Activity of Foreign Espionage Services in the USSR), part I. Moscow, 1940.

Nikulin, Lev Veniaminovich. *Mertvaya zyb'* (Groundswell). Moscow, 1965.

Penkovsky, Oleg. *The Penkovsky Papers.* London: Collins, 1965.

Peters, Yakov Khristoforovich. *Vospominanii o rabote v Vecheka v pervy god revolyutsii* (Reminiscences of Work in the Vecheka in the First Year of the Revolution). *Proletarskaya Revolyutsiya* (Proletarian Revolution) 10 (33), 1924.

Petrov, Ivan Mikhailovich. *Osoboye zadaniye* (Special Mission), An Anthology, pp. 296–309. Moscow, 1968.

Pimenov, Revolt I. *Kak ya iskal shpiona Reili* (How I Searched for the Spy Reilly). Radio Liberty Samizdat Archive, Munich, AS 1089, 1972, Leningrad, 1968.

Price, M. Philips. *My Reminiscences of the Russian Revolution.* London: George Allen & Unwin Ltd., 1921.

Rayevsky, V. *Latyshskiye revolyutsionniye deyateli* (Latvian Revolutionary Workers). Anthology, Riga, 1958.

Reed, John. *Ten Days That Shook the World.* New York: Random House, 1960.

Reilly, Pepita N., and Sidney Reilly. *Britain's Master Spy, Written by Himself, Edited and Completed by His Wife.* London: Elkin, Mathews and Marriot, 1931.

Reswick, William. *I Dreamt Revolution.* Chicago: Regnery, 1952.

Salisbury, Harrison E. *Black Night, White Snow.* New York: Doubleday, 1978.

Savinkov, Boris Viktorovich. *An Excerpt from My Reminiscences. Vozrozhdeniye* (Paris) 9 (1950).

———. *Kon voronoi* (The Pale Horse). Paris, 1924.

———. *Memoirs of a Terrorist.* New York: Boni, 1931.

Sayers, M., and A. Kahn. *The Great Conspiracy: The Secret War Against the Soviet Union.* Boston: Little, Brown, 1946.

Seale, Patrick, and Maureen McConville. *Philby: The Long Road to Moscow*. New York: Simon & Schuster, 1973.

Serge, Victor. *Memoirs of a Revolutionary, 1901–1941*. London and New York: Oxford University Press, 1963.

Sofinov, Pavel Georgievich. *Stranitsy iz zhizni F. E. Dzerzhinskovo* (Pages from the Life of F. E. Dzerzhinski). Moscow, 1956.

Solzhenitsyn, Aleksandr. *The Gulag Archipelago*, vols. 1–2. New York: Harper & Row, 1974.

Stepun, F. *A. B. V. Savinkov: otryvok iz vospominanii* (B. V. Savinkov: An Excerpt from My Reminiscences). *Vozrozhdeniye* (Paris) 9 (1950).

Ullman, R. H. *Britain and the Russian Civil War*. Princeton, N.J.: Princeton University Press, 1968.

Wolfe, Bertram D. *Three Who Made a Revolution*. New York: Dial Press, 1964.

Wrangel, General Baron Peter N. *Always with Honor*. New York: Robert Speller & Sons, 1957.

Wynne, Greville. *Contact on Gorky Street*. New York: Atheneum, 1968.

Index

Lavergne, J. (*continued*)
116, 119
Leeper, Rex, 109–10, 147
Left Social Revolutionaries, 40, 42, 44, 45, 48, 49–56, 88, 225–26
Lenin, 15, 45, 79, 80, 93, 151, 223; on Allied intervention, 62; attempted assassination of, 88, 227; and Brest-Litovsk treaty, 17–18; death of, 165, 166, 179–80, 230; at Fifth Congress, 47–48; and planned Allied coup, 81; Reilly requests meeting with, 1–2; Robins and, 13, 17; "sealed train" incident, 14
Lettish Rifles, 54, 60–61, 63–64, 72–78, 79, 80, 81–82, 83, 91, 117, 227
Litvinov, Maksim, 108, 109, 114
Lockhart, Bruce, 1, 2–3, 9, 24–25, 44, 54, 61, 62, 68, 70, 71, 81, 83–84, 93, 95, 113, 115, 116, 126, 128, 131, 225, 227, 234; and Archangel landing, 22, 68, 72, 92, 110; arrests of, 90, 94; on anarchists, 21; on Cromie, 41; and Brest-Litovsk treaty, 18; on Dzerzhinski, 24; exchanged for Litvinov, 108; fundraising role of, 70–71; Leeper and, 109; and Left SR uprising, 55; and Lettish Rifles, 64, 72–78, 104–6; meetings with Berzin, 73–78; Poole and, 111; Reilly and, 22, 91–92, 148, 152–53, 227–28; Robins and, 11, 17–19, 21; on Savinkov, 38–39, 166; trial in absentia, 115–31. *See also* Lockhart plot
Lockhart, Robin, 109, 133, 210, 219
Lockhart plot, 217; trial of participants in, 114, 115–31, 132–33

Marchand, René, 96–97, 117, 119, 125–26

Massino, Nadine, 7–8, 27, 84, 123. *See also* Reilly, Nadine
Maugham, W. Somerset, 84–85, 151
Mikhailovna, Yelena, 84, 86–87
Minayev, Vladislav Nikolaevich, 218–19, 228
Mirbach, Count Wilhelm von, 25, 42, 44–45, 49, 51–53, 58, 103, 185, 226
Monarchist Organization of Central Russia (MOCR), 157–59, 164, 182, 187–88, 196–97, 202, 203–7, 216
Monarchists, 29, 45, 59–60
Morans, Jeanne, 68, 115, 122, 125, 131
Moscow Municipal Association. *See* "Trust, The"
Muraviev, N. K., 125–26, 128, 129
Mussolini, 167

New Economic Policy (NEP), 151, 164, 212
Nicholas II, Czar, 26, 59
Nikulin, Lev V., 208, 209, 212, 213, 214, 216
Norwegian Legation, 97–100
Noulens, Joseph, 22, 37

OGPU, 177, 178, 183, 203; and "The Trust," 195, 199, 201–7, 211–12; and efforts to bring Pepita Reilly to Russia, 231–32; and Reilly's return to Russia, 208–11, 213, 218, 230, 231; and Savinkov's death, 185
Okhrana, 4, 5, 6, 23, 233
Opperput, Eduard Ottovich, 194–95, 196, 208, 213, 216; confesses to Schultz, 202; defection of, 207, 214, 215; on Reilly affair, 207–16; on "The Trust," 215–16; and Yakushev, 196, 202–3, 204–7
Orlovsky, Vyacheslav, 26, 174, 186

Otten, Dagmara, 89, 92
Otten, Yelizaveta Yemelyanovna, 27, 71, 89, 115–16, 122, 123, 124, 125, 130, 131

Paris Peace Conference, 133, 137–40, 228–29
Pavlovsky, Sergei, 151–52, 165, 167
Penkovsky, Oleg, 216–17
Peters, Jacob, 40, 87–88, 109, 232; and Allied nationals, 65–66; on attempted coup, 97–98; interrogates Lockhart, 90; Kalamatiano's capture and, 99–100; on Kaplan, 91; on Lettish Rifles, 60; and Lockhart's arrest, 94; and Reilly's contact with Latvians, 103–6; testimony at Lockhart plot trial, 117
Philby, Kim, 224, 225, 228, 231, 233
Pilhau, Pilar von, 168–69, 205, 212, 232
Pilsudski, Józef, 151, 196–97
Poland, anti-Bolshevik activity in, 153–54, 164–65
Polish "window," 164–65, 195, 201, 206
Poole, DeWitt C., 10, 25, 30, 33, 74, 75, 83–84, 116, 117, 119, 126, 129; and Allied intervention, 37–38, 66–71; attitude toward Reilly, 111, 134, 225; escape from Russia, 100–101
Poole, Sir F. Cuthbert, 59, 74
Popov, Aleksai, 53, 54
Potapov, Nikolai Mikhailovich, 164, 182, 198, 202, 207, 209, 210
Potemkin, Aleksey Vasilievich, 31, 122–23, 130, 131
Pravda: on Lockhart-Berzin meeting, 73; on planned Allied intervention, 41–42; on planned coup, 92–94; on Savinkov's suicide, 184–85; "Struggle with Hunger" reports, 101

Puzinsky, 211, 212, 213

Radek, Karl, 55, 61–62
Radkevich, Georgy, 179, 180, 186, 188, 189, 206
Rasputin, 86–87, 88
Red Army, 30, 59, 147
Red Guards, 45, 98–101
Reed, John, 96
Reilly, Margaret, 109, 144, 152, 155, 221. *See also* Thomas, Margaret
Reilly, Nadine, 109, 143–44, 152. *See also* Massino, Nadine
Reilly, Pepita, 177, 186, 231; efforts of OGPU to bring to Russia, 197–98, 231–32; and Kutepov, 198–200; and Schultz, 194–95, 199; and news of Reilly's death, 191–95, 221; Reilly's last letter to, 192–93. *See also* Bobadilla, Pepita
Reilly, Sidney George, 2, 5, 44, 54, 115, 116, 119, 124, 128, 131, 151; activities during World War I, 7, 8–9; as agent for Cheka, 223–34; and Archangel landing, 57–60; arrests of, 212–13, 223–24; arrival in Petrograd, 61–62; arrival in Russia, 1–3, 8–9, 22, 24–25; 223; assumes name, 6; attitude toward Bolsheviks, 225; attitude toward planned coup, 85, 97; Berzin and, 74–78, 81; on Cheka, 23; claim against Baldwin Locomotive Co., *see* Baldwin Locomotive Co.; correspondence with Boyce, 181–82, 184; correspondence with Churchill, 172–74; counterrevolutionary activities in Soviet Union, 25–35; and Cromie's death, 88–89; Cumming on, 107–8; death of, 214, 216–17, 218–21, 231, 232, 233; efforts to return to Soviet Union, 111–14; escapes from Soviet Union,

Reilly, S. (*continued*)
101–2, 227–28; false identities of, 27–28; family background of, 4–5; at Fifth Congress, 47–48; financial difficulties of, 154–55, 161, 163; and French Intelligence Service, 226–27; in hiding after Lockhart's arrest, 90–92, 94–96; and Houselander, 45–46; introduced to Churchill, 140; and Kalamatiano, 29–31; and Krassin, 161–62; and Latvian sharpshooters, 60–61, 63–64, 74–78, 227; and Left SR uprising, 49–56, 57, 225–26; letter from Boyce, 180–81; letter to Dukes, 156; letter on Savinkov trial, 171; letter from Savinkov, 174; letters to Lockhart, 111–12; and Lockhart, 22, 152–53; loyalty to Russia, 222–24; and Marchand, 96–97; meeting with Berzin, 79–81, 86–87; meeting with Bonch-Bruyevich, 223; meeting with Hill, 95–97; Minayev on, 218–19; in New York, 7–8, 143–44; obituary notice on, 194; Opperput on "The Trust" and, 207–16; at Paris Peace Conference, 137, 138, 228–29; personality of, 3–4; physical appearance of, 46; plan to steal Soviet art, 209, 210; and planned Allied intervention, 40–41, 42, 78–85, 92–94, 181–82; political beliefs of, 4–5, 223–25; rehabilitation of, 234–35; returns to Russia, 89, 134–37, 186–90, 208–11, 230–31; role of, 233–35; and Savinkov, 38, 146, 148–49, 150–57, 163–64, 166–68, 173, 226–27, 229; and Shmidkhen, 74–78; and SIS, 133–34, 228–29; and Sisson papers, 14; social life in England, 108–9, 112–13; and Starzheskaya, 78–

79; treatment in prison, 213–14; on trial in absentia, 115–31; and "The Trust," 181–83, 185–86; in U.S., 163–64, 177–78; and de Vertemont, 34–35, 36, 88, 226; visit to Berlin, 159; and Voynich, 5; wives of, *see* Reilly, Margaret; Reilly, Nadine; Reilly, Pepita; and Wrangel, 157; and Yakushev, 187–88; and Zinoviev letter, 174–76, 229

Rellinsky, Konstantin Georgievich. *See* Reilly, Sidney George

Renucci. *See* Artuzov, Artur Khristianovich

Reswick, William, 178–79

Robins, Raymond, 11, 13–14, 15–16, 17–19, 20–21, 109

Rosenblum, Sigmund Georgievich. *See* Reilly, Sidney George

Rosenblum family, 4–5

Russian Armed Services Union (ROVS), 157, 165

Sablin, Vladimirovich Yury, 45–46

Sadoul, Jacques, 17, 18, 22

safe houses, 27, 68, 79, 80, 84, 86, 87, 187

Savinkov, Boris, 25–27, 34, 38–39, 45, 57, 60, 161, 165–66, 187, 210, 225, 230; and Allied intervention, 36, 38–40, 42; anti-Bolshevik campaign, 150–57; arrested, 168–69; captures Yaroslavl, 56, 58, 59; and Churchill, 146–47; description of, 39; financial problems of, 154–55; and Lenin's death, 165; letter to Dzerzhinski, 185; letter to Reilly, 174; Lockhart on, 166; meeting with Mussolini, 167; morphine habit, 166; and Reilly, 146, 148–49, 163–64, 226–27, 229; Reilly on, 156–57, 173; Reilly on trial of, 171–72;